FROM THE CHILCOTIN TO THE CHILKOOT

Selected Hikes of Northern British Columbia

By Vivien Lougheed

Caitlin Press Inc
Prince George BC
2005

Library and Archives Canada Cataloguing in Publication

Lougheed, Vivien
From the Chilcotin to the Chilkoot : selected hikes in northern British Columbia / Vivien Lougheed.

Includes index.
ISBN 1-894759-02-8

1. Hiking—British Columbia, Northern—Guidebooks. 2. Trails—British Columbia, Northern—Guidebooks. 3. British Columbia, Northern—Guidebooks. I. Title.
GV199.44.C22B74 2005 796.51'09711'8 C2005-901046-0

Cover and test designed by Warren Clark Graphic Design
Cover photo by Vivien Lougheed, taken in Mount Robson Park
Photos throughout supplied from author's collection
Index by Kathy PleH

Caitlin Press Inc. acknowledges financial support from the Government of Canada through the Book Publishing Industry Development Program and the Canada Council for the Arts, and from the Province of British Columbia through the British Columbia Arts Council and the Book Publishers' Tax Credit through the Ministry of Provincial Revenue.

Printed and bound in Canada.

Table of Contents

Acknowledgements

As always, I must thank my husband John Harris for joining me on my mountain adventures. These trips often include rain, snow, difficult river crossings and bear sightings. All the while, he carries more weight in his pack than I do and still seems to have the energy to make me a "spiked" tea at the evening campsite. During the winters his adventures start again when he corrects my grammar and spelling mistakes. Facing me with these corrections is often worse than facing a female grizzly with a cub.

I must thank Jen Harris for the hundreds of weekends she has devoted to trudging up and down mountains or through icy creeks so we could test whether a hike would be suitable for this book or not. Her analytical brain was always able to figure out what difficulties or pleasures a trail might present.

I must also thank Paige Pedersen and Robin MacDonald, hikers in training, who have started following us into the wilderness. They are representative of the next generation of adventurers who will go even farther into the wilderness looking for the "can't be done" hike.

I thank Frank Peebles for hiking with me through some difficult terrain in the Tatshenshini and then editing the descriptions of those hikes.

I would also like to thank all the people who have joined me on hikes that often didn't end up in the expected place or time. I must mention the people who, after a few moments of discussion either at trailhead, mid hike or in a restaurant, have caught my enthusiasm and then gone with me. Then there are those who have traveled great distances to join me mostly on the northern trails. Elsebeth Vingborg from Denmark and Stephan Beiderman from Germany have come to hike with me often and now are far better bush persons than either John or myself.

I would also like to thank all the workers at the tourist bureaus across northern BC who fed me information, answered innumerable questions and offered suggestions about trails for this book. Their enthusiasm was refreshing.

Introduction

This book does not cover every possible hike in Northern British Columbia. Instead it tries to give you an introduction to the possibilities each area has to offer. Some of these areas like Tumbler Ridge and 100 Mile House are passed by without a glance by visitors to the province and that is a pity. I have attempted to describe a half-day hike, a full-day hike and at least one over-night trip for each area. On the other hand, some places are not great hiking areas and may have only one hike described while others are great and have many. In areas where there are established clubs, or where there are contact persons willing to give added information, I have named them. That way it gives you a hiking family, someone who can recommend other places or people to hook up with. If there are detailed hiking books available for an area, I mention them as well. Often hiking clubs, whose members make and maintain these trails, earn a large portion of their money from the sale of these books.

Northern British Columbia has thousands of acres of designated park areas where established and maintained hiking trails can be easily accessed. The north also has undeveloped land where the adventuresome (and skilled) hikers can punch their way into the alpines and wander for days. The Tatshenshini Provincial Park is one such area where established trails do not exist but the landscape is exquisite. Anyone with skill can enjoy it.

All hikes are categorized according to their degree of difficulty and the time and skill/equipment required to complete the trip.

Moose on the side of the road, Tumbler Ridge.

Degrees of Difficulty

The First Class hike will be an easy couple of hours or less, along a trail with little change in elevation. All you will need is some rain gear just in case, pepper spray just in case, toilet paper just in case and maybe a small snack. This can be carried in a small daypack or a shoulder bag.

The Second Class hike is a full day hike along a trail. You will need a first aid kit, tarp, pepper spray, light boots or good runners, rain gear, a change of clothing, matches, fire starter, food and water to last the day. This equipment can be carried in a regular sized daypack. You must always carry emergency equipment in the event of a change in weather or an accident.

The Third Class hike is a much more difficult day hike or a single overnighter. It will be the same as the second-class hike only you may go off trail, over rocks, and you may need to pick your route in some parts. Besides the equipment needed for the second-class hike, you will need a tent and sleeping bag for overnight, map and compass, and boots rather than runners.

The Fourth Class hike is more than one night but it will be mostly along a trail so getting lost will not be a huge problem. You will need everything for the third-class hike plus a sleeping pad, rope, stove, fuel, binoculars, dishes, and meals for the duration of the hike.

The Fifth Class hike is more than one night out, often along a suggested route rather than a trail. These hikes (there are only a few in this book) are only for the most experienced hikers. Fifth class hikers need no instructions on what to take.

How to Read this Book

Times in this book are approximate and when I give a suggested time, it is what the hike has taken me, under normal conditions (no snow, ice, bears, etc.) and when I am fairly well rested. You may be a much faster or slower hiker than me. Try one or two hikes and compare your time with mine. This will give you an idea of how long it should take you on other hikes.

The Distance I record for a trail or route is usually calculated by the distance measured across the map. It does not include the distance used to go up and down hills or around obstructions like fallen trees. Therefore, when I say that a hike of eight kilometers has taken me three hours up and two hours down, what I am probably saying is that, because I am walking a kilometer and a half per hour, the trail is fairly steep. However, if I say that an eight-kilometer hike has taken me two hours, then you can be certain the hike is along the flat.

Organization of this book follows the highways taken to reach each trailhead. The back of the book has information on trail etiquette, bear awareness, gear and food suggestions. Be certain to read the section called "Bear Country". Since you will be hiking in Northern British Columbia, seeing bears is a possibility. For your own safety and for the safety of the bear, be sure you know what to do.

Highway 97 describes the hikes that are reached off the highway between 100 Mile House and Prince George including the side trips on Highway 26 into Barkerville and Highway 20 into Bella Coola.

Highway 16 East describes the hikes between the Alberta border and Prince George plus those that follow Highway 5 south around Valemount, and Wells Gray Park.

Highway 16 West describes trails from Prince Rupert to Haida Gwaii.

The **Stewart Cassiar Highway** describes trails from Kitwanga on Highway 16 West, through Meziadin Junction and north to the Alaska Highway.

The **Alaska Highway South** describes the hikes reached from the highway between Prince George and Fort Nelson.

The **Alaska Highway North** describes hikes that follow the Alaska Highway from Fort Nelson to the Chilkoot but includes only the hikes that are totally or partially in British Columbia. This section also has hikes in the Tatshenshini Park that is accessible from the Haines Highway in the Yukon Territories.

Emperor Falls, Mount Robson

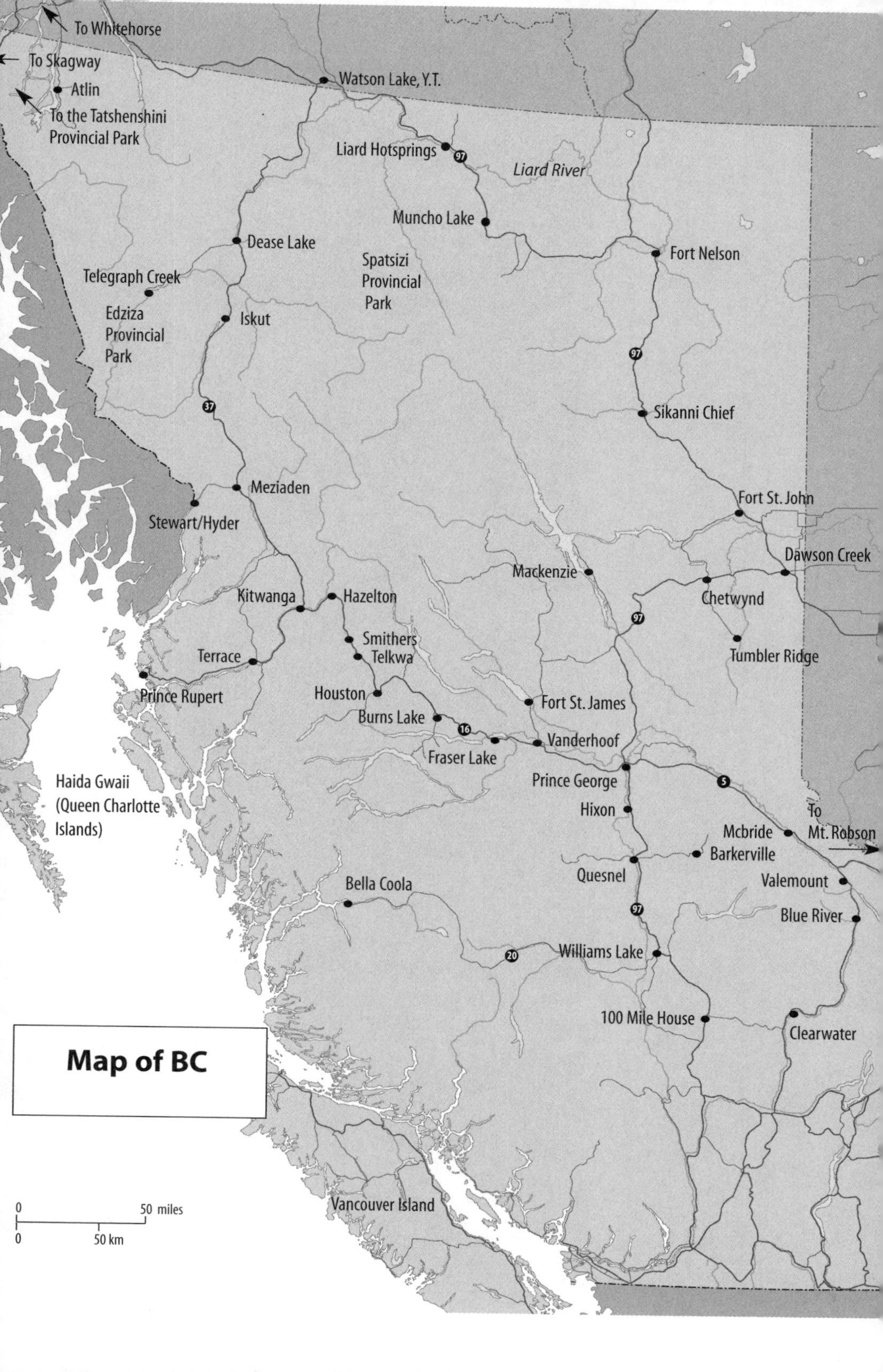
To Whitehorse
To Skagway
Atlin
To the Tatshenshini Provincial Park
Watson Lake, Y.T.
Liard Hotsprings
97
Liard River
Muncho Lake
Dease Lake
Fort Nelson
Telegraph Creek
Spatsizi Provincial Park
Edziza Provincial Park
Iskut
97
37
Sikanni Chief
Meziaden
Stewart/Hyder
Fort St. John
Dawson Creek
Mackenzie
Kitwanga
Hazelton
Chetwynd
97
Smithers
Telkwa
Tumbler Ridge
Terrace
Prince Rupert
Houston
Fort St. James
Burns Lake
16
Vanderhoof
Fraser Lake
Prince George
5
Haida Gwaii (Queen Charlotte Islands)
Hixon
To Mt. Robson
Mcbride
Barkerville
Quesnel
Valemount
Bella Coola
97
Blue River
20
Williams Lake
100 Mile House
Clearwater
Map of BC
Vancouver Island
0
50 miles
0
50 km

Highway 97

From 100 Mile House to Williams Lake

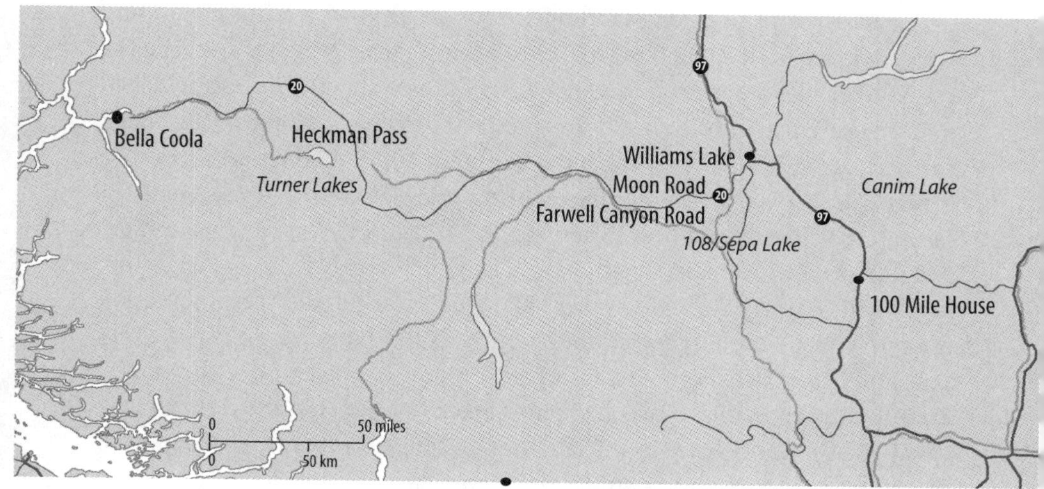

100 Mile House

Mile houses along the gold rush trail from Seattle to Barkerville became stopping places for travelers to eat and sleep. Mile zero in British Columbia was at Lillooet just 100 miles away from here, on the Fraser River. The name given to the lodge or house at that time was Bridge Creek House but the house was soon renamed to 100 Mile House because of its distance from Lillooet. The name has never been changed, only now the area is a town of about 2000 residents rather than just a lodge.

The original lodge was owned by many and was built up so that it eventually consisted of five adjoining buildings holding sixteen bedrooms in all. The last owner of the lodge was Lord Martin Cecil who came from England to run the place. However, shortly after his arrival in 1937, the buildings caught fire and burned so that nothing was salvageable.

100 Mile House is a friendly town that offers everything for the visitor from a doctor and dentist to bowling and golf. There are malls, restaurants, grocery stores, motels, campgrounds and lodges available. Most of the lakes located on or near Wells Gray Park, Mahood Lake Road or at Sheridan Lake also have restaurants and lodges or campsites. There is also a world-class

health spa just eight miles north of town. However, the area's reputation as a birding center is fast becoming the big draw and to date there have been 280 species identified during nesting season. The biggest draw for birds are the Sandhill Cranes who have nesting sites in the area. Ask at the Visitors Center where you may see them.

Cranes are regal birds, standing 1.3 to 1.6 m (4 to 5 ft) in height and have a wingspan of 2 to 2.5 m (6 to 7 ft). Mature males weigh about 5 kg (12 pd) and females are just a bit smaller. Grey in color, their most distinguished markings are their white cheeks and bare red foreheads. Cranes often preen themselves with clay thus changing the gray color of their feathers to a brown that helps them camouflage during nesting season. Cranes mate for life and they like to nest near water. In Canada, nesting season is around the end of April or the beginning of May. The females usually lay two eggs that hatch within thirty days and cranes keep their young under their protection for one year. Being territorial, they return to the same nesting spot every year and bring last year's hatchlings with them. However, once they are at their nesting sites, they chase the youngsters away and start the cycle all over again. When cranes leave in the fall, they go quickly, often flying 80 km (50 mi) an hour and up to 800 km (500 mi) in a day.

Cranes are sometimes misidentified and thought to be Blue Herons. One difference in the birds is the way they fly; cranes fly with their heads out straight while herons fly with their heads tucked in. Another difference is that cranes nest on the ground while herons nest in trees.

100 Mile House has the world's largest set of skis sitting outside the Visitors Center. They are 12 meters (36 feet) tall, weight 275 kilograms (600 pounds) and cost $3500 to make. Be certain to stop in. The municipal campground is one kilometer up Horse Lake Road on the bank overlooking the creek. The campground is next to the Centennial Trails.

100 Mile Demonstration Forest

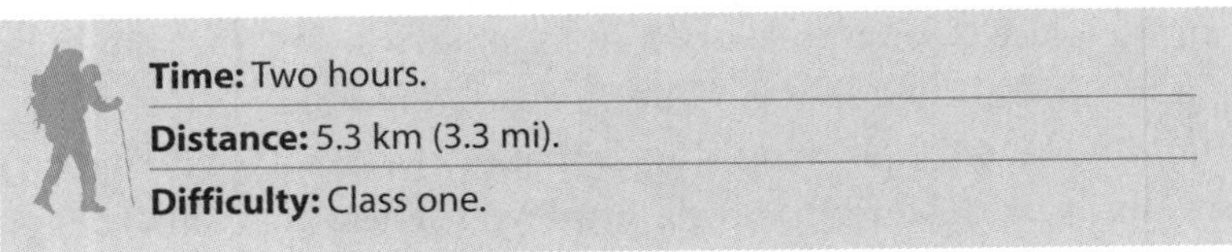

Time: Two hours.

Distance: 5.3 km (3.3 mi).

Difficulty: Class one.

The route: This is a looped trail that has interpretive signs along the way depicting the points of historical interest and some of the plants found in the area.

Trail access: There is a snowmobile road from the Visitors' Center to the Demonstration Forest. If driving, follow Highway 97 south of town for 1.6 km (one mi) to the bottom of 99-Mile Hill (the long hill at the south end of town). Turn right after the railway overpass onto the side road and drive for one km (0.6 mi) down this road.

The trail: The entrance to the trail has a map of the area and the first spot of interest is where the old Cariboo Wagon Road passed. Farther along the trail there is a sign describing the history of logging and there is an old mill site. The trail shows recent logging and the treatment that follows logging. The wetlands are the next point of interest with some birding opportunities. This is followed by Margaret Springs, which in turn is followed by spruce, fir and pine forests. The entire route is interspersed with descriptions of plants and trees that grow in this environment. Oregon Grape, a plant that grows abundantly in the area, was once used by First Nations people to create a yellow dye from the roots and inner bark. The berries are edible but quite sour.

Walking bridge at 108 Mile/Sepa Lake Trail.

Centennial Park and Bridge Creek Waterfalls

Time: Half an hour to the falls but an hour if going to the ridge.

Distance: One kilometer to the falls, 2.5 km (1.6 mi) if going to the ridge.

Difficulty: Class one.

The route: Centennial Park has numerous trails but the waterfalls are the most popular destination. The maintained trail is flat and easy to walk. However, if you are going up to the ridge and over to the campsite that is beside the power lines you will have a bit of a grunt. There are picnic tables and an outhouse at the campsite parking lot.

Trail access: From the Visitor Information Center, drive north along Highway 97 to Fourth Avenue. Turn right and follow Fourth for two blocks to Cedar Ave. Turn left onto Cedar and then immediately right to the parking lot that is located beside the Parkside Center for the Arts and Culture.

The trail: From the parking lot, follow the trail that skirts the creek. There is a second trail on the opposite side of the parking lot that has a picnic area and playground for children. This trail can be taken on the return trip from the falls thus making a loop. If you want to go to the ridge, take the trail to the right once you are at the waterfall. The trail continues up from the falls and makes a sharp right-hand turn at the top of the hill. The trail then loops back down to the parking lot while the trail that follows the left-hand fork (it looks more like it goes straight ahead) near the falls goes to the power line and campsite. There are wooden walkways over the wetter areas. While walking near the falls, look for signs of an old lumber mill that was located here until 1930. The pipe that is in the creek below the falls was used to funnel water and power the machinery used in the mill. There are more signs of the flume farther up, near the campsite. You can follow the creek past some rapids to a water hole where you can swim during nice weather. The trails continues up to the bridge on the road and is called the Bridge Trail. It goes under the bridge and skirts the subdivision on the opposite side of the highway.

Birds commonly seen in this area are ruby and golden crowned kinglets, red breasted nuthatches, mountain and black capped chickadees, woodpeckers, thrushes, grouse, crossbills, creepers and winter wrens.

For more information on these trails ask at the Visitors' Center or purchase *Trails of the Southern Cariboo* by Colin Campbell, also available at the Visitors' Center.

Hendrix Creek Waterfall

Time: Half an hour.

Distance: Half a kilometer one-way.

Difficulty: Class two.

The route: This is a non-maintained trail that has a lot of deadfall that must be navigated. This trail is for those wanting real exercise. The trail was built and was maintained by Weldwood of Canada and BC Forests. The waterfall, located at the east end of Canim Lake, has a 20 m (60-ft) drop and the area has good birding possibilities. This is a long drive for a short hike but if staying at Canim Lake for a night, the hike is a nice one.

Trail access: Follow Highway 97 north from 100 Mile House for about a kilometer (.6 mi) to the Forest Grove Road. Follow Forest Grove Road for about 15 km (9.3 mi) and then turn right onto the Canim Lake road. The road becomes gravel at this point. Follow this road for about 10 km (6 mi) and at the first fork, take the left hand one so that you travel along the north side of Canim Lake. At the next fork, midway up the lake, take the road on the right-hand side. You will pass road # 610 and # 620 and then at road # 60-18, take the right hand fork onto the road called 7000. As soon as you cross a bridge, take road # 7000 1/2 and follow it to the sign indicating the trailhead.

The trail: This is a non-maintained trail that leads to a 20-m (60 ft) waterfall that drops over a ledge and into a pool. Besides the scenery, birds are what you should look for while walking here. From May to September there is a good chance of seeing the Northern Loon, American Bittern, Marsh Wren, swallows, eagles and numerous song birds.

The name Canim Lake comes from the Indian word in the Chinook language meaning "canoe". Archeological discoveries have indicated that the area was occupied about 4300 years ago. The pristine lake that is 37 km (23 m) long is surrounded by low hills and meadows that have pine, spruce and Douglas fir trees. There are resorts and campsites on the lake.

108 Mile/Sepa Lake

Time: Three hours.

Distance: Ten km (6 mi).

Difficulty: Class one.

The route: This hike can include the entire ten km (6 mi) or it can be cut short to about 5 km (3 mi). Those wanting the shorter hike can walk around the east side of 108 Mile Lake and then skirt the rim of Sepa Lake on their return. Those wanting more can do the entire circuit around both lakes. Although water birds are the main attraction on these lakes, you may also see the downy and red-headed woodpeckers, loons, chickadees, nuthatches and red-winged blackbirds.

Trail access: From 100 Mile House drive north 18 km, past the 108 Mile Resort and the air strip. There is a farm, museum and a rest area at the heritage site and trailhead for this hike. From the heritage site walk back toward 100 Mile House and turn right onto the path that skirts the creek. Follow this to the covered bridge (it has swallows nesting under the roof) and continue. There are signs indicating which lake you are walking around.

The trail: Follow the trail that goes gently up and down around the lake and winds in and out of the bays to a beach and picnic site. From there, the trail comes to a fork where you can either go south and around Sepa Lake or cut across the top of Sepa Lake and then go north and around 108 Mile Lake. You may also go south at this point around Sepa Lake and back to the parking lot. This is a heaven for birders so if that is what you like, bring the birding guide and binoculars along with your snack and drinking water. Horses may be hired to ride around the lake if walking isn't really what you want to do.

108 Mile Heritage Site

This Heritage Site is as the name suggests, just eight miles (12 kms) north of 100 Mile House. After spending a few years trying his luck in the goldfields farther north, William James Roper decided to settle down and start ranching. He chose this spot for his homestead. Roper wasn't too successful at ranching so he sold his farm to an English couple, Mr. Charles M. Beak and his wife Marie Johnson. They operated the ranch for a number of years and expanded the buildings so there was a store and roadhouse. After a few years, they sold the farm. This pattern of working, expanding and selling of the land was repeated by other settlers until, in the early 1900s Captain Geoffrey L. Watson purchased it for the exorbitant price of $11,000. Watson was the last to work the land and operate the roadhouse before it was left to disintegrate. 108 Mile Hotel at the heritage site was built in 1867 but wasn't moved to this location until 1892 after the road was built.

Eventually, the people of the area saw the value of the property as a heritage site and raised money to restore the buildings. Now it is a popular tourist attraction where travelers visit the site and then walk around the lake.

You may also walk from the Heritage Site under the highway underpass for an easy stroll to a lookout point.

Highway 20 to Bella Coola

There are numerous lodges along this highway in which you can rent a room, pitch a tent or purchase a meal. However, during high summer season in July and August, it may be a good idea to book a room in advance.

Bella Coola, at the end of the road, offers every type of service needed plus some interesting tourist attractions. There are numerous day hikes in and around Bella Coola, most of which are not described here. Visit their tourist office or parks office for more information.

The road into Bella Coola starts its downward 1525 m (5000 ft) plunge to the ocean at Heckman Pass. The plunge goes for 43 km (27 mi) along a winding, narrow road. Commonly called "the hill", there is one ten-kilometer (6 mi) section that has switchbacks with grades of 18%. This hill makes a great downhill cycle but for motor homes or bigger vehicles, it can be a nerve-wracking challenge. All those descending this hill should have good brakes on their vehicles. Safety measures include stopping often to allow your brakes to cool and using only low gear. Those pulling trailers who are not comfortable with the descent can leave the trailers in a parking lot at the top of the hill.

Bella Coola is also where Alexander Mackenzie ended up after traveling across Canada in 1793. He painted his name and the date on a rock in the Dean Channel. For those wanting to follow part of Mackenzie's route along the three-week hike from the Blackwater River out of Prince George to Bella Coola, purchase *In the Steps of Alexander Mackenzie* by John Woodworth, a self published guide that includes maps for the trip. The Mackenzie Trail hike is not described in this book.

Doc English Bluff Ecological Reserve

Time: 45 minutes.

Distance: One kilometer (0.6 mi).

Difficulty: Class one.

Equipment: Carry water as there are no streams along the way from which to drink.

The route: This is a good uphill grunt to help weed out any weariness from driving. The hike goes 50 m (150 ft) up within one km (0.6 mi). But the exercise is refreshing and stopping to watch the birds that are so abundant along the trail also allows you to catch your breath.

Trail access: From Williams Lake drive along Highway 20 for about 30 km (19 mi). Moon Road is on the left just before a hill. Take Moon Road and drive for about three km (2 mi). Park under English Bluff, the hill you will ascend.

The trail: From the small parking area under the bluff, follow the trail up the mountain. This is one place where Golden eagles can be found. These magnificent kings of the skies nest along the cliff edge of English Hill. It was because of these birds and some rare plants found on the hill that the area was made into an ecological preserve. Dominant vegetation includes the Interior Douglas fir tree and bunchgrasses. Unlike grasses on the prairies or on your lawn, bunchgrass grows in circular bunches of tightly-packed growing stems. Each stem produces separate leaves and flowers above the ground. These systems die in the fall but grow again each spring. Vespers, sage grouse and grasshopper sparrows often build nests or hide from predators under the overhangs of bunch grasses. Bunchgrass covers less than 1% of the total area of British Columbia.

Be careful when near the top of English Hill and along the edge as there are no guardrails. The drop is steep. From the lookout you can see the Fraser River in one direction and the ranchlands spreading out toward Bella Coola in the other. There are also some caves on the hill but they are small.

Farwell Canyon

Time: Half an hour to one hour.

Difficulty: Class two.

Equipment: Boots are a must if going to the dune and water should be carried. Eye protection is recommended to protect your eyes from the sun and the sand if the wind is blowing (which it often is in this canyon).

The route: The canyon, known as the badlands of the Chilkotin, is near the junction of the Fraser and Chilcotin Rivers. The canyon walls and cliffs nearby have been admired for centuries. Some of the cliffs have ancient pictographs on them. The wind-sculptured sandstone and hoodoos in the area are well worth the visit. There is also a magnificent shifting sand dune that should not be missed. Bighorn sheep can be seen at the preserve before the canyon trailhead. For those into driving, you can do a 230 km loop from the turn off at Highway 20 back to Williams Lake.

Trail access: From Williams Lake drive south to Highway 20 and head west for 44.5 km (27 mi) to the Farwell Canyon Road. It is the first left after the Toosey Reserve. Other landmarks are the Old Riske Creek school house and general store. The gravel road right after that is the Farwell Canyon Road. Turn south (left) and drive for 15 km (9 mi) to the Sheep Range Provincial Park. Here there are not only large game animals but over 40 species of butterflies have been identified during their migration periods in the spring/early summer. The Farwell Canyon Bridge is 21 km (13 mi) from the turnoff at the Riske Creek general store and schoolhouse. Park before crossing the Farwell Canyon Bridge.

The trail: Walk across the bridge and along the road to the small trail on the left-hand side. This will take you to a rock face where you can see some pictographs. This canyon is the home to one-fifth of the world's California Bighorn Sheep. Also, looking across the Chilco River, you will see a large sand dune. This will/should be your next destination. To get there, go back to the road and across the bridge. Walk back toward town and away from your car until you see a large post. Cross the road at the post and head for the gully. There are orange ribbon trail markers along the way. After crossing a gully, you will start a half-hour uphill slog. There are prickly pear cactus and scree, sand and rocks to maneuver around. To be safe, you will have to climb diagonally because of the loose sand and rock. From the top, you will see one of Canada's largest moving dunes. You may climb on the dune and from there, the views of the Canyon are spectacular. Be certain to do this.

The loop: To drive the rest of the loop back to Williams Lake, continue along the Farwell Canyon Road to the Community of Big Creek. From there head north to Hanceville and follow that road back to Highway 20 at Lees Corner where there is a coffee shop and gas station. From there, turn east back to Highway 97.

Rainbow Range

Time: Two days unless doing the circle which needs five or six days.

Distance: 16 km (10 mi) to the Rainbow, 58 km (36 mi) for the circle.

Difficulty: Class five.

Equipment: Grizzly bears are numerous in the area and pepper spray is essential. So is a clean campsite.

Topo maps: 93C/12 and 93D/9

The route: The main objective of this hike is to see the Rainbow Mountains, a prism of colors that changes according to the season. Once out of the tree line (within four hours) the remaining sections of the hike are in the alpine. There are unnamed alpine lakes to camp beside and abundant wildlife to watch. There is also the option of going over to Crystal Lake and down to the Alexander Mackenzie Trail. From there you could continue along the A. Mackenzie trail and finish at Bella Coola or you could go back up the Tweedsmuir Trail that crosses the Octopus Trail and return by that trail to your car. For the longer hikes, please see the park wardens at the office located near the campsite in Bella Coola and get the latest information. You must have topo maps if doing the circle hike.

The Rainbow Mountains are located in Tweedsmuir Provincial Park that has an area of 981,000 hectares of preserve to explore. Tweedsmuir was the fifth Governor General of Canada and he traveled in the area during the 1930s.

Trail access: Drive Highway 20 to Heckman Pass about 360 km (225 mi) west of Williams Lake. Park at the picnic site on the pass. The trailhead for Rainbow Range/Octopus Lake is just west of the parking lot.

The trail: The Rainbow Trail veers off to the right (away from the Octopus Trail) shortly after entering the forest. There is a small lake seven km (5 mi) up the trail that takes no more than a four hours to reach and is good for camping. If going in and out on the same trail, camp at the lake and walk without a pack to the viewpoint for the Rainbows. To do this, continue to the pass that is straight ahead. This will take at least three or four hours to reach. Near the pass the Rainbow Mountains come into view and you will forget every huff and puff you took to get here. After the first lake, the way becomes clearer as the bush thins out and the terrain becomes tundra. Some may wish to spend a couple of nights up in the area.

There are three unnamed lakes to the west of the pass where you can walk, camp and spend a day looking around. To get to the three lakes from the pass follow the trail and the cairns. The third lake on the map, tucked between two hills is no longer on the landscape. Continue toward the lava cliffs and ledges where you can look down onto the Crystal Lake Trail or up at the Coast Range. The last mountain on your left is Mt Waddington, BC's highest peak.

From here, return by the same way that you came. However, for those wanting to do longer and more complicated hikes like joining up with the Mackenzie Trail, I would suggest speaking with the wardens at the park office in Bella Coola to to have the route marked out on the topo maps.

Octopus Lake trail starts at the same place as the Rainbow Range. The lake is 14 km (9 mi) from trailhead and takes five to six hours to reach. This is a straightforward walk and can be done as a very pleasant overnight trip.

The Circle hike that includes the **Crystal Lake Trail**, the **Tweedsmuir Trail** and the **Octopus Lake Trail** is a total of 58 km (36 mi) and takes about five days. The beginning of the trail is the same as the Rainbow Range trail except you must continue walking uphill and past the turnoff for the Rainbow. This is a horse trail and there is a horse camp about halfway along this trail 9 km (5 mi) from trailhead. At the junction of the Mackenzie trail and the Crystal Lake trail is a cabin where you can get shelter if needed. This can be reached by the end of the second day. From Crystal Lake it is a steep couple of kilometers down to the cabin and the Mackenzie trail. The cabin is also tucked in under the impressive Mount Mackenzie looming above at 2146 m (6975 ft).

The Tweedsmuir Trail goes up the creek and hill from the cabin at Mount Mackenzie to a small lake about six km (3.5 mi) away where you can rest but there is no camping there. It is about the same distance to the campsite at the western end of Octopus Lake. There is a second campsite at the opposite end of the lake. The mostly downhill hike back to the trailhead at Heckman Pass is 14 km (9 mi) and can be done in a short day.

Hunlen Falls and Turner Lakes

Time: Four to six days is required if you must walk the Atnarko Road (also called the Tote Road) and/or if you are going to canoe the lakes or explore other trails. If you are just walking to the falls and the Atnarko Road is dry, allowing you to drive the 13 km (8 mi) to trailhead, two days is enough. The walk to Turner Lake campsite is about 10 hours.

Distance: 17 km (10.5 mi) one way.

Difficulty: Class five hike.

Equipment: Water must be carried for the first 13 km (8 mi) if the Atnarko Road is walked. Grizzly bears are abundant and pepper spray is essential as are clean camping habits. Food should be stored in the bear caches available at each campsite. There is a charge for camping at the lakes.

Topo maps: 93C/4 and 93C/5

The route: This is a difficult hike and if you must walk the first 13 km (8 mi) that section is boring. Once at the falls, the exploring is endless. The lakes themselves are worth canoeing. There are canoes at Turner Lake available for rent. There are also numerous camping sites along the lakes.

Trail access: Follow Highway 20 past Heckman Pass 360 km (225 mi) from Williams Lake and park at the Atnarko Campground/parking lot and picnic site. During dry season, the Atnarko/Tote Road can be driven for 13 km (8 mi). If the road is wet or if you have not got much clearance on your vehicle (four-wheel drive is recommended) that distance will have to be walked. Driving time is just under two hours. Walking time is a full day.

The trail: Trailhead is at the confluence of the Atnarko and Hotnarko Rivers. Stillwater Lake is four km (2.5 mi) past the trailhead and is the last place where fresh water can be obtained until you are at the Turner Lakes so you should fill your bottles. Do not camp on the road or at the parking lot because the area is frequented by grizzlies. You should also walk this section in midday when the bears are resting. The trail follows a pack trail that goes up and down rockslides above the river. Three km (2 mi) into the hike, there is a trail to Stillwater Lake, the last source of drinking water before the Turner Lakes Campsite.

After crossing the large delta at the mouth of Goat Creek, you will cross the Atnarko River on a well-maintained footbridge. The next section of the trail includes 78 switchbacks that take you up about 2000 feet to a ridge above the Atnarko and Goat Creek valleys. The viewpoint offers great views of the Goat Creek canyon and some of the peaks in the Glacier Mountains. There are no camping spots along this trail until you get to Turner Lake.

Before reaching the Turner Lakes campsite, there is a turnoff to Ptarmigan Lake and Whistler Pass. The Turner Lake campsite is a good place to use as a base camp from which to visit the surrounding alpines. There are ten tent pads, a food cache, an outhouse, a dock and a canoe rental facility located at Turner Lake. There are cabins on the west side of Turner Lake about four km (2.5 mi)down. Each lake below Turner Lake has tent pads and primitive campsite facilities.

The viewpoint for the falls, that drop 260 m (853 ft) over a cliff and into the valley, is a short distance from the Turner Lake campsite. This is one of the highest waterfalls in Canada. From the north end of the campsite, follow the trail around the lakeshore to the bridge. Once across, follow the trail (to the left) for about 15 minutes. You will be walking on the rim of the cliff and across the valley the falls can be seen plunging endlessly into the abyss below. The falls were named after Hana-Lin, a Native trapper who worked the area. You can continue along the trail past another viewpoint that sits above Lonesome Lake. The trail continues around in a loop, eventually rejoining the main section leading back to Turner Lake.

Junker Lake Trail, 10 km (6 mi), follows the east side of Turner Lake down past Cutthroat Lake to Vista Lake. It will take three to four hours one way to get to Vista Lake. The trail is quite wet and overgrown in places but once down at Vista Lake, the trip will seem well worth the work. There is one campsite on Turner Lake part way down and then a second one at the top end of Junker Lake. This campsite is on a nice beach.

The six lakes sometimes called the Turner Lakes and at other times called the Hunlen Lakes can also be canoed. Rentals are available at the Tweedsmuir Wilderness Camp at the Turner Lake Campsite. Canoeing is an easier way to see all the lakes than hiking. There are primitive campsites along the lakes with food caches and outhouses. The caches should be used to help prevent a bear encounter. There are four portages between the lakes that are between one-half and one kilometer long. The portages are marked by white markers while the campsites, often on sandy beaches, are marked by red markers.

Ptarmigan Lake Hike is 12 km (7.5 mi) from the Hunlen Falls and 555 m (1800 ft) higher in elevation. This hike should take around five hours one way. The trailhead is about a kilometer north of the Turner Lakes campsite. Once through the pine forest, the walking becomes pleasant and there are cairns marking the way above tree line. These cairns are called "Stone Women" and were named by a girl's trail crew years before. Camping is at the north end of the lake. This is a splendid hike, mostly in the alpine, and can be done as a very long day hike from Turner Lake.

However, the recommendation is to camp at Ptarmigan Lake and hike over to Molly Lake or Echo/Gem Lakes as day hikes.

These can be hiked as day hikes from Ptarmigan or by taking packs and staying at the campsites at the respective lakes. These trails are also marked with"Stone Women". The lakes are both in the alpines and the walking is splendid although very steep in places. Hanging glaciers and hanging valleys on Glacier Mountain dominate the views. The lakes are about 14 km (8.5 mi) apart. Although the alpine areas are marked with cairns, a topo map and compass should be carried in the event of foul weather and poor visibility. For more information on these hikes visit the parks office in Bella Coola.

Valley View Loop

Time: Two hours or less

Distance: Five kilometers (3 mi) maximum.

Difficulty: Class one.

The route: This is a leg stretcher for those wanting to get out of the car for a while.

Trail access: Follow Highway 20 past Heckman Pass, down the hill to the Alexander Mackenzie Heritage Trailhead and park at the picnic site across the way. Both trailhead and picnic site are marked. If coming from Bella Coola, follow Highway 20 past Hagensborg to the AM Trailhead.

The trail: Follow the trail that starts at Burnt Bridge Creek for about ten minutes, until you come to a fork in the trail. The one to the left leads to the first viewpoint overlooking Stupendous Mountain and the Bella Coola River. The next stretch that continues to the right at the fork goes through a manure fir forest to a suspension bridge over Burnt Bridge Creek and to a picnic site. This walk will take about 45 minutes one way.

If going farther rather than returning by the way you came, continue along to the Mackenzie Heritage Trail another half hour or so and finally to the Burnt Bridge turnoff. This area has alder, cedar, cottonwood and fir trees. The next section requires that you cross two bridges over an arm of the creek and then over the main section of the creek. You then switch-back up the trail for great views of the creek you crossed a few minutes before. The last section of the road takes you back to the trailhead.

The entire loop will take about two hours to complete; depending on how much time you spend enjoying the views. The trees are beautiful, the river is clean and refreshing, the birds are abundant and the walk is rejuvenating.

Snooka Creek

Time: One to three hours.

Distance: East loop is 5.5 km (3.4 mi), West loop is 7.5 km (4.7 mi) and the South loop is 2 km (1.25 mi).

Difficulty: Class one.

Trail access: Follow Highway 20 from Bella Coola to Hagensborg and turn south onto the Snooka Creek Forest Road. Continue along this road for one kilometer and park at the parking lot. It is seven km (4.3 mi) from the center of town to the trailhead.

The trail: These hiking trails, developed by the BC Forest Service and located close to town, provide easy and moderate routes to follow. The trails are used by hikers, mountain bikers and horseback riders. The Snooka East loop is the easiest of the three. The other two are moderate in difficulty. Views of the four-mile subdivision and the Talleo Cannery on the North Bentinck Arm are seen from the trails. The signs indicate which loop you are on and signs at the trailhead show the routes.

Odegaard Falls

Time: Half day. Some of the half-day is used up driving.

Distance: Four kilometers (2.5 mi) return.

Difficulty: Class one or two.

Trail access: Five km (3.1 mi) east of Hagensborg turn west onto the first road after the Nusatsum River Bridge. Follow this for about 45 minutes to the Odegaard Falls Forest Service Recreation site. The distance is 24 km (15 mi) but the travel is slow and a four-wheel drive vehicle is recommended, especially if the weather has been rainy.

The trail: The walk to the foot of the falls is through cedar and balsam forest for about 1.5 km (1 mi). You then start the uphill climb to the falls that drop about 400 m (1300 ft) into the East Nusatsum Valley. The creek is fed by the Odegaard Glacier located at the top of the Nusatsum River. The waterfall is classified as a horsetail waterfall. The reason this waterfall is special is that it has a large volume of water pouring over the cliff; it spews about 200 cubic feet per second. This trailhead also gives access to Odegaard Pass and Purgatory Lookout. For more information on that hike, ask at the park office in town.

Highway 97

From Williams Lake to Quesnel

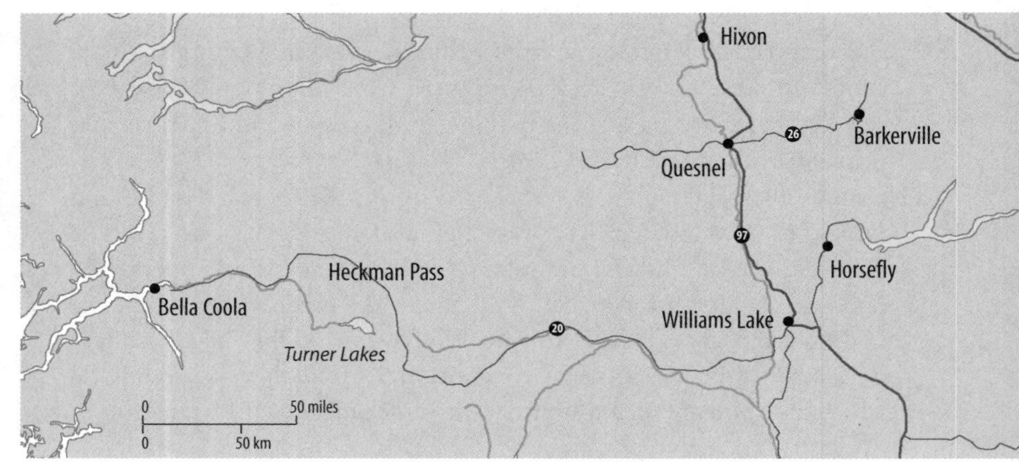

Williams Lake

Before the Europeans came, Williams Lake was called Colunetza. The name means "place of the lordly ones". The name was changed in 1860 to honor Chief William who was the leader of the Sugar Cane Indians. Chief William became famous for encouraging his followers to ignore the Chilcotin War that was started in 1864.

Highway 97 bypasses the center of Williams Lake. However, if you take the road west at the traffic light, you will reach down town and find some food that may be a welcome change from the franchise specialties found along the highway. There are campsites at the lake and numerous hotels and B & Bs in town. The Laughing Loon Pub on the highway is great for pub food. It is also used as a landmark when getting/receiving directions.

For more trails in this area and Highway 20 toward Bella Coola, please purchase *Trails of the Southern Cariboo* by Colin Campbell, published by Rocky Mountain Books, 1998.

Walking Tour of Williams Lake

Time: One hour

Difficulty: Class one

Equipment: Can of pop/water

The route: This is a walk that can be done in part or in its entirety but is mostly within a six block area.

Trail access: Going north on Highway 97, turn left at the traffic lights. This is Oliver Street. Follow it down the hill, past the mall and stampede grounds to 8th Ave and park.

The trail: At 8th Ave and Oliver St. is the Pinchbeck House and at the far south end of 8th Ave, next to the stockyards is the Pinchbeck Grave. William Pinchbeck was an early settler who had a pack train service to the gold fields farther north. He did well. He also built a ranch, hotel, stopping house and brewery and he had a whiskey still.

8th Ave stockyards service the cattle industry for the area between Clinton and Quesnel, Horsefly and Bella Colla. The Williams Lake Stampede was started in 1919. In all the years of competition, there has been only one death at this stampede. In 1932 Lloyd Cyclone Smith met his death while trying to steer off a runway horse. Cyclone's horse collided with the wid horse and Cyclone's horse fell, his foot got stuck in the stirrup. He was crushed under his fallen horse. After Cyclone's death, his wife built a chapel and mortuary in his honor. The mortuary was built because there was not one available at the time of Cyclone's death and his body had to lay in wait in the local garage.

8th Ave, north of the old stockyards, is what was once called Tent City. This is where locals from around the area came and pitched their tents, sat around telling yarns by the campfire and discussed the merits of the day's rodeo events. The newspaper in Vancouver dubbed the area"City of Tents" in 1921 and the name stuck. Squaw Hall was also on this site but it got a bad reputation over the years and was eventually torn down. Too bad. There were lots of wild memories attached to the building.

Sacred Heart Church on Yorston Street and 4th Ave was first opened as a mission by Father Modeste Demers in 1842.

Lakeview Hotel on Mackenzie Ave between Yorston and Oliver was first built in 1920 and was owned by Jack Chow, an early resident of

Williams Lake. The hotel burned to the ground in 2005 (just at print time of this book) and no decision as to its fate had been made. The Mackenzie Store next to it was built during the same time and both hotel and store were burned during a fire on March 9th, 1921.Two men, George Weetman and Johnny Salmon died in the fire.

Log Cabin Hotel, Oliver St and 1st Ave was built in 1920 by Archie Campbell and Bill Smith. It had 13 rooms, a lobby and a dining room but its real claim to fame was that it had the first bathtub in Williams Lake even though it had only cold water. Rooms and meals were 50¢ each.

Williams Lake River Valley

Time: Six hours if you stop often. This trail can also be enjoyed on a bicycle.

Distance: Seven kilometers (4.3 mi).

Difficulty: Class two.

Equipment: Bring water and bear spray as bears are common in the area. Keep dogs on leash so they won't disturb cattle in the area.

The route: This walk takes one through forests rich in bird life, past a dramatic canyon to the Fraser River.

Trail access: Follow Mackenzie Ave north for four km (2.5 mi) and then turn left onto Frizzi Road. Cross the BCR tracks and turn right. Follow this road past the landfill dump and a small industrial site. The road continues for seven km (4.3 mi) or so; when at the forks, take the right hand fork. Continue for one kilometer more. Park. This road is not recommended for motor homes or for any vehicles when it is slippery from rain.

The trail: The valley starts at the north end of Williams Lake and just west of the city. This is where the valley is the widest. As you head towards the river, the valley narrows and the cliffs and gullies become a dramatic landscape.

The trail is rich in birds that like a forest of cottonwoods, birch and Douglas fir, along with marshlands and of grasslands. There have been 252 species of birds recorded in the valley with pygmy owls, kingfishers, herons and dippers being common. Mule deer, black bear, bobcat and moose can be spotted along the trail and muskrats, mink and beaver live along the river. Pink salmon at one time ran the full length of the river up to Williams Lake and on farther north. Recently there have been pink salmon again found in the waters of Williams Lake River, about one kilometer upstream from the Fraser River.

As the trail narrows closer to the Fraser, it passes cliffs that sit 150 m (500 ft) above and in other places the trail sits 200 m (600 ft) above the river. Along the way, you will pass about 24 bridges made mostly from boxcar floors. Some have fallen into disrepair so caution must be taken when crossing.

The valley was designed about 10,000 years ago. Then, glacial ice cut through the rock depositing gravel along the way. The ice eventually dammed the Fraser River and formed Williams Lake. Near the top of the valley there are deposits of shells that indicate the lake was once much larger. Much of this has been eroded by wind and rain.

Jimmy Fox Trail

Time: Two to six hours, depending on where you turn back.

Distance: 13 km (8 mi) return if going to Signal Point but half that distance if going only to the viewpoints.

Difficulty: Class two.

The route: This is a long stroll with views of the lake and surrounding hills as your payoff. This mountain is a common mountain bike haunt with many side trails going back down the hill.

Trail access: Follow Highway 97 north from town for 2.5 km (1.5 mi) to the Fox Mountain Road. Follow it for the same distance to an unnamed gravel road that is just beyond the gas line. Take that road for a few hundred feet to where the road widens and then park. Do not drive around the curve. The trailhead is marked.

The trail: The trail passes through forest to the edge of the plateau that overlooks the town and lake. Turn to the east (left) and follow the trail for as long as you wish. If you go all the way down the steep slope you will end up back in town near Broadway Ave. I suggest you go to where the trail starts to descend and return the way you came and back to your car. This is an excellent walk where children can also enjoy some exercise.

Eureka Peak

Time: Three to four days.

Distance: 25 kilometers (15.5 mi) one way.

Difficulty: Class five.

Topo maps: 93 A/7. A map must be carried in the event of bad weather and poor visibility.

The route: This route is almost completely in alpine. The only complication is that a car must be left at each end of the trail; one for drop off and the other for pick up. It is not recommended to hike the trail starting at Crooked Lake because that end of the trail is very steep and finding the route from east to west is more difficult. The steep part is best walked when packs are a bit lighter.

Trail access: From Williams Lake follow Highway 97 south for 15 km (9.4 mi) and turn east onto the Horsefly Road. Follow this for 60 km (37.5 mi) to the community of Horsefly. From Horsefly, follow the Black Creek Road for 45 km (28 mi) and then follow the left hand fork onto 100 Road. Once at the Crooked Lake Road, stay left again for about 5 km (3 mi). When you cross a series of bridges over the Horsefly River (called Whiskey Bridges) turn right onto a secondary road. Follow this to the marked trailhead. For pick up, go back to the Crooked Lake Road and follow it to the lodge on the lake or to the MOF recreation site. If planning on having a beer, a meal, a room and a shower at the lodge, they will let you park your vehicle there while you hike.

The trail: At the start of the trail and the end of the road where you park your car, you will see a large steel tripod. From there, follow the skidder trails to the forest. Follow the alpine slope heading east and then traverse up the hill and below the ridge. A radio repeater tower is on a hill to the northeast. There is a campsite beside a small alpine lake at kilometer five (mi 3), before you pass the tower. The next section of the trail follows the ridgeline to the top of Eureka Peak and crosses a series of passes. There is another recommended camping spot at kilometer12 (mi 7.5). The climb from this camping place will take you to two alpine lakes and another camping spot. The last 11 km (7 mi) is almost totally downhill. From the lakes, take the old mining road that skirts the south edge of the lake to the Crooked Forest Service Road. It is about another half a kilometer to your car.

Quesnel

Quesnel is a clean mill town with a great coffee/muffin shop just a block off the main highway. The shop is called Granville's and is highly recommended for a visit both before and after your hike.

Because it is part of the Gold Rush Trail to Barkerville, Quesnel has historical artifacts dotted around the town that are related to that period in history. Billy Barker Days, held every third weekend in July, are a blast. People dress in period costume and celebrate with a rodeo, children's festival, tournaments and the comical Biffy-raft race.

Should you want more information about hiking in Quesnel or Barkerville area, purchase *Hiking the Cariboo Goldfields* by Garry Edwards, Dorthea Funk and Ken Stoker, published by Rocky Mountain Books, 2002.

Camping at Ten Mile Lake Provincial Park just north of town offers toilets, telephone, sani-station, water, firewood and showers. In Quesnel, there are hotels and B & Bs for the visitor along with numerous restaurants.

Walking Tour of Quesnel

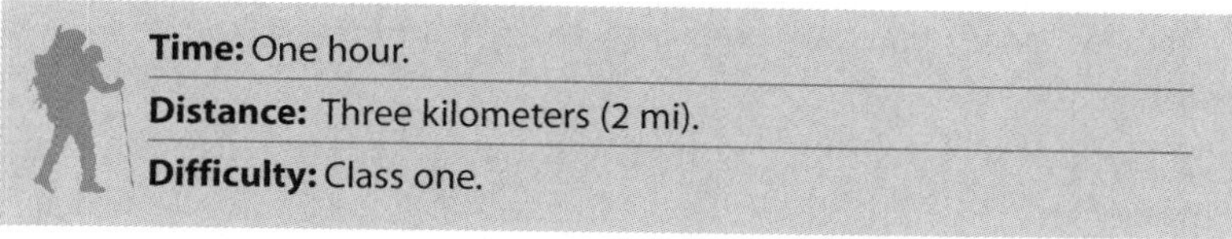

Time: One hour.

Distance: Three kilometers (2 mi).

Difficulty: Class one.

The route: This is a self-guided walking route through the town and the route passes historical places of interest. It also connects to the River Front Trail (see below). The booklet called "*An Historic Walking Tour of Quesnel*", published by the Quesnel Museum & Archives, the City of Quesnel, UNBC and the Quesnel & District Credit Union is available at the District Museum. The booklet has a good map and the historical descriptions (more than what I have given here) are excellent.

Trail access: Go to Quesnel & District Museum and Archives where the pamphlet can be purchased. It is located on Highway 97 at the LeBourdais Park just at the foot of the bridge over the Fraser River and the hill going south out of town. It is also across from the BCR yards.

The trail: LeBourdais Park was named after a local pioneer and MLA for the district who worked for the municipality from 1937 to 1947. The park was originally a racetrack. The **bell tower** beside the museum has a 400-pound bell purchased from the T. Eaton Co. in 1911.

The **railway station** across the street was built for the Pacific Great Eastern Railway in 1921. Walking toward town you will see the **creamery**, built in 1925. Because of its production of good-quality butter, the creamery made Quesnel famous during the 1920s and 1930s.

The trail continues along Carson Avenue, named after a local blacksmith. The **cemetery** is on this street and the oldest grave is dated 1865. The museum has historical information about those presently residing in the cemetery.

St. Andrew's United Church is on Carson and Kinchant St. It was built in 1911 and has a bell in the tower that weighs 600 pounds. I wonder if there was a competition during those early days as to who would ring the heaviest bell. Continuing west, the next stop is the **cenotaph**, built in the 1930s to commemorate those killed in WW I. It later included those killed in WW II and the Korean War.

Behind the cenotaph, on McLean Street, is the **Helen Dixon School**, built in 1936. It is now used by the Continuing Education Department.

The **automobile dealership** was originally the location of the Johnson Brothers livery stables that operated between 1909 and 1922. The location then became a car dealership and remained so, operated by the same family until 1999.

On Carson and Reid Sts., is the **Cariboo Observer** office. The building was built by the Royal Bank in 1928. At the time, the bank was managed by a Mr. Commons and was called by locals, the House of Commons.

The **Wheel Inn Restaurant** was built in 1863 first as a residence but in 1919 it became a boarding house run by a local spinster. On the corner of Carson and Front Streets is a log building that was the **Hudson Bay Company's** original building. It was constructed in 1863 but not sold to the Hudson Bay until 1882. It is believed to be the oldest HBC post still on its original site in the country. Farther along Front Street is the **Cornish Water Wheel**. Originally located in Barkerville, the wheel was placed here in 1930.

Farther up Front Street is the **Quesnel Hotel** that has been in operation since 1913. Prior to that, this was the site of the Occidental Hotel. Barlow Avenue is where the Chinese had their businesses and homes dating back to the 1860s. Now however, most buildings are of a newer era. At the eastern end of Barlow Street is the **Vaughan Restaurant**. It was built in 1934 by C.D. Hoy, a photographer who lived in the house with his wife and ten kids.

The **Billy Barker Hotel** and the **Quesnel Court House** were both built in 1961 although the sites originally had historical buildings dating back to the turn of the century.

Riverfront

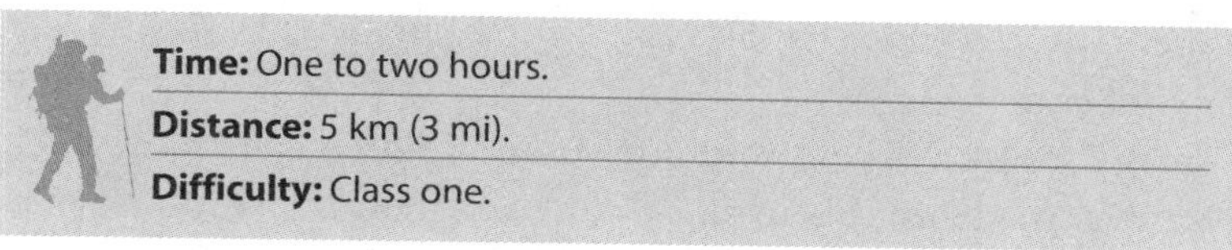

Time: One to two hours.

Distance: 5 km (3 mi).

Difficulty: Class one.

The route: This is a pleasant five-kilometer (3 mi) walk around the edge of town. The trail crosses the Fraser Bridge that was first built in 1928. It is now a walking bridge.

Trail access: Ceal Tingley Park, where the Quesnel and Fraser Rivers meet is the start of this trail but it can be picked up along other sections. The trail crosses the historical Baker Creek at the Fraser Foot Bridge. The trail is very well marked.

Pinnacles Peak

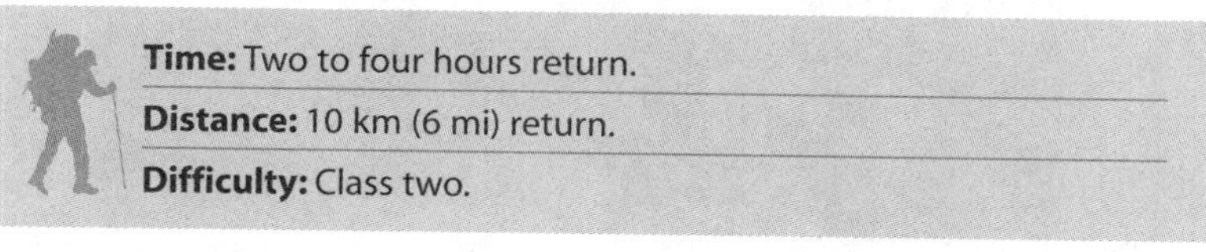

Time: Two to four hours return.

Distance: 10 km (6 mi) return.

Difficulty: Class two.

The route: This is a paved trail for the first section, following a ridge above Baker Creek. If you go all the way to the amphitheatre, you should carry class-two equipment. Since there is little change in elevation, it is not a difficult hike.

Trail access: Cross the Moffat Bridge over the Fraser River into West Quesnel and turn right at the first set of traffic lights onto Baker Drive. Follow Baker Drive for about 5.6 km (3.5 mi) up to the plateau. The road name changes to Pinnacles Road. There is a parking lot on the south side of the road, at the park entrance.

The trail: Follow the paved trail to the edge of the plateau overlooking Baker Creek. The edge of the cliff is barred by a chain-link fence all the way to the hoodoos, those wind and water sculptured rock formations created about 12 million years ago. This is really what you came to see. At the end of the fence, there is a trail leading down an arm to a spot that has better views of the hoodoos.

Beyond the fence and along the edge of the plateau, the trail crosses a cattle guard and passes through a field sometimes inhabited by cows. The path then crosses a creek and continues along the canyon rim, sometimes very close to the rim, and eventually goes downhill to the amphitheatre.

This is a wonderful walk and one young children can enjoy. Be careful once past the fence if bringing children as there are sections where the side of the hill is slipping into the valley below and the drop is steep.

Pinnacles Peak Park.

Deserter's Creek

Time: Four hours.

Distance: Nine km (5.5 mi) return.

Difficulty: Class two.

Equipment: Boots are recommended as there is some scrambling around the rocks.

The route: This trail follows a creek up to a wall of rock that has an amazing open-topped cave complete with waterfall. This maintained trail is good both summer and winter.

Trail access: Cross the Moffat Bridge into West Quesnel and continue straight ahead along Anderson Driver. The road soon changes its name to West Fraser Road. Follow it for about 20 km (12 mi) from the bridge to Narcosli Creek. Stop before the bridge over Narcosli Creek. There is a parking lot on the south side of the road.

The trail: The well-maintained trail starts across the road from the parking lot. There are signs. The path follows the Narcosli Creek to the confluence of Deserter's Creek.

You will walk through forest to an arm of the mountain where there have been steps carved into the rock for your convenience. I am not certain if it was the deserter or the club who carved the steps. The height of the arm is the greatest change in elevation for the entire walk.

Once over the steps, you will go down a trail that leads to Deserter's Creek. The trail winds through the forest most of the time. There is one section where some scrambling is required to get up from the creek level onto a shelf above the creek.

At the end of the creek there is a rock wall with a cleft where the waterfall drops about 150 m (500 ft) from the plateau above. Entry to the cave is possible. In winter there is an ice wall inside. If you want to reach the plateau above, I suggest you scramble up the south side of the wall (not inside the cave). I have not done this so I do not know if it is possible but it looks like it is.

This is my favorite hike in the Quesnel region and a great trip for kids. The waterfall is such a bonus.

Highway 26 to Barkerville/Wells

Barkerville is a provincial park that, during the summer months, has people dressed in period costume acting out the days of the gold rush. There is a charge to enter the park. However, if hiking in the mountains beyond the town-site, there is no charge to pass through town. The best book to purchase if wanting to hike in the area extensively is *Hiking the Cariboo Goldfields*, by Garry Edwards, Dorothea Funk and Ken Stoker, published by Rocky Mountain Books, 2002. Besides trail descriptions, the book has a lot of historical information pertaining to the trails.

In Barkerville and Wells, just 10 km (6 mi) apart, there are three campsites in which to stay plus numerous B & Bs and a heritage site hotel in Wells.

Groundhog Lake

Time: Eight to nine hours if returning on the same day. If only going to the Richfield Courthouse, the walk is about an hour.

Distance: Nine km (5.5 mi) to the lake, two km (1 mi) to the Courthouse. If you are going to listen to Judge Begbee hold court, check in town for times.

Difficulty: Class two to the lake, class one if going only to the Courthouse.

The route: The trail follows the old wagon road above the creek, past the Courthouse, past Cooper's Cabin and then up a steep section of Mount Agnes to Groundhog Lake. There is a cabin at the lake where hikers may stay for the night although it is patronized mostly by motor-powered enthusiasts.

Trail access: If hiking to the lake, you need not pay the entrance fee to the park. However, if just going to the Courthouse, you must pay the fee. The entrance to the park is located at the parking lot next to the town-site of Barkerville and at the eastern end of Highway 26.

The trail: From the park entrance, walk through town and follow the trail that skirts the creek. The trail ascends the mountain with a gentle incline. Along the sides of the trail are post markers indicating historical events that occurred at those places. The first stop is where Billy Barker struck gold and started the biggest gold rush north of California. See the local hiking guide for details on the claims staked along the road.

Black Jack Creek flows into the canyon from the right shortly before you come to the Courthouse. Just a few meters before the Courthouse is a tumble down log house known as Lucky Swede's cabin. Lucky was a miner who found fortune in the gold fields but, like so many others, soon lost it.

Continue up hill, along the road. The first creek past the courthouse is Walker Gulch. Continue ahead, following the ski signs to Summit Rock. There are other trails coming from the sides. These are generally used in winter for snowmobiles. Stay on the main trail. Summit Rock is about 2.5 km (1.5 mi) from the courthouse. The rock is about 3 m by 3 m (9 ft by 9 ft) in size so it is hard to miss and is located beside a meadow. A short distance beyond the rock is a sign pointing to Johnson's Bar, the local relief station.

Cross the meadow to a junction where the trail goes across the creek

Children find cave on the way to Richfield, Barkerville

or veers to the right (with a ski symbol). Follow the trail to the right along the remains of a ditch that was built during the gold rush days to channel the water flowing in the creek. There is a washout next that needs to be skirted but the way is fairly clear.

Cooper's Cabin, your next landmark, was built in 1897 and is no longer habitable. However, this is a good place to rest and refuel with a snack before doing the last 2 km (1 mi) grunt up the mountain.

Half a kilometer up the mountain, Groundhog Creek joins the Jack of Clubs Creek (the one you've been following) and then the trail is crossed by another snowmobile trail. Continue up. The lake itself is located in a cirque and was formed when the creek was dammed so the miners could control the flow of water down to the town. The cabin overlooks the lake.

Although there has been conflict between skiers, hikers, bikers and snow mobile operators as to whose domain Agnes Lake really is, the local clubs are trying to find an amiable solution for all. Please be protective of the delicate environment and courteous to those who enjoy a different sport to yours.

Murray Cabin/Waverly Cabin

Time: All day or overnight.

Distance: Three km (2 mi) to either cabin and 10.5 km (6.5 mi) if doing the Yellowhawk/Jubilee loop.

Difficulty: Class two or three. There is almost 700 m (2100 ft) in elevation change if doing the circuit.

Topo maps: Spectacle Lakes 93 H/3

The route: The most popular walk is to Murray Cabin and back out the same trail. However, you can also branch off and go to the tiny Mount Waverly Cabin. Those wanting a full day hike can do the loop going in at Yellowhawk Creek and coming out on the highway where Jubilee Creek crosses the road another 2.5 km (1.5 mi) from the Yellowhawk trailhead. For the loop, you should purchase the hiking guide for the area (see introduction to Wells/Barkerville). I have never done the loop.

Trail access: Drive from Wells toward Barkerville and turn left onto the Bowron Lake Road. Cross the Williams Creek mining operation and turn left onto the main road that leads to the Bowron Lakes. Drive just over 3 km (2 mi) to the parking lot of the Yellowhawk Trailhead. There is a large sign indicating the spot.

The trail: The trail goes into the woods, crosses a ridge then descends into a swampy area. Across the bog the trail climbs a second ridge. There is a drop toward Yellowhawk Creek about a kilometer up the trail. It then crosses the creek and starts the traverse up the mountain.

At the junction of two trails, there are signs. One sign indicates the summer trail, another indicates the Yellowhawk Summit. The trail leading to the right goes to the Mount Waverly Cabin and the trail to the left goes to Mount Murray Cabin. Both trails wind steeply up the mountain for a bit.

The trail to Murray levels out and then descends to the creek and eventually to the cabin. This is a clear and fairly easy trail to follow.

The trail leading to Waverly Cabin does not go quite as steep as the Murray Cabin Trail at the beginning but it is much farther (6 km (4 mi) from trailhead) and far more difficult to follow once past Mount Greenberry. A topo map is essential when going to Waverly Cabin.

To get there, follow the trail to the right (south) from the junction, through open forest and then across a flowered meadow. From the meadow follow a deep ravine downhill and in an easterly direction. There are ribbons along this part of the route but they are sparse. The trail follows Empire Creek for a short distance and trail work is obvious. Where the trail maintenance ends, the trail turns to the right and up a hill out of the ravine. Parts of the trail have grown over but there are ribbons on some trees showing the direction. Generally, from the creek up to the cabin, the trail is difficult to find. The cabin is on the north face of Waverly Mountain at an elevation of about 1700 m (5500 ft).

Those going to Mount Murray (the Yellowhawk loop) and Jubilee Creek must branch off before the junction to the cabins. For this circuit route, purchase the local hiking guide.

Two Sisters Mountain and Lookout Tower

Time: Nine hours.

Distance: 14 km (8.75 mi) return.

Difficulty: Class two.

Equipment: Once up the trail two kilometers, there is no easy access to water. At the top of the mountain, there are no water, firewood or toilet facilities. If you plan on spending the night, water and stove will have to be carried up.

Topo maps: Wells 93 H/4 and Spectacle Lakes 93 H/3

The route: This is a straightforward hike to a lookout tower on the highest peak in the Quesnel Highlands. From the top, parts of the Bowron Lakes can be seen. This hike is a favorite of mine.

Trail access: Drive from Wells toward Barkerville and turn left onto the Bowron Lake Road. You must pass through the Williams Creek mining area to a stop sign. From there turn left and follow the Bowron Lake Road for 17 km (10.6 mi) to the Ketchum Creek Road. Turn left and follow Ketchum for just under 5 km (3 mi). There is a sign indicating the Two Sisters Trailhead on the side of an abandoned tertiary road.

The trail: Follow the road up hill forever (it seems). The walk has sections that are less steep than others but for the most part it is up hill all day. However, it does not take long before the views supersede the need for oxygen. Within a couple of hours you will be in the alpine meadows with Chisel Lake and Little Atan Lake below.

Once near the top, the saddle, visible from the trail allows you to reach the south peak rather than staying on the road and going to the lookout tower. The scramble up to the south peak is difficult and occasionally requires handholds on outcrops to get higher. However, the climb is well worth the effort as the views are second to none in the area.

If you stay on the road to the tower, you will come to the most difficult part of the hike. The road is steep and littered with loose rocks making the footing unstable. However, once at the tower (which is open and provides shelter), the views are worth every panting breath. More of the Bowron Lake chain comes into view along with the Mowdish Range, Tediko Peaks and McLeod Peaks.

There is no water, firewood or toilet facilities at the tower so if you are planning on staying overnight, you must bring it all with you.

Highway 97 Quesnel to Prince George

Hixon Creek Waterfall

Time: Ten minutes.

Distance: Half a kilometer.

Difficulty: Class one.

The route: This is a rugged waterfall that is located just beyond a well-used picnic site. There is also a second trail near the parking lot, at the top of the hill that leads down to some rapids on the creek where bird watching is very good.

Trail access: Turn left 0.9 km (0.5 mi) south of the Hixon Bridge; east onto the Hixon Creek Road. This road is between the store (gas station and bus stop) and the bridge. Take the left fork when you come to it and follow the road for 3.6 km (2.25 mi). There is a parking lot on the north side of the road.

The trail: At the back of the parking lot there is a sign that leads to the trail down the hill to the rapids. This is for those wanting to see birds.

To get to the waterfall, walk east along the road (downhill) for about 200 m (600 ft). Follow the marked trail along the creek to the canyon. These waterfalls drop about 100 m (300 ft) and in high water are quite spectacular. This is also a nice picnic spot.

Buckhorn Lake/Frost Lake

Time: One hour to all day.

Distance: A few kilometers up to 25 km (15 mi) if going to Frost Lake.

Difficulty: Class one or two.

Route summary: Should you need a leg stretcher, the trail from Buckhorn Lake up hill through the forest is lovely. If you want a full day's excursion, a walk or cycle to Frost Lake is nice. It has a moderate amount of up and downhill. If walking, it will take at least ten hours to return but if cycling, it shouldn't take more than five hours.

Trail access: Drive south on Highway 97 from Prince George to the Buckhorn Lake Road. Turn left and follow the road for about 20 km (12.5 mi) and park at the lake. There is a Forest Service camping site and, in the summer, it is possible to swim in this lake. It is stocked with rainbow trout and motorboats are allowed on the lake.

The trail: Cross the road from the lake at the east end (near the outhouses) and walk along this road and the skidder trail, up hill, through thick deciduous forest. There are about three creeks which cross the trail but they offer no challenge. There are some very old cars along the side of the trail. This skidder trail eventually runs into the Frost Lake road. If you don't mind walking on a road, the walk into Frost Lake is nice. Once on the Frost Lake road turn left and continue uphill. At the top, you get a good view of the surrounding hills. The lake has a nice picnic area. In spring and fall this is a very silent walk. During summer months there are occasionally vehicles along this road and in winter there are snowmobiles.

Frost Lake trail adjoins the Buckhorn Lake Trail

Francis Lake

Time: Eight hours.

Distance: 23 km (14 mi).

Difficulty: Class two.

Elevation change: Almost none.

Trail summary: If you need a nice walk in the woods during the fringe seasons this is an excellent choice. There are creeks and swamps, hills and forests where wildlife abounds. Except for Perspiration Pass, these trails are also good for cycling.

Trail access: Drive south on Highway 97 to the Buckhorn Lake Road. Follow the road for about 25 km (15 mi) to Francis Lake. There are forestry signs indicating to which lake the side roads lead. If there is snow, parking at the side of the Buckhorn Road is fine.

The trail: The walk from the road leads over a creek and to the west side of Francis Lake. In summer, this road can be driven. To walk to Frost Lake, take the fork to the left before reaching the picnic tables and campsite.

You may also go straight ahead, over Perspiration Pass and down to the Frost Lake trail. This is a nice little grunt to the top. On the Frost Lake side of the hill, the trail disappears so you must head down through the bush. Once on the road, turn left and walk back to the Buckhorn road. Turn left again to get back to Francis Lake.

If you are not going over Perspiration Pass take the first left hand fork before the campsite at Francis Lake and then take the first right hand fork and follow that trail. It eventually comes to a creek/swamp area where a bridge over the creek is partially in place.

About three hours after leaving the car, you will come to another road. Going left and back to your car would be a very long day unless you are on a bike. Turning right will eventually take you to the campsite at Opatcho Lake and in turn back to the Buckhorn road, albeit a long way from your car. Walking back the same way you came is recommended. The scenery is not exceptional but because it is low in elevation, it can be walked early (or late) in the season and wildlife is fairly abundant; especially birds.

Highway 16 East

From Prince George to the Alberta border

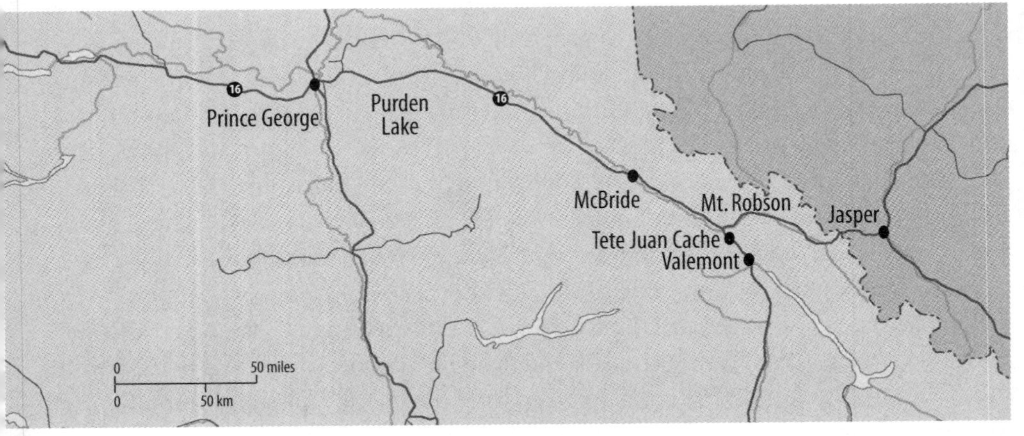

Prince George

Prince George, with three pulp mills, can be rather unattractive at times. However, the friendliness of the people makes up for any missing glamour. Located in the center of the province, the town is a good base from which to hike either in the McGregor Mountains to the north, the Western Rockies to the east or the eastern foothills of the Coast Mountains to the west.

There are hotels and restaurants to suit almost any taste/budget. Café Voltaire at Books and Co. on 3rd Ave is reputed to be the best bohemian hangout in Western Canada. There is the Second Cup at Parkwood Mall. There are many non-franchised coffee shops in the down town area. The Achillion Restaurant, that has stayed in business for more than twenty years because of the delicious food, is conveniently located in the heart of the city. The Vietnamese and Indian restaurants available are so good they could compete with restaurants in their own countries.

If you enjoy hiking in the area, purchase the *Prince George and District Trail Guide*, edited by Dave King and Bob Nelson, published by the Caledonia Ramblers (now in its 8th edition). Although the production looks like a homemade job, the trail information is accurate and the price is right. The book is a money raiser for the local hiking club, the Caledonia

Ramblers. They do most of the work on the trails and they lobby for the preservation of land. If you wish to join the Ramblers for any of their hikes, visit the web page at www.unbc.ca/~ramblers/.

Beaver Lakes

Time: One hour.

Distance: Two km (1 mi).

Difficulty: Class one.

Trail access: Follow Foothills Blvd (located at the end of 1st, 5th or 15th Ave. and take the Cranbrook Hill Road located between 5th and 15th. The road is steep. Follow it for 1.5 km (1 mi) and turn left onto Kueng Road. Follow that to the end and park.

The trail: This trail is also accessible from behind the university and is part of the Greenway Trail (see below). Follow the mud/gravel road straight ahead and through the clearing that is rapidly growing over. Walk for about 20 minutes, some times uphill. After about half an hour the road divides. Take the right hand fork to the first lake about half a kilometer farther. This is a pretty spot with views of the Prince George bowl from a few places. The lake is surrounded by bush and often beaver or ducks can be seen on the water. There is a picnic table and a dock at the lake.

Greenway

Time: Half an hour to five hours.

Distance: One km (0.5 mi) to 18 km (11 mi)

Difficulty: Class one/two.

The route: This system of connecting trails is on Cranbrook Hill and behind the university. You can walk to a couple of tiny lakes, the water tower that overlooks the city or all the way to Otway, 18 km (11 mi) away. At Otway there is another group of connecting trails although they are used mostly in winter for skiing. No dogs are allowed on the Otway section. Prince George skiers are a bit uptight about doggie dodo.

Trail access: Follow 15th Ave uphill to the first right-hand turn off after the road leading to the university campus. Follow this road (it goes behind the university student residences) for a few hundred feet and park in the parking lot. There are trail signs and maps indicating where you can go and where you are in the trail system.

There is a public bus that runs from down town to the university so that is an option if a car is not available.

The trail: The trails to the two little lakes are fairly clear and can take anywhere from half an hour on up to as long as you want to stay. One trail goes to the campsite on Highway 16 West.

The walk to Otway takes about five or six hours in all. However, the Otway walk passes mostly through forest and does not give any appreciable views. The plant life is interesting and there is the chance of seeing a moose. This walk is a good spring break-in because it is not across high elevations. This trail is popular in the winter for cross-country skiers.

The first two km (1 mi) is fairly flat and comes to the junction of the trail leading to the Forestry lookout. Continue to the left. There are signs and kilometer markings all the way along the trail but no resting benches. The trail is wide and well maintained.

At about km 8, you may turn to the left to a lake that is rich in bird life. At about kilometer eight, there is a creek and swamp. Then a steep up hill which is quite muddy during the run-off season and during high rains.

Once near Otway you will pass a farm, cross a road and then enter the Otway Trail system. At the Otway cabin there is a phone should you need to call a taxi or friend to pick you up.

Tabor Mountain

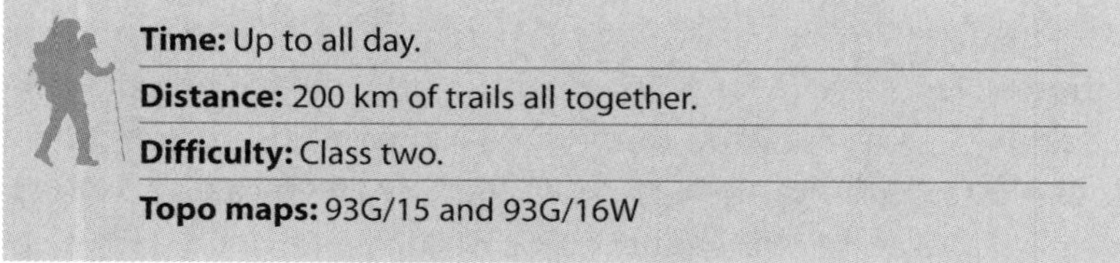

Time: Up to all day.

Distance: 200 km of trails all together.

Difficulty: Class two.

Topo maps: 93G/15 and 93G/16W

Trail summary: This mountain is used in both summer and winter. There are trails going everywhere and even one that goes across the mountains over to Frost Lake (accessible by vehicle from Highway 97 South (see

Buckhorn Lake/Frost Lake Trail). There are also three cabins on the mountain that make good destinations for a stop or overnight stay.

Trail access: There are numerous ways to get to the mountain with two accesses off Highway 16 near the Tabor Mountain Ski Hill. The first is at the Caledonia Nordic Ski Club cabin and the second is at Bowes Creek. Both have parking spots and signs indicating where they are.

The other access area is from the west side of Tabor Mountain. To get there, follow Highway 16 east to the Tabor Lake turn-off where the Log Cabin Restaurant is located. Follow Highway 16A past Bonnet Hill to Groveburn Road. Follow Groveburn (turn south, the only way you can turn) and follow this to areas that look like trailheads. They are. Or you can follow Groveburn that turns into MOT Road all the way up to the top of Tabor Minor (in summer).

I cannot begin to describe the trails on this mountain. However, no matter which way you decide to go, be certain to take note of your direction because you could end up a long way from your car when you finally decide to go home. The other alternative is to purchase the local hiking guide with its detailed map of Tabor Mountain. All trails are marked and intercross each other. This is a spectacular exercise area and highly recommended for those wanting anything from a short few hours to a full day going to Frost Lake.

Willow River Interpretive Trail

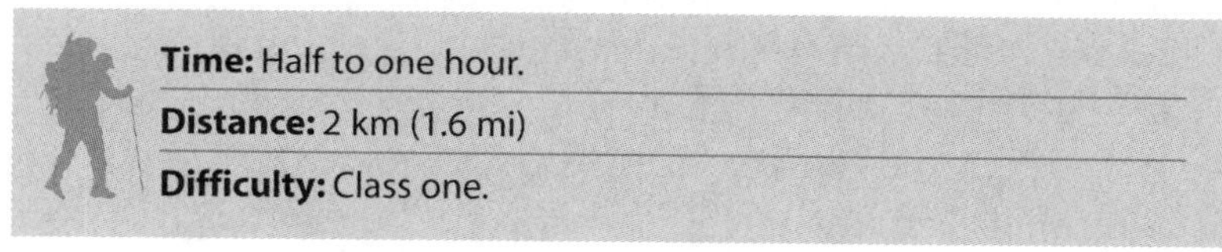

Time: Half to one hour.

Distance: 2 km (1.6 mi)

Difficulty: Class one.

The route: This trail follows the Willow River south through a new forest to a canyon that in the mid 1970s took the lives of eight canoeists. A fire went through the area in 1961 and the new growth has both deciduous and coniferous trees of substantial size.

Trail access: Drive east on Highway 16 for 32 km (20 mi) to the Willow River bridge. Stop just before the bridge and look for the trailhead on the north side of the highway.

The trail: This is an easy trail with no substantial ups or downs. However, the lookout over the canyon section where eight high-school students lost their lives in the 1970s is an impressive sight. During canoe season, you may often see kayakers going along the river to the pullout just under the bridge.

Raven Lake/Grizzly Den

Time: Nine to 10 hours if doing the circuit. Two and a half hours to either Grizzly Den or Raven Lake cabin from Eight-mile cabin near the car park.

Distance: 4 km (2.5 mi) to either cabin, 12 km (7.5 mi) for the circuit.

Difficulty: Class two/three.

Topo maps: 93H McBride (1:250,000)

The route: The hike has been a popular destination for over 30 years for those living in the area. In order to help keep it pristine, it has recently been made into a park. There are three cabins on this route, all available for hikers to overnight. The Eight-mile cabin, just one quick jog up a hill, is close to the parking lot. However, the road from Highway 16 East to the parking lot is open only in summer. If going in during the snow season, you must ski/hike the 12 km (7.5 mi) in.

Trail access: From Prince George travel 89 km (55.6 mi) east to Hungry Creek Road. The road is about 200 m beyond the Hungry Creek sign and 28 km (17.5 mi) past Purden Lake. Turn right and follow Hungry Creek road for 13 km (8.1 mi) to a spot where you may park (there is a sign) if going to Grizzly Den. If you wish to go to Raven Lake Cabin, continue along the Hungry Creek road for another 2.5 km (1.6 mi) to a landing on the left where vehicles may park. There is a sign showing the way through the bush, across a log over the creek and up the trail.

The trail: To Grizzly Den, from the parking spot, head through the thick willow following the markers on the trees, to a log that crosses the creek. From there continue up the hill along the trail to Eight-mile cabin. This will take about half an hour. The cabin has recently been fixed up and staying here is comfortable. In August, the huckleberries are abundant both on this trail and the one going to Raven Lake.

From Eight-mile cabin follow the trail through the bush and up the mountain. There are creeks running across the trail where drinking water can be obtained. There is a swamp that must be crossed about 45 minutes before you reach Grizzly Den cabin. Often people carry rubber boots to get across this spot but during dry spells, the "meadow" is quite dry.

For those doing the circuit, continue behind the Grizzly Den cabin and up to the pass that is visible to the west (behind the cabin). It will take about 45 minutes to get to the pass. On the west side of the pass, head to the lakes below and continue along the trail. There are some trail markers but the section between the lakes and the avalanche slope on the side of the hill on the west is occasionally difficult to find. Go slowly and watch for markers. Raven Lake is tucked into a cirque and the ridges around the lake are good to climb. This is one of the prettiest lakes in the region.

The cabins are bare bones so you must bring all your equipment with you. If they are full, you will have to use a tent.

Longworth Lookout Tower

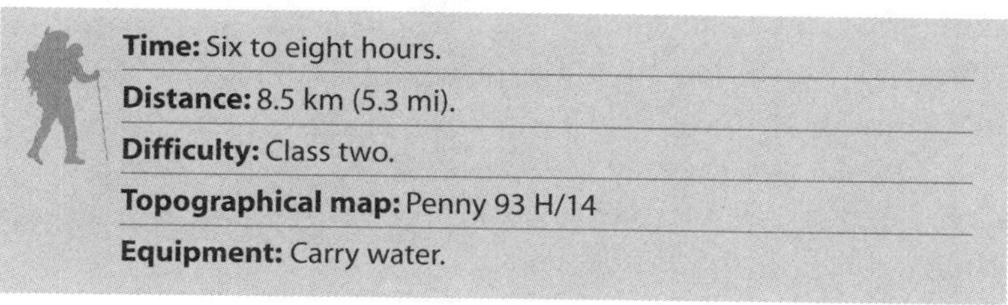

Time: Six to eight hours.

Distance: 8.5 km (5.3 mi).

Difficulty: Class two.

Topographical map: Penny 93 H/14

Equipment: Carry water.

The route: This is an interesting trail that starts in forest and takes you to enticing alpine. There are two abandoned cabins and the lookout tower to explore. There is also a creatively designed lawn chair just waiting for you to plop into once you make it to the top. Because of the elevation gain, this is not an easy hike.

Trail access: Drive east along Highway 16 to the Bowron Lake Forest Service Road. Turn north and follow the road until you reach the washed out (at time of writing) Fraser River bridge. Continue to the right passing both McGregor and Sinclair Mills. When you come to a four-way junction, turn left onto Longworth South Road. There is a large log cabin on the corner. Follow the road across the tracks to an old gravel pit. Park here.

The trail: Follow the road leading into the trees through the cedar forest. Some of the trees are huge. The trail moves gently for a while and then has a spurt of serious up hill. The trail is well marked.

At the junction that takes less than an hour to reach, follow the right hand fork and start up the hill. The trail is wide and clear. The switchbacks are long and pleasant. You will pass one small spring that has a muddy base. Best to carry water.

Cabin on the way up to Longworth.

Once into the sub alpine, you will come to an abandoned cabin that was occupied by the early forestry workers who wanted a change of scenery from the tower. The cabin would not offer shelter in bad weather. The trail continues up from the cabin and moves onto an arm of the mountain that leads to the tower. Below the arm you will see a second abandoned cabin but this one is in poorer shape than the first. You also must go downhill to reach it.

The lookout is in good shape and offers warmth during bad weather. There are many ridges that could be explored beyond the tower. The only downside of staying up here is that water must be carried.

If you are interested in hiking to old fire lookout towers, purchase *Fire Lookout Hikes in the Canadian Rockies*, by Mike Potter, published by Luminous Compositions in Banff.

Ozalinka

Time: Six hours return.

Distance: 12 km (7.5 mi).

Difficulty: Class two or three.

The route: This trail follows a creek before breaking into the open. From the meadows it is another 30 to 45 minutes to the cabin. During bad weather, the cabin is difficult to find.

Trail access: Follow Highway 16 west of McBride to the Dore River Road. Turn south on the Dore River Road and follow it. The pavement ends about 2 km (1 mi) after the turnoff. Within a short distance the road crosses Dore River. At 6.3 km (3.9 mi), take the right fork. After crossing Dore again, the road climbs uphill while veering to the right. Stay on the main road until a fork at 15 km (9.4 mi). Take the right-hand fork that crosses the Dore again and continue another 4 km (2.5 mi) to trailhead located on the right hand (west) side of the road.

The trail: The trail follows the creek through the bush, along the bank for at least an hour's walking time. It can be wet and muddy and at times you must scramble over deadfall and debris. You will eventually cross the creek and come into an open meadow. The trail is clear to the meadow. From the beginning of the meadow to the cabin is less than an hour. Stay in the main valley going uphill. Once at the cabin, the exploration possibilities are endless. There are lots of animal tracks in the area.

Going into the Ozalinka cabin.

Dunster

Time: Eight to ten hours.

Difficulty: Class three.

Equipment: Water must be carried.

Topo map: 83 E/4 Croydon

The route: This is a long steep hike (it goes up 1250 m/4100 ft) that should be done on a clear day so the views of Rocky Mountain Trench and Mt. Robson can be appreciated. There is a lake and a tiny cabin at the top. The cabin should not be a destination after the snow falls. By the time the snow has reached the Robson valley floor, the cabin would probably be covered and finding it would be impossible. This is my favorite hike in the area.

Trail access: Follow Highway 16 east to the Dunster turnoff, located on the south side of the highway between McBride and Tete Jaune Cache. Follow the road down and across the Fraser River Bridge, also known as the Flower Bridge. Locals decided to decorate their bridge with flowers to make it far more attractive than what government officials want. The government sent painters in to cover the flowers. The locals repainted the flowers. They are still on the bridge today.

Bob Lake at the top of Dunster Trail.

Continue, turning left at the end of the road. Turn left at Pepper road and then within 100 meters turn right. There are signs indicating Raush Valley.

You will not go through the town of Dunster when going to the mountain. However, it is recommended that you do visit the town, have ice cream and meet some of the locals.

Park in the gravel pit at the end of the road (after you have made the right turn). The trail starts at the far end of the gravel pit. You may also start walking on an old road that is beyond the trail but it takes a longer route and eventually joins the main trail further up the mountain.

The trail: Once on the trail above the gravel pit, continue up for about two hours where you will come to the first viewpoint. The trail is mossy and steep but well maintained. Sandals are not recommended for this hike. When I decided to do this one, I had all my gear on the front steps of my house while I waited for my friend to pick me up. We threw everything into the trunk of her car and headed out. At trailhead, I realized that I had left my boots on the front steps. My friend gave me her boots and hiked up in Tiva sandals. Not easy.

Ten minutes after the first viewpoint, the trail descends a bit before climbing up again on the opposite side of a small gully. It takes about three and a half hours to get above tree line.

Once above tree line you must cross a rocky slide area and then go down to the lake. At tree line, the views of some walls in Kakwa Park come into view as does Mount Robson massif.

Past the slide area, follow a dry creek bed around the side of the mountain until Bob Lake comes into view. There is a tiny cabin on the north side of the lake. Since the views are so impressive, this hike should only be done during good weather.

Beyond the lake you may continue up valley for views of the Raush Valley and River. It is well worth the walk. If you take this hike during the shorter days of autumn, the colored leaves of the trees and the soft light of early evening will help make your photos spectacular.

Little Lost Lake

Time: Two hours.

Distance: 4 km (2.5 mi).

Difficulty: Class two.

Equipment needed: Water and a snack.

The route: This is a nice leg-stretcher or lunch break to be enjoyed when traveling along Highway 16 east and wanting a walk that is not inundated with tourists. The trail also has one of the biggest fir trees in the area, a waterfall and a picnic table near the lake.

Trail access: Follow Highway 16 east past the Highway 5 turnoff about 1.5 km (1 mi) and park at the avalanche gate east of the weigh scales. The trail starts at a BC Forest Service trail sign about 100 m (300 ft) back of the gate and on the north side of the road. The Fraser River is to the south.

The trail: Follow the trail from the Forest Service sign up through fir, spruce and aspen to an old roadbed that continues for a short distance. The road was built as a fire fighting access in the 1960s.

At a fork in the road just before the lake is the largest Douglas Fir tree ever spotted by Art Carson (see introduction to Valemount) in all his years of exploring the area.

Either direction at the fork leads you through a lush avalanche slope. If going right, the trail will take you on a circle tour around the lake beginning with a view of the waterfall. Continue around the lake and arrive at the picnic table. Should you want to continue up the hill after the first waterfall, there is a trail going off to the right. Follow it to a second waterfall. The views from here are excellent.

On the way down, should you miss the branch of the trail that leads directly to your car, do not worry. By continuing along the trail, you will end at the weigh scale along the highway.

Swift Current Creek

Time: Two to three hours to the gravel flats; overnight to the cabin and headwall. If going to the cabin and back, at a very fast walking speed, it would take a minimum of eight hours. You may also mountain bike to the cabin.

Distance: 3 km (2 mi) to the gravel flats, 8 km (5 mi) to the cabin.

Difficulty: Class one and three.

The route: This trail goes through a corner of Mt. Robson Provincial Park and then turns up Swift Current Creek Valley. Although not difficult to the cabin, the exploring beyond the cabin is not for the inexperienced.

Trail access: From Tete Jaune Junctions, follow Highway 16 east to the Swift Current Creek Bridge just beyond the weigh scales. Immediately before the bridge is a road to the north. Follow this road to an area of young trees. This was a sawmill years ago. There is a trailhead sign in the opening. Park here.

The trail: Follow the old road for 2 km (1 mi) to the Mt. Robson Park sign. Shortly after the sign is a bridge over a stream. The road then disappears. At km 3 (2 mi) you will be at the gravel flats. Many people hike only to the flats. If you wish to explore the flats, keep to the left of the main creek. When facing upstream you will see a beaver pond at the base of an avalanche slope. To go upstream, you will have to cross the stream at least twice. During hot weather, the stream, because it is fed by a glacier, rises quickly during the day.

To the Cabin: From the flats the exact distances are not available. Beyond the beaver pond the road can be found again along the gravel flats. This is easy hiking. Nestled between the east branch of the creek and a rocky cliff at the very end of the gravel flats is a small cabin built originally by former residents of the area. The cabin is tiny but open for public use. It is first come, first served so if the weather is good and it looks like others may be there, be certain to have a tent in which to sleep. Please keep the cabin clean.

To the Headwall: There are more gravel flats and a spectacular headwall farther up the valley. First climb the pole ladder up the cliff near the cabin door, then traverse upstream parallel to the creek, descending to the creek when you are beyond the cliffs. Here, a cottonwood tree has been felled across the creek. Cross the creek on the tree and make your way through the forest to the base of the mountain. Animal trails may be picked up that will lead up the valley and along the base of the mountain until it is possible to return to the creek again. Proceed upstream through increasingly open streamside areas to the headwall. This is a great spot with the water cascading down from the top of the mountain.

Note that it is not advisable to return to the cabin along the west side of the creek (right facing downstream) because steep cliffs drop straight into fast water at some points along the creek. Once at the cliffs you will have to turn and walk back to the cabin by the same way as you came.

The above description was provided by Art Carson of Valemount (see below for further contact information).

Yellowhead Pass/Mountain

Time: 4 – 6 hours.

Distance: 10 km (6 mi).

Difficulty: Class two.

Topographical maps: Rainbow 83D/15

Equipment needed: You must carry water.

Yellowhead Pass Trail.

The route: Used for about 150 years, until the railway was built, this was the main walkway for fur traders and gold seekers to cross the Canadian Rockies. Today, the early part of this hike is a popular hangout for elk. The trail is mostly through poplar, birch and pine forest and is fairly wide and well cleared. This is a nice walk if camping at the Lucerne Campsite and in need of an after lunch leg stretcher.

Trail access: Drive east along Highway 16 beyond the Highway 5 turnoff for Valemount. From the Lucerne Campsite on the north side of the road, drive for for 1.6 km (1 mi). Turn north onto a gravel road, to the railway tracks. There is a small parking spot on the south side of the tracks.

The trail: Cross the tracks and follow the road west to the trailhead. The walk is mostly up hill and fairly steep for about 45 minutes. Along here you will get your first views of the Yellowhead Lake and Mount Fitzwilliam.

The next noticeable landmark is a grove of wind-toppled pines where a freak tunnel of wind in 1985 blew through and left its devastation. The trail continues along the ridge.

The next 45 minutes takes you through a wet swamp and after another half hour the trail disappears. On the trees there are markers to follow across the swamps (positive types call this a meadow). From the swamp (some call this a meadow) continue toward the west and up the valley for as far as you wish to go. Be sure to watch for elk, especially if coming down at dusk.

Mount Fitzwilliam

Time: Long day or overnight.

Distance: 26 km (16 mi) return.

Difficulty: Class three.

Topographical maps: Rainbow 83D/15, Jasper 83D/16

Equipment needed: Carry water to the top and overnight gear if staying the night.

The route: This is a steep hike but once on top of course, the rewards are well worth the effort. I was lucky the last time I came up this trail. It was pouring rain and quite cool so the alpines were covered in mist. Once on top, the sun came out and stayed out until I was partway down again.

Trail access: Drive east for 3 km (2 mi) from the Lucerne Campsite and turn north into the Yellowhead Boat Launch. Park here. Cross the highway on foot and follow the sign that directs you to the trail.

The trail: Once on the base of the hill on the south side of the highway, follow the old roadbed west to a park trail sign describing some of the wildlife found in the area. This is where you start the long upward climb. The trail is wide and well maintained. There is no drinking water until the campsite and Rockingham Creek.

At about kilometer five, there is a branch in the trail. If you take the left-hand fork, you will come into the campsite from the creek. On the right-hand fork it will take longer to reach the same spot. The right-hand fork is better groomed. The campsite has flat pads for tents and a few rings for campfires. The wood does appear to be getting a bit thin so I would suggest using a stove. There are many comforts here like cut logs for stools, poles for tarps, and trails to the water.

Rockingham Creek Bridge is a bit rickety but certainly safe enough and it beats fording the creek. It rages here at certain times of the year. The trail is no longer a highway but now becomes a rocky path, slippery when wet. There are some small creeks to maneuver and a swampy area to cross. At the swamp, watch for markers to help you through the scrub willow.

From the swamp head toward the wall of rock, cross a slide area that is inhabited with picas, and then turn south to get to the Fitzwilliam basin. Once on top, you will find signs at the end of the slide area indicating a campsite. Continue past the second slide area under Mt. Fitzwilliam, past Bucephalus Peak, and Kataka Mountain. There are small alpine lakes (still frozen in June) and wonderful little coves to tuck into that are out of the wind. The hike down is by the same route as you came.

Mount Robson

At 3954 meters (12,850 ft) above the sea, Mount Robson is the highest point in British Columbia's Rocky Mountains. Records indicate that the mountain was named in the early 1800s after Colin Robertson who was a factor for the Hudson's Bay Company. Mt. Robson Park was formed in 1913, the same year that the difficult peak was conquered by Conrad Kain.

Since this is the most popular backpacking route in the Canadian Rockies, park officials feel that visitor control is necessary which means they

Mount Robson, the highest peak in the BC Rockies.

permit only a predetermined number of people per day to go up to Berg Lake. They accept some reservations (I believe 20% of the available campsites can be booked in advance). Leave yourself a day or two lee-way just in case you can't go up the day you arrive.

No dogs are permitted on this trail but there is a kennel in the area where you can board your dog while you hike. There are no open fires allowed so a stove and fuel is necessary. However there is a comfortable shelter at Berg Lake where meals can be cooked and you can warm up if the weather is foul. There is a daily camping fee ($8 per person) that may be paid at the information center or collected by a visiting warden after you have set up camp.

In our English/French bilingual country, there was once a sign posted at the washbasin outside the shelter at Berg Lake written in English, German and Japanese, informing people about the rules. It has since been removed.

There are campsites with running water, showers and shelters near the base of Mt. Robson. The restaurant near the Park Office serves expensive cafeteria-style food that is not worth the price. I guess this means you should bring your own and eat at a picnic table.

Mount Robson/Berg Lake

Time: Minimum two days for the very strong and five days for those wanting to explore more than just the lake.

Distance: 40 km (25 mi) return to Berg Lake.

Difficulty: Class four.

Topographical map: Mt. Robson 83E/3

Equipment needed: If you can manage it, take a bicycle to the far end of the Kinney Lake flats. There is a rack where bikes can be chained. I have never heard of a problem with anything disappearing and I personally have never had a problem.

The route: The first 8 km (5 mi) may be cycled which makes the trip seem much shorter. Some choose to make the campsite at Kinney Lake their final destination while others like to spend days going to the passes beyond Berg Lake. After Kinney Lake there is a steep climb through the Valley-of-a-Thousand-Falls, Mt. Robson's most beautiful passage way. This upward section continues for a total of 7 km (4.5 mi) although not all of it is steep. The top is crowned by Berg Lake often dotted with chunks of ice falling from the glacier that spews down from Robson's peak.

Trail access: The park is 100 km (60 mi) west of Jasper town site. Greyhound buses will stop at the view point/information center and the walk from there to the trailhead is only two kilometers.

The trail: Cars can be left at the parking lot next to the trailhead. The trail is wide and well maintained and follows the Robson River up valley to Kinney Lake. The first section passes through lush, semi-rain forest caused from the moisture that passes from the Pacific and collects on this high peak. This also means bring good rain gear.

A little bridge crosses the water being drained from Kinney Lake. The lake's green color is caused by the rock that has been ground to flour by the moving glaciers located above. The lake is named after George B. Kinney, one of the first mountaineers who tried to scale the peak in 1907 and again in 1909. This section of the trail, still well defined, goes through the trees.

The Kinney Lake campsite at kilometer seven has numerous tent sites that are well spaced in the forest thus insuring some privacy. There is also a covered shelter and outhouses near the lake. Wood is no longer available and the stove in the shelter has been removed. Open fires are not permitted. From the campsite continue along the side of the lake through the trees, to the flats. Just before the end of the valley is a bicycle parking lot. The outwash of the flats is the result of spring run off from the Robson River when it drains the upper reaches of the valley.

If cycling, this is the end of the easy part. The next 3 km (2 mi) is along the Robson River through the Valley-of-a-Thousand-Falls. It is straight up (450 vertical meters) and by far the most difficult part of the trip.

Whitehorn Campsite, at kilometer 10.5 is just over the suspension bridge that gets hikers across the Robson River. This is a good campsite for those wanting to take two days to reach the top. A kilometer past the campsite is another suspension bridge that leads back over the Robson River.

A second set of steep switchbacks start about a kilometer past the campsite. Just half a kilometer up the steep part is the first of three waterfalls known as White Falls. These are the least impressive of the three.

Emperor Falls, Mount Robson

Falls of the Pool (the second waterfall) is my favorite waterfall on the trip and is mid-point between the three. Looking down (there is a fence) you can see how over the years the water has carved a deep hole into the rock.

Within the next kilometer and a half you will come to Emperor Falls and its viewpoint. Leave your pack along the trail and follow the trail to the right through the trees to the falls. These are the most dramatic of the falls along the valley and you can even walk in behind them if the outflow is not too heavy. Plan on getting wet if you do this. There is a campsite just beyond the falls but it is often damp and although not as crowded, it doesn't offer the same degree of comfort as the chalet at Berg Lake.

The trail flattens from Emperor Falls onward and the views of Mt. Robson and Berg Glacier draw you toward the lake. Once at the lake the trail follows the north side through the trees to the chalet and campsite.

The end of the day is at about kilometer 20. There are two far less populated campsites just half a kilometer and two kilometers farther up the trail past the chalet.

Side trips: Two kilometers up the trail from the chalet is the park boundary, a little lake and the height of this walk, **Robson Pass** at 1652 m (5370 ft). Behind the chalet is a lovely hike along the creek up to **Toboggan Falls**. Follow the trail north from the chalet on the west side of the creek. **Snowbird Pass** is another favorite, long day hike from the chalet. To get there, walk toward Robson Pass. There is a sign indicating the direction of Snowbird Pass. The trail crosses over a flat washout area and a lake holding some of the melt water of the Robson Glacier. The trail finally follows the ridge of the lateral moraine along the side of the mountain to the pass. There are some difficult spots that have been reinforced and made safe with hand rails. If you are quick and want a really long day, you can go down into the Snowbird Valley on the east side of the pass over to another trail that will connect into the North Boundary trail and back to Berg Lake. Going to Snowbird Pass is my favorite walk from the chalet.

Highway 5

South to Clearwater

Valemount

Valemount is a community that caters to the outdoor enthusiast. The town is surrounded by snow-capped mountains, which are used for hiking in summer and heli-skiing or snow mobiling in winter. There are numerous cafés and motels, a campsite and outfitters who will go to extremes to give you the outdoor thrill you want.

If you find the area irresistible and want to know more than this book provides about hiking in the surrounding mountains, please go to the tourist information office. They will either give you detailed information on your desired routes or put you in touch with Art Carson, the hiking guru of the area. Art is also the man with whom I conferred for trail descriptions around Valemount and the Robson Valley. His descriptions are accurate and to be trusted. He is a strong hiker so judge yourself accordingly when using his descriptions. I found that my times were much longer than his.

Should you want information about hiking in the area from Art before you arrive please e-mail him at acarson@vis.bc.ca. You may also visit his website at www.carsonelectronics.ca. for other trail descriptions not recommended in this book. Since Art is a very busy man, he may take a few days to answer your e-mail questions. Be patient.

The Yellowhead Outdoor Recreation Association has maintained cabins in the mountains that are always a draw for hikers. These cabins may be booked through the Raven Office Service in Valemount, phone 250-566-4225. The town has also produced a visitor's map that has many of the smaller trails marked on it. You may obtain one at the Visitor Center in town.

RW Starratt Wildlife Refuge Trail

Time: Up to two hours.

Distance: Up to 4 km (3 mi).

Difficulty: Class one. This is an easy walk with a high chance of seeing wildlife, especially at dawn and dusk.

The route: The trail follows a dyke built in 1983 around the marsh near town where bird life is especially plentiful.

Trail access: Follow Highway 5 south of Valemount to the edge of Cranberry Marsh. There are signs indicating the trailhead and a parking area is available. However, this is so close to town (I'd say in town) that a vehicle is not needed to get to trailhead.

The trail: The trail follows the dyke built for Ducks Unlimited to enhance waterfowl habitat in the marsh. At the end of the dyke, trails lead to the right via another dyke and back to the highway or to the left through patches of wetland forest to a viewing platform. There are many interpretive signs along the boardwalks.

Following the left fork will take you around the marsh. Continue to and through an abandoned farm field, then follow the road on the far side. At a prominent trail sign, turn left onto a trail paralleling McKirdy Road, past a picnic site to a set of stairs. Climb the stairs and walk west on McKirdy Road to Aspen Street. It is paved. Follow Aspen in a southerly direction to 17th Avenue. Signs point out the trail. Walk west along 17th to Ash then turn south again and walk toward the marsh. At the south end of Ash a trail leads to the west and back to your vehicle.

Mount Terry Fox

Time: Minimum ten hours.

Distance: 6 km (3.5 mi) one way.

Difficulty: Class three.

Equipment needed: Water must be carried.

The route: This is a difficult hike up steep terrain, covering a substantial vertical and horizontal distance. The elevation gain to the peak is about 1800 meters (6000 ft). You should be fit if wanting to get to the top and back in a day. Do this hike during the longer days of summer rather than during the fringe seasons when the days are shorter. There is no place to camp or to obtain water on the way up. The trail follows an arm or ridge between two creek valleys. Terry Fox was a Canadian hero, a young man afflicted with bone cancer who, with one prosthetic leg, ran part way across Canada raising money for cancer research. On his last run, he was stopped by his disease at Thunder Bay, where he died.

Trail access: Follow Highway 5 north from Valemount to Stone Road, across from the Mount Terry Fox rest area. Turn right onto Stone Road and then left onto Tinsley Road. Cross the tracks and follow the signs to the off-limits gravel pit. Turn left before getting to the pit.

The trail: There are seventeen switchbacks along the first section of the trail that leads to a ridge that is below tree line. Once at the ridge, you are less than half way to the summit. Near the tree line are some dead standing trees, covered in a luminous moss that makes this spot look like a Disney creation.

Mount Terry Fox, a hell of a grunt.

The ridge you have followed separates Teepee Creek on the right (going up) and Hogan Creek on the left. Teepee actually looks like it could also be a nice creek to follow to get near the summit.

At tree line, the trail opens but becomes less distinct. Note the outcrop above and slightly to the left. Stay to the right of the outcrop and work your way up and around. There are cairns to guide the way. Your destination is beyond the next sub peak that has the radio tower on top.

Once at the radio tower, the peak of Mt. Terry Fox comes into view. Past the radio tower (and heading to TF peak) with Teepee Creek still on the right and Hogan below, you will dip a bit to some tiny lakes. These are the headwaters of Terry Fox Creek that flows into the Fraser River.

To get to the summit, follow the slope beyond the lakes until you can go no higher. Should you want to continue exploring these mountains for a multi-day hike, please contact Art Carson in Valemount. He will give you detailed information about what is beyond the peak.

Return by the same route as you went up or work your way in a north westerly direction along Jackman Ridge and toward Tete Jaune Cache. If you choose that route to descend, you must bushwhack down to the road once you are back in the trees and then you must walk back along the road to your car. Regardless of the way you return, I hope you have a beer in the trunk of your car waiting for your arrival.

Wells Gray Provincial Park

Wells Gray Park was named after the Honorable Arthur Wellesley (Wells) Gray who was born in New Westminster in 1876. He became the provincial Minister of Lands in 1933 and died in 1944.

The park has three roads leading into its treasures. The most common entrance is through Clearwater from Highway 5 at the east end of the park. This highway can be accessed from Valemount in the north or Kamloops in the south. Highway 24 south of 100 Mile House will take you past numerous lakes not in the park and over to Little Fort. From there you can take Highway 5 to Clearwater and the park. There is also the Mahood Lake Road that leaves Highway 97 north of 100 Mile House. The 88 km (55 mi) of gravel road will take you to Mahood Lake that is in the park and where there is some limited hiking. See 100 Mile House section. Regardless of how you enter this park, it is worth taking the time to check out some of the sites. For a complete hiking guide that includes all the trails, descriptions of the flora and fauna, and some historical information, purchase *Nature Wells Gray Hiking Guide* by Trevor Goward and Cathie Hickson, published by Lone Pine, 1995. This is a well-organized and easy to follow book.

Spahats Creek

Time: To the Plunge Pool, three hours; to the Eye of the Needle, six hours return.

Distance: 2 - 6 km (1 – 3.75 mi) return.

Difficulty: Class two.

Equipment: Boots must be worn as the rocks are slippery and good grip is necessary. At the falls there is a lot of mist so if the weather is chilly, a rain jacket is recommended.

The route: The Plunge Pool is at the base of a waterfall and the Eye of the Needle is a canyon. Both are nice walks. The pool is often visited by tour groups.

Trail access: Just over 10 km (6 mi) from Clearwater is Spahats Provincial Park and the viewing point. The falls seem to drop from between the cracks of two mountainous rocks into a pool far below. To descend to the valley, walk from the viewpoint, following the fence along the rim of the canyon downstream until you come to the end of the fence and a fork in the trail. Take the left-hand trail downhill.

The trail: Once you have dropped about 150 m (500 ft) into the valley you will come to a second trail that goes in two directions (left or right). The one to the left will take you to the pool just a short distance away. The trail passes through a canyon that eliminates most of the sun's rays. Continue across the rocks carefully. The waterfalls thunder into the pool. There is nothing to visit beyond the waterfall. This hike should not take more than three hours to return and if you are very fast, you can do it in just over two.

When you arrive at the fork and take the right hand trail (see above), it will take you to the Eye of the Needle. This is a circle route that will take about six hours to complete. The trail gets its name from the geographic formation on the canyon; a widening at one end so the canyon has the shape of a needle. The walls of the canyon rise on one side almost 200 m (600 ft) and on the opposite side, 650 m (2000 ft). However, at the "eye" the distance across from each wall is about 500 m (1500 ft) thus diminishing the dramatic effect. The trail follows the lower, eastern side of the canyon to a small creek and then it follows close to the canyon wall for a bit. At the lower end of the canyon, the trail ascends along a talus slope where you will have to negotiate around some fairly large outcrops. Once past the talus slope watch for a natural rock bridge about 10 m (30 ft) below the trail. Continue ahead to the plateau and flat ground where you will be less than an hour from your car. At the fork on the plateau, take the left one that goes back to the parking lot.

Trophy Mountain Meadows

Time: Three hours to the meadows.

Distance: 6 km (3.75 mi) return.

Difficulty: Class two.

The route: This trail takes you to a flowering meadow within a short distance. Because this is such an exceptional flowing spot, it is popular with local hikers. Others who would like to camp overnight above the meadow may continue on to Sheila Lake where there is a primitive campsite. The section to the lake is called the Skyline Trail and offers the best views in the park.

Trail access: From Clearwater, follow the highway for 11.5 km (7.2 mi) and turn east onto the Trophy Mountain Road. There are clearly marked signs. Follow the road for 4 km (2.5 mi) and take the left hand fork. It is another 13.4 km (8.4 mi) to trailhead and in that distance the road rises about 300 m (1000 ft) in elevation – better to drive it than walk. At 7.7 km (4.8 mi) there is a sign stating that you are at Sheep Track Bench. Turn right at the sign and proceed through a logged-off area for another five or so kilometers (2+ mi). There is a sign at the trailhead.

The trail: From the logged area, walk through forest for about an hour. The trail will open into a meadow laden with wild flowers of every description. If you arrive at the meadow early in the season (before July), you will be welcomed by an ocean of yellow glacier lilies. These are a favorite of grizzlies so be on the lookout before entering the meadow. If coming later in the year, you will find flowers such as lupines, cow parsnips, bog orchids, mountain daisy, alpine veronica and Indian paint brushes. Those are the most obvious, but there are many more.

Please stay on the trail or if resting, on the rocks rather than in the meadow. This is a delicate area.

For those continuing on to Sheila Lake, walk north, veering to the left. Along this trail, the Skyline, on a very clear day, you may even see the peak of Mount Robson to the north. For detailed information on this trail, purchase *Nature Wells Gray Hiking Guide* by Trevor Goward and Cathie Hickson or ask the park wardens at the park office in Clearwater for detailed information.

Philip Lake

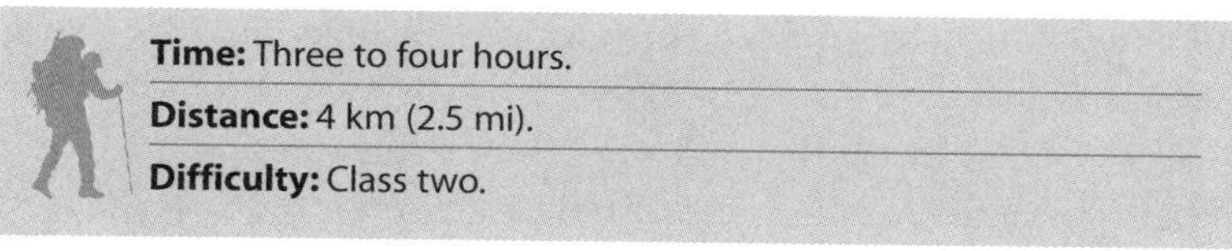

Time: Three to four hours.

Distance: 4 km (2.5 mi).

Difficulty: Class two.

The route: This trail is the start of routes to a number of destinations. For longer hikes, please purchase the *Nature Wells Gray Hiking Guide* (see above).

Trail access: Follow the Wells Gray Park Road from Clearwater for 26.8 km (16.75 mi) and turn right onto the side road. This is a steep road that goes for 7.5 km (4.7 mi) to the trailhead. There is a small parking spot about 2.5 km (1.6 mi) before the trailhead where those with low clearance on their cars can park. You will have to add time to the expected hiking time to walk the distance from this parking lot to the trailhead.

The trail: There is a primitive campsite at the lake for those wanting to stay overnight. The trail to the lake at the beginning is steep and full of rocks that have been made smooth in the polisher of a glacier thousands of years ago. The steepness levels a bit after about 45 minutes (if carrying a full pack) and continues at that grade to the lake. From this campsite you can do a day trip up to Caribou Meadows or a full three-day trip over to the campsite at Flight Lake and then the circle trail out along Battle Creek. Speak to park wardens for this information or purchase the hiking guide for the area.

Green Mountain Viewing Tower & Foot Lake

Time: One to two hours return.

Distance: 2 km (1.25 mi).

Difficulty: Class one.

Equipment: You must carry water.

The route: You can drive to the tower and then walk to the lake. The tower offers splendid views of the surrounding countryside. It is also a nice place to have a picnic.

Trail access: Drive along the park road from Clearwater for 36.1 km (22.5 mi), just past the park entrance. There is a sign for the tower. It is 3.5 km (2 mi) up the hill.

The trail: Once you have enjoyed the views around the tower, follow the trail in front of the tower. This trail leads to the lake. This is an excellent little walk and you can be back to your car within an hour if you hurry.

Whitehorse Bluff

Time: Four to six hours.

Distance: 12 km (7.5 mi).

Difficulty: Class two.

The route: This is a half-day hike that goes to a bluff overlooking the Clearwater River. You must descend on your way there and ascend on the way back.

Trail access: Follow the road to the Green Mountain Lookout Tower (see above) but branch off and park about a kilometer before the tower. The trailhead is marked.

The trail: The trail is flat for the first half hour. When you come to a fork, veer to the right and start down the hill. The trail flattens again and when you come to the next fork, take the right hand one again. The one to the left will take you down to the river. Follow the trail to the edge of the bluff. If you go down to the river, it will take another two to three hours and then you have to come back up which will take even longer. This bluff is actually an old volcano that originally erupted while it was under a lake that dominated the plateau thousands of years ago.

Dawson Falls Viewpoint

Time: Half an hour.

Distance: One km (0.5 mi).

Difficulty: Class one.

The route: This is a stroll along a well-maintained trail to a waterfall that is often called the "Niagra" because of its expanse across 60 m (175 ft) of arched rock. Although the distance of the drop is not much, the falls are impressive.

Trail access: Follow the park highway north from Clearwater for 40.2 km (25 mi) to a pullout where there is a sign indicating the falls.

The trail: There are two trails or lookout points. Follow the trail to the right and you will see the falls from the side and the left fork will lead you to a face-on view of them. The left fork view is more dramatic.

Helmcken Falls and Rim Trail

Time: Half an hour to the viewpoint and three hours to the rim.

Distance: Under 2 km (1.5 mi) to the viewpiont, 8 km (5 mi) to the rim.

Difficulty: Class one/two.

The route: These falls plunge over a precipice for 140 m (465 ft) into the river below. They drop three times farther than Niagara Falls and are what made the park famous. Everyone visiting the park should see them at least once. Walking the rim to see the falls from another vantage point is also recommended.

Trail access: Follow the park highway north from Clearwater for 43 km (27 mi) and turn onto the Helmcken Falls Road. There are signs. The viewpoint is 4 km (2.5 mi) up the secondary road.

The trail: It takes about ten minutes along the fence line for a good view of the Myrtle and Clearwater Rivers that flow around 175 m (500 ft) below. Be aware that going beyond the fence can be dangerous as you are on the edge of a cliff. Those wanting to go farther along the rim should be experienced and have good boots, water, snacks and raingear. The trail beyond the lookout goes down to the Myrtle River and follows it downstream, first past a few riffles, then rapids and then the precipice.

Clearwater Lake

At the lake, there are a number of campsites accessible by car. There are also picnic tables, a boat launch and numerous hiking trails one can take. I will mention only one, the most interesting for me. However, if you would like to do a longer two- or three-day hike, there is a trail to Kostal Lake. There is also a canoe route up Clearwater Lake and over to Azure Lake. Please talk to the park wardens for this information or purchase *Nature Wells Gray Hiking Guide* by Trevor Goward and Cathie Hickson, published by Lone Pine, 1995.

Dragon's Tongue

Time: Three hours.

Distance: 4 km (2.5 mi)

Difficulty: Class two.

Equipment: Good boots should be worn, as you will be walking on lava beds (sharp rocks).

The route: This is a lava flow that erupted from the Dragon Volcano located at the top of Falls Creek. For this hike, you can go all the way to the top of the lava flow or just partway.

Trail access: Clearwater Lake is 65 km (41 mi) from Clearwater along the park highway. From the campsite at the south end of the lake walk back along the highway to the Falls Creek Bridge. There is a trail at the north end of the bridge going into the bush (east). Follow this trail.

The trail: The trail is uphill to begin with but soon goes down the other side of the hill to Falls Creek. The first notable thing you will see is the Grotto, a cut deep in the lava. This was formed when the lava reached the ice of a glacier and stopped flowing. When the ice melted, the grotto was left. Continue along the trail, over the next hill, and you will find more of the lava flow. The next notable spot is called the Dragon's Teeth, where more lava formations are found. These resemble serrated teeth. This formation was caused from lava flowing over tree trunks.

Continue along the main trail until you come to a clearing. Cross over to the middle of the flow and explore more of the formations. It is a fascinating area.

Highway 16 West

From Prince George to Haida Gwaii (Queen Charlotte Islands)

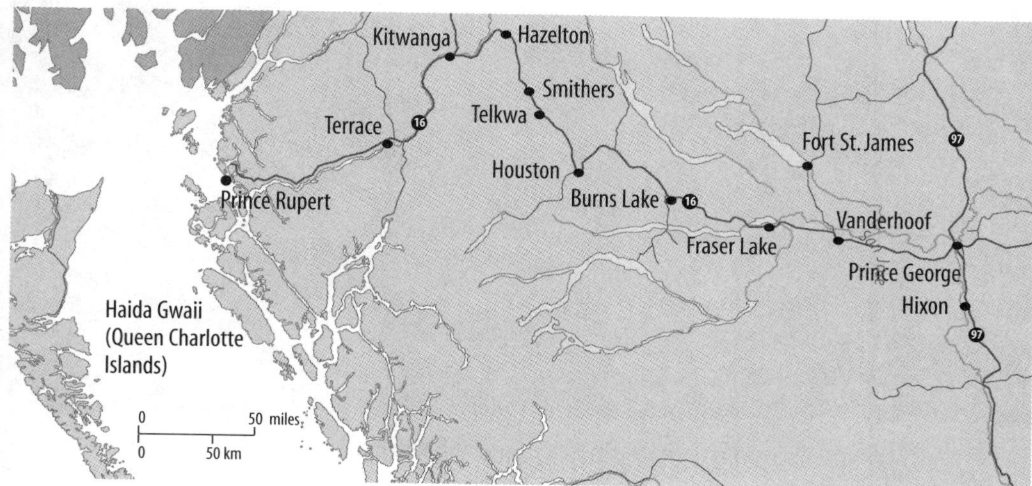

Fort George Canyon

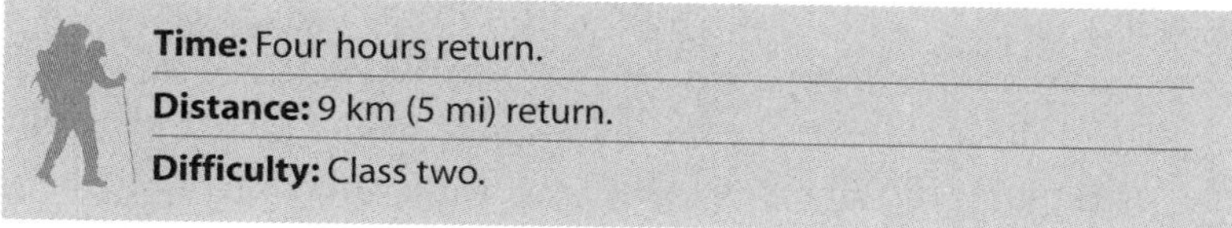

Time: Four hours return.

Distance: 9 km (5 mi) return.

Difficulty: Class two.

The route: This is an easy trail with interpretive signs along the upper section and historical remains on the lower part. It is a good, all-day (including driving time and a stop for coffee) walk for anyone over the age of six or seven.

Trail access: Follow Highway 16 west to the Blackwater Road. Turn left and follow it to the West Lake Road, about 12 km (7.5 mi) from Highway 16. Follow West Lake Road past the lake and a total of 9.5 km (6 mi) beyond. Take the left fork(at 9.5 km) and follow it for almost 2 km (1.25 mi) and then turn left onto a tertiary road. Follow this for almost 2 km (1.25 mi) to a parking lot. There are signs from the lake to the parking lot. There have been numerous car break-ins at this parking lot. Some

Fort George Canyon where sternwheelers were hauled up-river.

leave their cars open with nothing in them; others have alarm systems set loud.

The trail: There are outhouses and picnic tables at the parking lot and a gate to discourage any motorized vehicles from entering the area.

The walk is fairly level with interpretive signs indicating the flora of the area along the upper section. The signs indicate things like pine cherry tree, Douglas fir, yarrow, columbine, white spruce, dogwood, Oregon grape, Douglas maple, Saskatoons, mountain ash, kinnikinnick and much more. Part way down the trail there is a bench at a viewpoint overlooking the valley.

Once at the river, you will see across the way a reddish outcropping. This rock was used as a marker in the days of river travel to indicate the beginning of the canyon just below.

In the canyon itself, there are three channels that were used for the different sized boats used. The sternwheelers pulled up to the west shore (where you are standing) and the passengers had to disembark and walk up stream to a landing beach. Much of the freight too had to be unloaded and moved over skids to the beach where the boats could be reloaded. There is an iron post near the shore that was used to tie the headline from the sternwheelers so that they could be winched up the canyon. The bigger sternwheelers had to power their way up the river and used the far channel to do so. Return by the same way you came.

Vanderhoof

This is a farming community with interesting cafes (in town, not along the highway) and good hotels. Vanderhoof's historical fame comes mostly from the Baptist Church, originally built in 1834 by Mary and Cornelius Vanderhoof. At the time of building they established the church, a school and a cemetery. Cornelius came to the area from the states in 1804 and after starting his homestead, he returned to get his family. They were the first members of the community. Although the history is scanty and the site of the original church is unknown, its many names have been recorded. It was called the Tuppers Plains Baptist Church and then the Salem Baptist Association. It went back to Tuppers before finally becoming the Vanderhoof Baptist. The church has been on its present location since the mid 1800s.

In 1900 the church had the bell tower added. But then interest in the Baptist religion waned and the church fell into disrepair. Because of this, there were no services from 1923 to 1930 except for one funeral. In late 1929 the people of the community decided to repair the church. A new roof was put in place and walls were repaired. The windows were added and the front got two doors on either side of the main one. The church remained like this until the mid 1950s when a new bell tower was built and then in 1979 the floor was replaced. The final result is an eclectic building but one that still attracts worshipers.

There is a private campsite along Highway 16 just west of the main road leading into town.

Home Lake

Time: Four hours.

Distance: 6 km (3.75 mi) to the lake and about 35 km (22 mi) to the Kenny Dam Road.

Difficulty: Class two to Home Lake and Class four if going to Kenny Dam Road.

The route: This is an easy walk to a nice little lake where there is a government recreation site and a cabin open for the general public. From this lake you can walk to Little Home Lake, Paddle Lake and on to the Kenney Dam Road. The area is dotted with numerous unnamed lakes. However, most of this walk is in the forest, so views are minimal.

Trail access: Drive south of Vanderhoof on the Telegraph Road to the Kluskus Forest Service road that is between the Tatuk Lake and the Kenney Dam roads. There are signs indicating Finger-Tatuk Provincial Park. Travel along Kluskus for 42.5 km (26.5 mi) and park.

The trail: This is a straightforward trail. Walk through the trees on the well defined and marked trail to the lake. It will take a few hours to get there. If little lakes are your thing, I would suggest taking a few days and crossing over to the Kenney Dam road. The trail is not well defined once past Paddle Lake. It becomes easy to follow again near Crystal Lake. For detailed information on this trail, visit the information center, 2353 Burrard Ave, phone, 567-2124 or 800-752-4094. During the summer there is also an information center at the museum on the highway.

Omineca

Time: Three to four hours.

Distance: 6 km (3.75 mi) one way.

Difficulty: Class one/two.

The route: This is an old Indian trail that goes down to the Stuart River. Long ago, the locals took canoes over this trail and then paddled the river to Stuart Lake. There are two trails at trailhead. The one going in the opposite direction to the river will take you back into Vanderhoof but that is close to 20 km (12.5 mi). The trail down to the river and back is an excellent walk.

Trail access: Follow Highway 27 north toward Fort St. James for about 14 km (9 mi) to the Blue Mountain Forest Service Road. Follow it for about the same distance, past a little lake on the north side of the road, and about one km (.05 mi) past a creek that crosses the road. There is a sign indicating the trailhead. If walking from Vanderhoof take the Striegler Pit Road about 8/10 km (1 mi) after the Nechako River Bridge. Turn east (right) and follow it to the marked trailhead sign.

The trail: From the Blue Mountain Forest Service Road to the river, it is an easy 6 km (3.75 mi) walk with a lot of it downhill. However, that makes it uphill on the way back. This is a popular trail with a few lookouts that make it fun to walk. If walking back to Vanderhoof, the trail starts on the opposite side of the road to the river trail and goes south for 20 km (12.5 mi). Another option is to walk to the river by finding the trail at the end of Striegler Pit Road (see trail access) in Vanderhoof. These trails are also trails that the gold miners used to get to the Omenica Goldfields in the late 1870s.

Fort St. James

Located on Stuart Lake, the fort is about two hours from Prince George and one hour from Vanderhoof. The town is on Highway 27 and the turnoff is at the weigh scales just west of Vanderhoof. The restored Hudson's Bay Co. Trading Post in Fort St. James is a huge tourist draw and if you are there between mid May and mid September, I suggest you take time to visit the fort. There are actors dressed in period costume who take visitors on tour.

The fort was originally a post built by the North West Trading Co. in 1806 and taken over by the Hudson's Bay Company in 1821. James Douglas, the first governor of BC, was one of the chief factors at the fort. Fort St. James admits in their historical documents that the coming of the Europeans was both beneficial and damaging to the local residents. The Europeans brought metal tools and guns that helped make life easier but they also brought whiskey, disease and Christian schools that did not make life easier.

The name of the fort was originally Na-Kra-ztli which means "arrows floating by". The name comes from a legend where the Indians fought a battle with dwarfs that resulted in arrows floating in the Stuart River (the river that flows out of the lake toward Prince George). Simon Fraser came in 1806 and called the fort the Stuart Lake post. In 1822, the name was changed by the Hudson's Bay Company to Ft. St. James. For more history about the fort, visit www.fortstjames.com.

There are three campsites on the lake and numerous lodges in the area, most on the lake. One, Douglas Lodge is especially interesting as it was built in 1924. The restaurants in town are not numerous and pizza is about the best to settle for. There are grocery stores if you wish to make your own meals.

Mount Pope

Mount Pope is named after Major Franklin Pope who worked as a surveyor on the telegraph line in 1865. There are caves in the mountain, on the bluff that faces the lake. To date, there has been no exploration of the caves.

Time: 4 to 6 hours.

Distance: 13 km (8 mi) return trip.

Difficulty: Class two

The route: This is a well-maintained trail that has a few much-appreciated benches along the way. At the top, there is a covered shelter overlooking Stuart Lake in one direction and Pinchi, Tezzeron and Trembler Lakes in another. The views are worth the work it takes to get here.

Trail access: Drive north through Fort St. James to the Stone Bay Road. Turn west and follow it for 3 km (1.8 mi). There is a large parking area on the right shortly before the road ends. There is a sign.

The trail: This is a steep climb to begin with and then there is a bit of a level section where you skirt partway around the side of the mountain that faces the lake. It is

Mount Pope, Fort St. James.

along one of the level sections that remains of the old telegraph line can still be seen. A bench overlooking Stuart Lake has been placed just past the telegraph line. Then the trail starts winding to the top. If it is a miserable day and cold on top, there is a bench below the lookout that is sheltered from the elements to some degree. There are some who, once a year, run this trail just to get in shape for the summer of outdoor adventure.

Nyan Wheti

Time: Five days – less if you are fast, strong and good at reading maps.

Distance: 50 km (30 mi).

Difficulty: Class five. This trail must not be done unless you have spoken with the people at Fraser Lake Information Center for the latest details on the route. You should also have all topographical maps of the area and be skilled at using a compass.

Topo maps: 93K/1, 93K/2, 93K/7, 93K/8

The route: Hiking this trail is only for the experienced and adventuresome. This is a historical route used mainly by the native people traveling and hunting between Fort Fraser and Fort St James. The name means "Trail Across" in the Carrier language. Prior to the establishment of the fort, the people used the trail as a trade route with other tribes. The trail is not used much now so some bushwhacking may be necessary. I have not done this trail myself.

Trail access: At Ft. St. James, drive 13 km (8 mi) along Sowchea Road and when you come to Baker Drive turn west. The trailhead is at the very end of Baker Drive. After hiking for roughly five days you will arrive at the Nautley Reserve on the north side of the Nechako River just out of Beaumont Park. For your pick up vehicle, travel to Beaumont Park and follow the road beyond that goes toward the Nautley Reserve. Continue along the Dog Creek Forest Road through the reserve and then turn north (left) onto the Etcho Lake Forest Service Road. Continue past the gas pipeline. About 2 km (1.25 mi) past the pipeline there is the Pack Trail (Nyan Wheti Trail) sign. Leave your vehicle here or better still, have someone pick you up five days after you start the hike. I am not sure how safe it would be to leave your vehicle there for that length of time.

The trail: I have not done this route so the information here has been gathered from other sources. On the first day, you must pass Pitka Mountain standing at 1460 m (4745 ft). This includes crossing numerous creeks. Sutherland Lake is tiny and located at about 20 km (12.5 mi) from trailhead. If you can make it this far, it is best for camping. Shortly after Sutherland Lake there are numerous logging roads that you will pass, including Marie's Forest Service Road. You could go down to Pitka Creek and hook up with the Dog Creek road that runs into Highway 27 if you wanted out at this point. However, just beyond the Marie Forest Service Road is Marie Lake and the trail goes to the north of Marie Lake (much better than logging roads), past Mt. Rosetti and hooks up with the Cunningham Forest Service Road that will take you down to the Nautley Reserve.

Dickinson

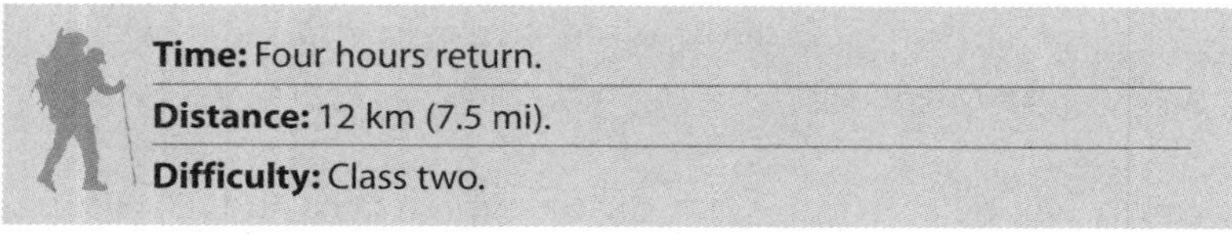

Time: Four hours return.

Distance: 12 km (7.5 mi).

Difficulty: Class two.

The route: This is a leg stretcher that can be done in half a day or less. The trail is a good place to get a view of Fort St. James, the lake and the surrounding mountains. The first part of the walk is mostly in forest but it doesn't take long to get to the top of the hill. It is also a good place to look for birds.

Trail access: Follow Stuart Drive to Pineridge Way Road just before the hospital. Follow that road for half a kilometer and park behind the secondary school. Walk along the dirt road to the trailhead – there is a sign. Follow the well-maintained and marked trail.

Fraser Lake

Originally Fraser Lake was built to accommodate construction workers building the Grand Trunk Railway. This was in the early 1900s. In the 1960s it became a mining village and most of the residents worked at the Endako Mine a few kilometers to the west. During its boom days, the hard working, hard drinking miners kept the town jumping. But a strike that broke the union and closed the mine in the 1980s left the town almost deserted. Once the mine opened again, without the union, the miners slowly moved back into the area. They are now a calmer bunch, drinking less and keeping a lower profile.

The town is pretty, located between Highway 16 and Fraser Lake. There is one old house, built before the mine opened, that has a river-stone fireplace. Otherwise the homes are new. There are two hotels and a few restaurants along the highway bordering the town. There are no campsites right in town; you need to camp at Piper's Glen near the east end of the lake or at Beaumont Park 15 km (9 mi) east of the town. The best coffee can be purchased at the gas station.

Mouse Mountain

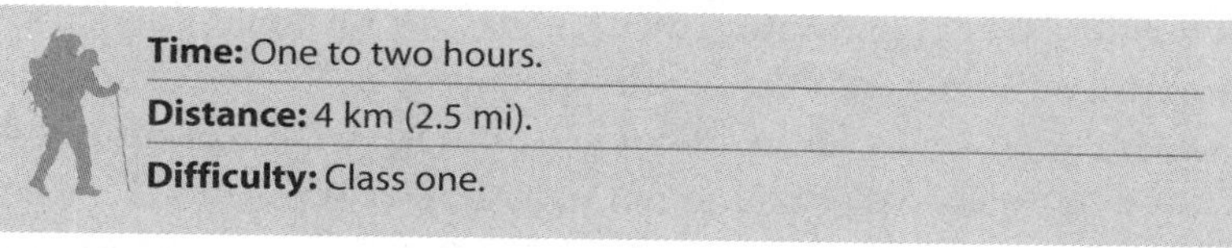

Time: One to two hours.

Distance: 4 km (2.5 mi).

Difficulty: Class one.

The route: The mountain, with trails going in many directions, is used both summer and winter. It is not possible to get lost – to go in go up and to return go down. The views of the lake are superb from the top.

Trail access: Follow the main street into town and turn east (towards Prince George) at the first road. Follow it past the recreation center over to the base of the mountain – the one that looks like a mouse hunched down.

The trail: From the parking lot continue in an upward direction until there is no more up. There are numerous trails from which to choose, none better than the next. Eventually, all trails will merge near the top. This is a good trail to take kids as the way is not difficult (just a bit steep) and the rewards are excellent.

Ormond Creek

Time: Overnight.

Distance: 26 km (16.25 mi) return.

Difficulty: Class three.

Route summary: This could be a very long day hike but is best as an overnighter. Since the area is isolated and the population low, the chances of having others at the lake are small. And if by a slim chance there are others at the lake, they will want the same sense of seclusion as you.

Trail access: Follow Highway 16 to the west end of Fraser Lake near Stelako or to the east end near Beaumont Park and follow that road around to the north shore of Fraser Lake. Just west of Pederson's Point Campsite you will see a sign indicating the trailhead for Ormond Creek. Park off the road or in the campsite parking pullout area.

The trail: The first part of the trail passes through a Douglas fir forest that is over 300 years old. This in itself makes the trip worthwhile. The hike follows Ormond Creek all the way to Ormond Lake. The most interesting part of the trail is the Oona Canyon that is about 150 m (500 ft) long and 20 m (65 ft) deep. There is one spot where there is a lovely waterfall but it is not visible from the trail. You must go through the bush to see it. The indication that it is close is the sound of the water. The trail continues and is fairly difficult even though the lake is not on the top of a mountain. There is a cabin at the lake that can be used for some shelter. I have not been to the cabin so I do not know how well maintained it is.

Houston

This little town sporting the biggest fishing rod in the world is a company town (sawmill) and like Fraser Lake, the residents for the most part are hard working. However, it is their community spirit that is to be commented on. In order to attract tourists in the early 1980s Warner Jarvis, a local fly fisherman, came up with the idea of the world's largest fly fishing rod. With his enthusiasm he managed to get Andrew Knappett to draw up the plans for the construction of the rod and then with the help of numerous volunteers, they built the rod. It took a total of six local shops 470 hours of donated equipment time and 576 hours of donated labor to complete the rod. By the time it was finished, 41 companies participated in the project.

The rod is constructed of aluminum and anodized bronze to simulate graphite. It is 1830 cm (720 in) long and weights about 800 lb (365 kg). The reel is 36 in (1 m) in diameter. The fly on the end of the line is a 53 cm (21-in) Skykomish Sunrise. When the rod was completed, those who helped in the construction carried the rod on their shoulders from the industrial park in town over to Steelhead Park on the highway across from the mall.

Child on hike in Houston

There are numerous hotels in town and an A & W, a deli, a Mr Sub, numerous pizza places, numerous restaurants including two Chinese restaurants. The best camping area is at the By-Mac Park, nine kilometers west of town on the Walcott Forest Service Road. Follow Highway 16 for 4 km(2 mi) to the Morice River Road (by the Canfor sign). Turn left and follow this road for five km (2.5 mi) to the Walcott Forest Service Road. Follow that for less than a kilometer to the campsite.

Buck Flats/Old Pine Nature Trail

Time: One to two hours.

Distance: 2 km (1.25 mi) return.

Difficulty: Class one.

Route summary: These trails are for skiing in the winter and hiking in the summer. The walk is a nice leg stretcher through pine forests with no elevation change. The trail passes near the shores of Beaver Pelt Lake, past a beaver dam and some wetlands that are rich in bird life. The trail eventually ends at a small waterfall. This is an excellent place to take children.

Trail access: From Houston, continue west on Highway 16 to Buck Flats Road and follow it for about 12 km (7.5 mi). Do not take any of the turn-offs. There is a picnic table at the parking spot and the area is called the Morice Mountain Nordic Ski Trails and the Houston Community Forest area. Walk from here to Beaver Pelt lake.

The trail: The trail is at the southeast end of the parking lot and passes Silverthorn Lake and then continues to a side trail that leads around Beaver Pelt Lake. This is the birding area. There is a lookout point at the south end of Silverthorn Lake. These trails are used for skiing in the winter and are well maintained. Mosquito repellent will be needed near the beaver dam. There is a total of 40 kilometers of trails in this area. Take note where you have walked so you aren't hopelessly lost for hours.

Nadina Mountain

Time: One night is recommended. It is a minimum of eight hours to the summit of the mountain.

Distance: 14 km one way.

Difficulty: Class four - this is a difficult hike because route-finding skills are needed for part of the hike.

Route summary: This is a strenuous hike to the summit of a mountain that looms out of nowhere to an elevation of 2300 meters (7550 ft). There are difficult sections and because the area is not highly used part of the trail before the alpine is difficult to follow. A compass and map should be used. The name Nadina means"Great Rock" in the local native language.

Trail access: Turn south onto the Morice River Road west of Houston and follow it for 39 kilometers past Owen Lake to the Nadina Wilderness Lodge. You must ask permission to enter the trail that starts at the back of the lodge near their shed. There is camping at Owen Lake for those wanting to get an early morning start (or to stay at the end of the hike). However, I would suggest trying to get a room at the lodge after the hike or at least purchase a meal.

The trail: Walk behind the shed and follow the partly overgrown road through the forest toward the mountain. It will take about three to four hours to reach Base Lake (you passed the opposite side of this lake driving in) where often campers spend their first night. Continue along the trail up the mountain. From Owen Lake to the summit is the most strenuous section and difficult if carrying a heavy pack. It will take four to five hours to get into the alpine. There are many mountain goats making this mountain their home. The terrain around the top of the mountain includes hoodoos, shale areas and swamp and should take about four hours to circumnavigate. The mountain has snow in the shadows of outcrops almost year around so water is not a huge problem.

Telkwa

Telkwa means the meeting of waters. The name was derived from the two rivers, the Telkwa and Bulkley, coming together in the center of town. Originally built on the bluff overlooking the river, the town was first called Aldermere and was a shopping center for those working and following the Telegraph Trail. By the early 1900s the town had a hotel, post office, general store and newspaper. In 1914 there was a huge fire and many of the business people who lost their buildings decided to rebuild in Smithers because that was where the boom had moved. The rest moved closer to the water. Telkwa didn't grow much after that. The church on the highway, St. Stephen's Anglican, was built in 1910 and the Telkwa Museum, a good place to visit, is located in the old school house that was built in 1920.

There are so many hikes in this area, a complete book is required and is available. The recommended book is *Trails to Timberline in West Central British Columbia*, by Einar Blix, published by Fjelltur Books, Smithers, 1989.

The best camping for those staying a few days is at Tyhee Lake just up the hill from town. The best restaurant is in the old train station and the best ice cream is across the street from the restaurant. There are also a few motels.

Trails in town

The three trails below are short and easy to do. None of the walks take more than an hour to complete.

Cariboo Trail or the Telegraph Trail follows the old telegraph line and in the days before the brush took over, you could walk from here to Quesnel. Today you can walk from the parking lot behind the school on Hankin Ave to the stairs leading up to Tyhee Lake just a kilometer away. It takes about half an hour to walk to the stairs. Starting at the school, you will follow the Heritage trail to Tower Street. Turn right on Tower and follow it a little way to the Telkwa Wagon Trail. Once in the Aldermere town site where there are benches for resting, the trail makes a sharp left and follows the Cariboo Trail. From the town site you may also follow the Aldermere trail back to the highway.

Telkwa Wagon Trail at one time joined present day Telkwa to the old community of Aldermere. From the school parking lot, follow Hankin Ave. along the Heritage trail until you come to Tower Street. Turn right on Tower and follow it a short distance to the Wagon Trail. Turn left and follow that to the Aldermere town site. Return as you came.

River Grade Trail was the original highway between Houston and Telkwa. It follows the Bulkley River for many miles but the maintained section is the part located in town. To get there, turn west on Hankin Ave and drive to the river where there is a parking spot and tourist information center. You may go either upstream or downstream along the river. Going upstream will take you to Eddy Park and going the other way will lead you around the bend in the river to a set of stairs and finally Highway 16 just across from the Aldermere Trail.

Hankin Plateau

Time: Minimum one night but if exploring the plateau then at least two days should be spent here.

Distance: 10 km (6 mi) one way to the plateau.

Difficulty: Class four/five.

Topo maps: 93L/6 Thautil River, 93L/11 Telkwa, (these may be purchased and laminated at the map store in Smithers).

The route: The plateau is one of the best in the area with spectacular views of the Coast Mountains in all directions. If you have food and time, there are a number of options. You can go over to Hunter Basin or to Webster Lake (a very steep trip up) or just play around the plateau. The plateau is not difficult to get to and is a good spot if you want to explore the eastern Bulkley Ranges.

Trail access: From Telkwa turn south at the lights and cross the Bulkley River and the railway tracks. This is the Coalmine Road. Do not turn left and follow the Bulkley River but continue straight ahead for about 6 km (3.75 mi) and then take the left-hand fork off Coalmine Road. Ascend a steep hill and check your odometer. About 3.5 km (2.2 mi) from the top of the hill is a zero marker for the Goathorn Creek road. Cross Goathorn Creek within 2 km (1.25 mi) and then take the left fork up the hill, away from the creek. Do not take the first road to the right after the km. 7 sign; this is Hunter Basin Road. Instead, continue along the Goathorn Creek road. It will drop down to Cabinet Creek and then up the other side. At km 9, there is a landing in which you can park. The area near the creek where there is a winter road (bushwhack) is the trailhead.

The trail: Follow the winter road for about a kilometer then turn onto an old mining road on the right. Follow this along the side of Webster Creek to a washout formed by a tributary creek about another kilometer along. Make a sharp left onto a clear trail and then a few minutes later turn right onto a better trail up through the trees. This is the ridge above Webster Creek. Continue on this trail as it goes up then down and then up steeply. You will come to other trails heading back to the road but don't take them. Continue up and up and up. After about 45 minutes the trail levels out a bit and then finally it gets onto a ridge. You will continue to a ledge overlooking Webster Creek and the entire Bulkley Valley. Once on the plateau, go as you wish. There is nice camping near the headwaters of Goathorn Creek.

For those wanting to go to Webster Creek rather than the plateau, take the trail that crosses Webster Creek. It is within the first two kilometers of where your car is parked. For this section, use your map and compass.

Smithers

Fur traders first started coming to the area in the 1860s with missionaries close on their heels. The most famous of these was Adrien Gabriel Morice who went to the Moricetown area and after learning the local language, translated the Christian prayer book into Carrier.

In 1866 the Telegraph line went through the area helping to open it up. It was then that the Bulkley Valley was named after the engineer, Colonel Charles Bulkley, who was in charge of the Telegraph line at the time. Farmers in their search for new land soon followed the telegraph line workers. Gabriel Lacroix was the first to come in 1900 and Fred Heal settled three years later on Tyhee Lake. The community was founded in 1913 as a divisional point for the Grand Truck Railway; the town was named after one of the directors, Sir Alfred Smithers. In 1921 Smithers became the first incorporated village in BC and in 1967 its status was raised to incorporated town.

Today Smithers is the town for all seasons with great skiing in the winter and hiking/canoeing/fishing in the summer. There are numerous hotels, motels, restaurants and outfitters able to help with any outdoor activity you may want to do.

Glacier Gulch

Time: 6 to 7 hours return.

Distance: 2 km (1.25 mi) one way.

Difficulty: Class two. Take a walking stick to help with both going up and coming down.

Topo maps: 93L/14 (not needed except for reference information)

The route: This is a steep hike that, as the glacier recedes, gets longer each year. The change in elevation for the two kilometers is about 1000 m (3000 ft). The views, of course, are exceptional and if you have no chance of seeing another glacier up close, this is a good one to explore. Do not climb onto the glacier as this one has some crevasses that could be dangerous if you are not roped and with experienced people.

Trail access: Follow Highway 16 west and turn south (left) onto the Lake Kathlyn Road about 4 km (2.5 mi) along the highway. There are signposts indicating Glacier Gulch and Twin Falls. After crossing the tracks, turn left onto Glacier Gulch Road and follow it for 4 km (2.5 mi). Park at the Twin Falls Recreation Site and look for the sign indicating the start of the Glacier Gulch Trail.

The trail: Before going up to the glacier, take a look at the falls. They are only a few minutes along a well-maintained walkway and the falls are quite spectacular, dropping down the side of the mountain from the toe of the glacier. The trail to the glacier is steep but it crosses open scree slopes from which the views are good. Near the top of the trail the glacier and the mountains behind come into view. This is when my camera can't stop clicking. If you need walking around Smithers, this trail is a must.

Babine Mountains Provincial Recreation Area

Located on 32,400 hectares/80,063 acres of parkland, the area holds numerous species of animals such as bears, wolverines and moose. However, the most desired animal to spot is the mountain goat.

Originally the park was occupied by Joe L'Orsa whose father had moved "back to the land" during the 1930s. Joe grew up there. During the 1970s he tried to make the area a park but the government didn't think this should happen. Joe won the favor of Rick Careless who founded the BC Spaces for Nature. He was able to convince the Ministry of Parks that the area should be kept as a managed area. This did happen and the area remained a recreation management area for ten years before it was elevated to a recreation area. Finally in the 1990s, after thousands of hours of lobbying time, the area was elevated to park status.

Today the 10 trails in the park are enjoyed by both the day-tripper and the dedicated back country hiker. Below, I have written about the two trails that traverse the park and encompass five of the 10 trails. You may do these in total or in part. For the longer trails a topo map should be purchased. This may be done in Smithers.

The most common access to the park is just 16 km (10 mi) from Smithers and five km (three mi) past Driftwood Canyon Park. Since the park has no developed facilities, it is especially good for those wanting isolation.

Cronin Creek

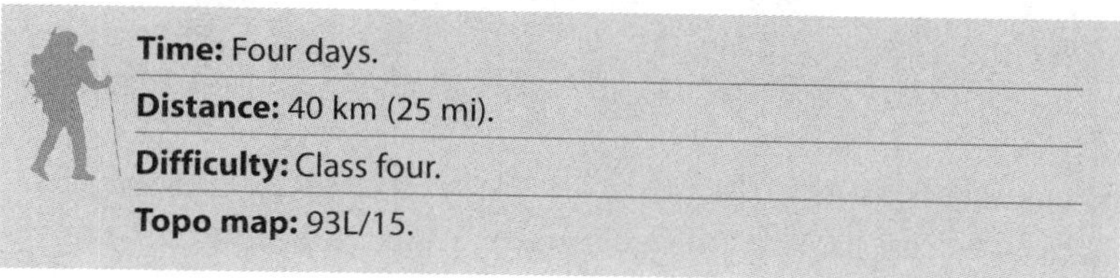

Time: Four days.

Distance: 40 km (25 mi).

Difficulty: Class four.

Topo map: 93L/15.

The route: This is the longest trail in the park and it starts on an old mining road. The trail then traverses the entire park from east to west (or the other way), joining with the **Hyland Pass Trail** and then the **Silver King Basin** trail and finally coming out at the Driftwood Creek Road. The walking distance is about 40 km (25 mi) in all with one cabin at Hyland Pass where there is also an abandoned mine site. If doing a traverse, you will need to have a pick up at one end.

Trail access: From Smithers take Highway 16 east and turn north on the Babine Lake Road. Follow it for some distance and then branch off at the Cronin Creek Forestry Road that is about 4 km (2.5 mi) past the Little Joe Creek Trailhead. Those with four-wheel drive can drive along the Cronin Creek Road for about 7.5 km (4.7 mi) to Cronin Creek. Those without will have to walk that distance.

The trail: Walk along the road that follows Cronin Creek (not the road straight ahead). You will pass Higgins Creek about a kilometer in and then Cronin Creek about 2 km (1.5 mi) farther. Once past Cronin Creek, continue up the trail another kilometer to a road going north (right). This goes to the Cronin Lookout. Continuing straight ahead will take you to the Hyland Pass Trail and past Mt. Cronin standing at almost 2400 m (7800 ft). The distance is 16 km (10 mi) to the Hyland Pass Trail. From here the next 15 km (9.5 mi) of trail is considered difficult due to its remoteness.

Once past Mt. Cronin you will pass an abandoned mine site and, a bit farther along, a shelter that sits in the shadow of Mt. Hyland. It is at the shelter that you will hook up with the Silver King Basin Trail. This is a popular trail that is used by many so the next 10 km (6 mi) may be populated.

Little Joe/McCabe

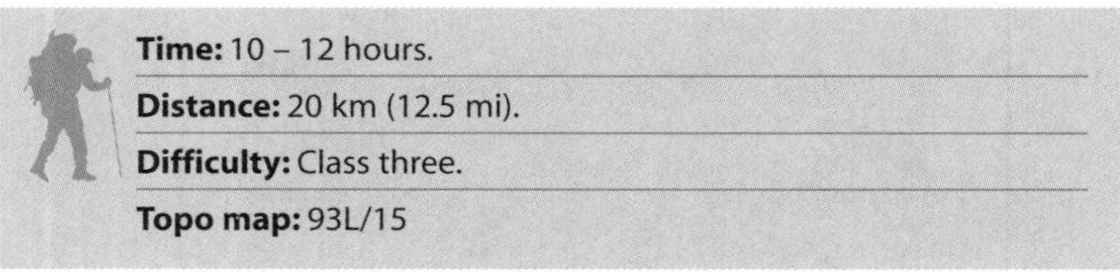

Time: 10 – 12 hours.

Distance: 20 km (12.5 mi).

Difficulty: Class three.

Topo map: 93L/15

The route: This route includes two trails that together cross the Recreation Area from east to west but closer to the south end rather than the northern Cronin Creek hike. There are two alpine lakes in the middle of the Little Joe/McCabe Trail where I would suggest spending the night before finishing the traverse. This trail may be done from either end.

Trail access: From Smithers take Highway 16 east and turn north onto the Babine Lake Road. The Little Joe Creek trail is off the Babine Lake Road just 10 km (6 mi) or so past the Burnt Cabin Road junction. You must park along the Babine Lake Road. If going in from the west, take the

Telkwa High Road north and turn east at Driftwood Creek Road. There are signs directing you to the Driftwood Canyon Provincial Park. Follow the road to its end and park in the parking lot. The McCabe Trail starts here.

The trail: The first section of the trail, traveling from east to west, is very steep and considered difficult. However, once in the alpine, less than 4 km (2.5 mi) into the hike (3 hours) the walking gets easier. Part way across the alpine you will cross the McCabe Trail. It is now only 8 km (5 mi) to the end of your route. Another option (for those wanting more) is to take the Lyon Creek Trail that is 20 km (12.5 mi) to its end at the Driftwood Road. Either trail has a gentle down through forest.

Twin Bridges Lakes

Time: Three to four hours one-way.

Distance: 10 km (6 mi) one-way.

Difficulty: Class three.

The route: The trail quickly reaches the alpines so the rewards are fast in coming. You must register at the trailhead for this hike. There is a box in which to place your registration.

Trail access: Take the Telkwa High road and turn east at Driftwood Creek Road. There are signs directing you to the Driftwood Canyon Provincial Park. Follow the road to its end and park in the parking lot.

The trail: This trail starts in the forest but soon climbs into the alpine. You follow Reiseter Creek all the way up to the lake. When you reach a fork in the trail about 8 km (5 mi) in, take the left hand fork. The next fork will take you into the lake. The route out is the same as the one going in. There is great camping beside the lake and many ridges that can be explored. One of the better ones is at the first fork in the trail. If you take the right hand fork, it will take you to a spot overlooking the lake and up onto a rocky ridge.

Hazelton

The scenery around Hazelton is so spectacular and the Indian villages so interesting that this area is a must for exploration. There are actually three Hazeltons; New Hazelton, South Hazelton and Old Hazelton, with Old Hazelton located about 7 km (4.3 mi) off Highway 16 along the banks of the Skeena River. There are ancient totem poles in Kitwanga, Kitwancool and in Hazelton. The Ksan Indian village, located at the confluence of the Skeena and Bulkley Rivers, is a must to visit and the Kitwanga Fort at Kitwancool is also a must.

The area has been the home of the Gitxsan and Wetsuweten people since long before recorded history. The name Hazelton comes from the hazel bushes that line the rivers and creeks in the area.

The people are friendly and helpful. I was cycling from Prince George to Prince Rupert and stopped at a store in New Hazelton to purchase some water. When the owner of the store learned where I was going she gave me my money back and told me that since I was going such a long way, I needed a gift from her for good luck. I made it to Rupert without getting rained out so I guess I did get the good luck. For those wanting to purchase Indian art, Hazelton is a good stop.

Ksan Indian Village, Hazelton

New Hazelton Lookout

Time: Less than one hour.

Distance: 2 km (1.5 mi).

Difficulty: Class one.

The route: This is a nice little walk to a waterfall. From the falls you can continue uphill to overlook the town.

Trail access: When traveling Highway 16 west toward Prince Rupert, make a left-hand turn at the Rainbow Restaurant/Geraco Industrial Supplies. This is Laurier Street. Follow it just beyond 13th Ave. and park.

The trail: Follow the road, veering to the east (left) until you see a bridge. Cross the bridge if you want to go up the hill to the lookout. The trail here is mostly in forest and there are benches on the way up. There are many trails going every which way so if you feel lost, head downhill. You will eventually come to the creek with the road on the other side.

If going to the waterfall, do not cross the bridge but go straight ahead. The waterfall is impressive. The road during high rains gets a bit muddy so runners or rubbers should be worn. If it has been dry for a while, sandals will do.

Thoen Basin

Time: Three to five hours return.

Distance: 5 km (3 mi) return.

Difficulty: Class two.

The route: This is a steep climb to alpine meadows along a ridge just above timberline. The views of the mountains are spectacular from the ridges.

Trail access: From New Hazelton, travel along Highway 16 east toward Smithers for 12 km (7.5 mi). Turn left (north) onto the Suskwa Forest Service Road that is located just after the railway overpass. Drive to the 21 km marker and turn right onto the Parker Main Road. Follow this for 15 km (9.4 mi). The trailhead is on the left hand side and at the far edge of an old cut block.

The trail: The first 4.5 km (2.8 mi) is through forest and sub alpine vegetation. The climb is steep and there is one creek crossing to navigate. However, once on top, the ridges are open. This is an excellent hike.

Thomlinson Mountain

Time: Six to seven hours return.

Distance: 15 km (9.4 mi).

Difficulty: Class two.

Topo maps: Hazelton, 93 M/5 and Kisgegas, 93 M/12.

The route: This is a quick way to get into the alpines and view the Skeena Valley from a good vantage point.

Trail access: From New Hazelton, drive about 6 km (3.75 mi) north towards Old Hazelton. At the Kispiox Valley Road turn right and drive for another 3 km (3 mi). Turn right onto the Salmon River Road and follow it over the Shegunia River. The road becomes the Babine Slide Forest Service Road. Follow this to the 30 km marker that is just before Sterritt Creek. Turn right and follow the logging road for 2 km (1.5 mi). Park wherever you can. The trail starts on an overgrown road about 200 m (600 ft) farther up. It is obvious.

The trail: This is an old mining road so walking or biking is good. It is a steady upward climb for about 7 km (4.4 mi) with the road switch backing often and sometimes ascending quite steeply. The grades are between 15% and 30%. You will climb about 300 m (1000 ft) in elevation to the alpine within that 7 km. Once in the alpine, the hill becomes quite steep and the exploration of the ridges is up to you. The upper portion of this hike is for experienced hikers only. There is no water in the alpine but water bottles can be filled at the streams that cross the road on the way up.

Blue Lake

Time: 9 hours or overnight.

Distance: 6 km (3.75 mi) one-way

Difficulty: Class three.

Topo maps: 93M/3 and 93M/4.

The route: This is a lovely walk, steep in parts and easy in others. The trail is clear although washed out in places. There are lots of goats on this mountain plus a great waterfall. Doing the return route in one day is possible but it is a long day. You can park/camp at the gravel pit near the trailhead so that an early morning departure is possible. There is no water available at the trailhead so you'd need to have some in your vehicle. Once at the top, there is the chance that you could cross over from the Blue Lake Trail to the Station Creek Trail but that would be only for the most experienced. This trail cannot be done early in the season due to snow at the higher elevations.

Trail access: From Smithers drive 54 km (33.75 mi) west along Highway 16. Just after Mudflat Creek crosses the highway, turn left and stay to the right at the next two forks. Park in the gravel pit. From Hazelton, travel east along Highway 16 about 9 km (5.6 mi) and turn right onto the gravel road just before Mudflat Creek. Although it looks possible, I would not drive past the gravel pit as the road is washed out and turning around would be difficult.

The trail: The trail that follows Mudflat Creek has an elevation gain of about 650 m (2000 ft) within 6 km (3.75 mi) and the climb is constant rather than steep sections interspersed with flat sections. The trail is on an old logging road up to the first lake. As you traverse up the mountain before the lake, you will come to a viewpoint overlooking the waterfall

Blue Lake Trail, Hazelton.

that drains Blue Lake above. Continue around the mountain along the road. There are often goats in this area. Once in the sub alpine Blue Lake will become visible. There is a second lake above it. You can camp in the bushes below Blue Lake but, during high water, this campsite is quite wet and sometimes washed out.

Continue past Blue Lake, staying on the west side of it and head up the hill to the next tiny lake near the Silvertip Glacier. Camping near Blue Lake is not possible. Once past Blue Lake you leave the trees and the walking is excellent. From the Silvertip Glacier, your options are unlimited and days could be spent up here. The one peak sticking out of the glacier is Red Rose Peak – how it got its name is beyond me.

Since 1910, the entire Rocher Deboule Range has been prospected. This includes the Red Rose Mine (named after the peak) where copper and tungsten were the main metals that were being sought. The trail to Blue Lake was originally constructed to service the Black Prince and the African Queen mining claims. Although the infrastructure has been put in place, there has never been active mining along this valley.

Terrace

Terrace was first settled by Europeans between 1889 and 1912 and mostly by those interested in mining, farming or working on the railway. Eby's Landing, on the Skeena River, was the original landing point for those settling here. Henry Frank built a house at the landing. His farm was called Kitsumkalum by locals.

The Grand Truck Pacific Railway arrived around 1910 and moved the "landing point" to the center of town. This was due to the donation of land by George Little, a local businessman, to the railroad company. Thus Kitsumkalum became history.

Terrace is deep in the Coast Mountains where outdoor recreation is the way of life. The town has an excellent museum, daily air service, bus service, numerous outfitters and great restaurants.

Kitselas Canyon

Time: Four hours.

Distance: 8 km (5 mi).

Difficulty: Class two.

The route: To get to the canyon you must stop at the Kitselas Band Council and ask for directions and permission to pass to the canyon.

Trail access: Follow Highway 16 east from Terrace about 20 km (12.5 mi) to the community of Usk. Take the ferry across the river and walk along the tracks.

The trail: Follow the tracks for about 4 km (2.5 mi); an hour more or less, depending on how much time it takes for you to explore the old totem poles that dot the landscape between the tracks and the river. There are also iron rungs secured in the rocks of the canyon wall that were used to hoist the sternwheelers through the canyon. If time is short you can return from this point. Those wanting to see the canyon gorge farther along the trail should stop at the band council office and get directions and permission. This second section of the hike will take you through old-growth forest and archeological sites where there is evidence of humans having lived here for thousands of years.

Gunsight Lake & Peak

Time: Full day.

Distance: 11 km (7 mi) return.

Difficulty: Class three.

The route: This is a great day hike into the alpine and to a group of lakes. For the more adventuresome (strong), the peak above the lake is a good destination. If you wish to carry gear, you can spend the night at the lake.

Trail access: Drive south along Highway 37 for 17 km (10.6 mi) to the Lakelse Provincial Park Campsite. You can park at the campsite or the gravel pit across the highway. There is a trail from the back end of the gravel pit to Hatchery Creek where the trail continues.

The trail: Once on Hatchery Creek, follow the trail upstream. As you walk along the creek you will pass foundations of old buildings belonging to the long-gone fish hatchery. Stay on the creek for about 2.5 km (1.6 mi). Cross the creek and then start the steep climb into alpine. There is a clear trail all the way to the Gunsight Lakes. If you want to go to the top of the mountain, it is another three hours uphill. The views of course are spectacular.

Sleeping Beauty Mountain

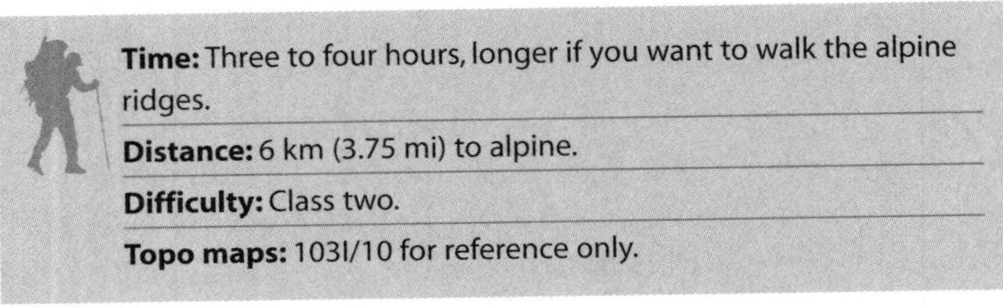

Time: Three to four hours, longer if you want to walk the alpine ridges.

Distance: 6 km (3.75 mi) to alpine.

Difficulty: Class two.

Topo maps: 103I/10 for reference only.

Trail access: Drive west of Terrace about 100 m (300 ft) past the Kalum River bridge and turn north onto the West Kalum Forest Service Road. Drive for 8.5 km (5.3 mi) and turn west (left) onto a secondary road. Drive 4.1 km (2.6 mi), cross the Erlandsen Creek Bridge and start up hill. Take the right hand fork at the 7 km (4.4 mi) mark and then take the left fork and drive another kilometer. If you have a two-wheel drive with low clearance you must park here. Otherwise, drive to the end of the road another 1.5 km (1 mi) farther.

The trail: This hike is a grunt from the start. The trail begins in a young forest but soon enters an older one. Once in the mature timber, you will find that the trail levels out a bit. Continue along the trail to a couple of lakes that are just below the alpine. From there the trail continues to a ridge in the alpine that overlooks the face of Sleeping Beauty. Follow the ridge as far as you wish. Return as you came. This is a spectacular hike.

Thornhill Mountain (Vicki Kryklywyj Memorial Trail)

Time: Five to six hours return.

Distance: 5 km (3 mi) one-way.

Difficulty: Class two.

Trail access: Follow Highway 16 east for half a kilometer from the junction of Highway 37. Turn right onto the Old Lakelse Lake Road and drive for almost 6 km (3.75 mi). Turn left onto the Thornhill Mountain Road and drive past the garbage dump to the bottom of the hill and take the next road where you can make a left hand turn. Follow this road for 2.3 km (1.4 mi) to the trailhead sign.

The trail: The trail starts with a creek crossing. Follow the walkway up the stairs and then walk along the old mining road. It is just under 5 km (3 mi) to the alpines and the grade is gentle. Once in the alpine, you will see a small alpine lake surrounded by stark gray rocks. From the lake you can do a bit of exploring or look across at the rest of the mountains looming in the distance. Vicki Kryklywyj, for whom the trail is named, was a local hiking enthusiast.

Maroon Mountain

Time: Eight hours return.

Distance: 12 km (7.5 mi) return.

Difficulty: Class three.

Topo map: 103I/15 is needed only for reference.

The route: This is an old prospectors' route with artifacts from that era scattered around the alpine. Evidence of previous human existence in an isolated area is always comforting. There are some lakes just below the alpine where one could camp.

Trail access: From Terrace, drive west along Highway 16 and turn north onto the Nisga'a Highway (Kalum Lake Drive). Continue for 33 km (20.6 mi), cross the Maroon Creek Bridge and then turn right a kilometer later onto the Wesach logging road. Follow this road for 3.2 km (2.1 mi), always veering to the left when you come to a fork until you cross Hall Creek. At the next fork take the right-hand road and go for another half a kilometer to its end. The trail starts here. There are signs all the way to trailhead (and beyond).

The trail:: Like many trails, this one starts with a steep climb and then a few minutes later it becomes moderate. The entire walk is about 850 m (2760 ft) up. The trail is well marked through the forest to the alpine. When you are just about through the forest, the trail splits. One goes directly to the alpine and is for those with excess energy as it is very steep. Those with less energy can head over to an old mining claim before going to the top. This second option, although less direct, is far easier than the first. Once on top, you will pass some tiny lakes and then dip down a bit to the remains of a few cabins. If it is clear, you will see Wesach Mountain to the north, a rugged piece of rock that is great for photo backdrops. Also watch for goats.

Nisga'a Lava Beds

The lava flows are about 10 km (6 mi) long and 3 km (2 mi) wide and the park where they are located covers an area of 17,683 hectares. The eruption that left these beds occurred some 300 to 400 years ago and caused the death of about 2000 locals living in the area at the time. The lava has four very different formations besides the usual large black chunks of rock. The formations are fun to identify. One is the tree-cast holes that were left when tree trunks were burned out after the lava covered them. Another formation is called the lava tube that was formed when the top layer of lava cooled and formed a crust that kept the lava inside flowing rather than hardening. This resulted in tubes being formed. The pahoehoe can be identified by its rope-like appearance. Rough and jagged rock formations are called AA's. For the more advanced geologists, there are also cinder cones, caves, spatter cones and a lava lake.

There are numerous local legends attached to the area and the most popular is the one that describes the birth of the volcano. It was due to some naughty children who showed disrespect to the salmon. The mountain became angry and spewed its wrath onto the villages where the children lived.

The area is treacherous to walk around except when on the trail because there are crevasses covered with vegetation. There are also unstable rock slabs and sharp rocks that could tumble onto you. There are five interpretive trails around the park but should you want to visit the crater, you will need to join a guided tour offered by the Nisga'a people. The hike to the cone is about 3 km (2 mi) one-way across a moonscape of black rock. The hike passes most of the volcanic features mentioned above. It is a moderate hike that goes up and down uneven terrain so good boots are recommended. The cost of a guide in 2004 was $12 Cdn.

There is a campsite at Vetter Creek and picnic facilities along the north shore of the Lava Lake. There is a charge for camping at the sites.

Trail access: To get to the park, take Highway 16 to Terrace and then travel north on the Nisga'a Highway (Kalum Lake Drive) for 100 km (60 mi). It is paved for the first 70 km (44 mi). You will pass Kalum Lake (a destination in itself) and then Rosswood where the Lava Lake is found. The road to the right, beside Ross Lake, goes to the Volcanic Cone Trail. Farther into the park you will find New Aiyansh, a village with a large visitor center. The other way to approach the area is to go from Kitwanga north along Highway 37 (Stewart Cassiar) to Cranberry River. From there, turn onto the Nass Forest Service Road and go for 86 km (54 mi) to the park.

Kitimat

The area was first inhabited thousands of years ago by people who fished for oolichan and traded its valuable oil with neighboring tribes. Some still practice fishing and extracting oil for trade today.

The 1950s brought modern industry to the area with the Kemano Project, the building of the Alcan plant where aluminum could be processed and exported. Alcan needed electricity for this project so, in 1954, they built a generating station. It was a monumental task that created a huge reservoir with a 16-km (10 mi) tunnel linking the reservoir to the plant at Mount DuBose (in Kemano). The company then had to run an 82 km (53 mi) transmission line over rugged terrain that included the Kildala Pass, sitting 1500 m (4875 ft) above sea level and always covered in snow. The plant had 35,000 construction workers employed for years. It became the largest aluminum plant in the western hemisphere. Then, the town started to grow. First employees for the plant came to the area. These people needed banks, housing, restaurants, entertainment and commercial goods so others came to fill those needs. By the late 1950s, the town had it all.

Some environmental studies have shown that toxic chemicals, possibly from the plant dumping its effluent into the waters, is causing the fish to die. Recently, the company has been forced to practice more environmentally sensitive methods of effluent disposal.

Mount Elizabeth

Time: Full day.

Distance: 12 km (7.5 mi) return.

Difficulty: Class three.

Topo maps: 103I/1 and 103I/2 for reference only.

The route: This is a long steep trail to alpine with an elevation gain of about 1350 m (4500 ft) in less than 5 km (3 mi). More than half the way up is in the forest. However, once out of the trees, the peaks are splendid.

Trail access: From Kitimat town center, drive north along Highway 37 toward Terrace for 8 km (5 mi). Just after the power lines, turn right onto a gravel road that has a sign indicating the way to Mt. Elizabeth. Drive for 14 km (8.75 mi), cross Elizabeth Creek and turn left onto a secondary road. There is another sign indicating the trailhead. Go a short distance up a steep hill and then turn left. There is a sign. Drive another 1.5 km (1 mi) and park beside the sign indicating the trailhead.

The trail: You will go up almost 1350 m (4500 ft) within 5 km (3 mi). That is steep. The first part of the trail switchbacks through the forest and takes about two hours to ascend. The trail follows an arm of the mountain and the arm has a steep drop off on both sides. Be careful if the fog comes in as a tumble off the arm of the mountain could mean serious trouble. Once above timberline, you will be on Little Elizabeth Mountain with the summit ahead and a saddle in between. The return trip is by the same route only it is twice as fast to get down (usually).

Prince Rupert

The town is named after the first Governor of the Hudson's Bay Company who was the son of Fredrick V of Bohemia and Elizabeth Stuart, daughter of King James I of England. Charles Hays of the Grand Trunk Pacific Railway chose the town site. It was to be the railway's most western terminus. By 1910, when things were progressing as he wished, Hays went to England to raise more money for his town that he believed, on its completion, would outclass Vancouver. Hays started back to Canada on the ill-fated RMS Titanic.

After the death of Hays and the decline of the railway, Prince Rupert turned to fishing. Salmon, halibut and herring became the economic backbone of the town. However, the people of Prince Rupert not only fished but they canned the fish so today, old canning sites can still be seen. After the boom of World War II, when the town became a military center, Prince Rupert moved into the pulp and forestry industries. Today it is a busy shipping harbor for goods going to the Orient.

The town is pleasant to visit, easy to get around and equipped with numerous services for the tourist. It is also the spot to catch the ferry to the islands.

Park Ave Campground

There are three routes going toward the city that you can take along these easy, well-marked and maintained trails. There is another trail heading out to the ferry. All trails are through the thick rainforest where deer and birds may be seen. The one starting at the Tsimshian Cedar Bridge follows the Pipeline trail and leads to the Moresby Lagoon where birding is a rewarding pastime. Once at Moresby Park you can go along trails to the center of town or down to the waterfront (where there are excellent restaurants).

If going to the ferry terminal follow the spruce pedestrian bridges, turn right at the old road and go toward the quarry, then the water-pipeline and finally the ferries.

Butze Rapids

Time: One hour.

Distance: 5 km (3 mi).

Difficulty: Class one.

The route: This is any easy trail to follow. It starts a short way out of town and goes through old growth forest for part of the way. Wildlife is abundant.

Trail access: Follow Highway 16 east for 6 km (3.75 mi). There is a parking lot on the highway and trail signs.

The trail: This walk has a few short steep sections and goes to a bay where you can watch reversed tidal rapids. There are interpretive signs along the way and the trail passes through old growth forest. Wolves are known to be in this area. You may also cross the road and walk the Mt. Oldfield Meadows trail that goes for 5 km (3 mi) through forests. If you want an all day hike, walk from the campsite (or your hotel) all the way to trailhead, around the trail and then back to town again. It will warrant a stop at the waterfront for dinner and beer.

Haida Gwaii, formerly called Queen Charlotte Islands

These islands consist of more than 150 islands on the edge of the continental shelf along the west coast of British Columbia. Besides kayaking, anthropological trips, cycling and hiking, one can enjoy the distinct modern art of the locals, the delectable foods in the restaurants and a restful night at one of the numerous camping places. This area is often a vacation destination in itself for both Canadians and foreigners.

Juan Perez was the first European to travel around these islands in 1774 and then in 1787 Captain George Dixon came along and named them after his ship, the Queen Charlotte.

By the 1900s Europeans came to farm and prospect for gold but by the depression of the 1930s, most, unable to eke out a living, abandoned the area. The inhabitants of the islands lived quietly until the late 1970s when adventurers, photographers and writers discovered the place. Word got out and now it is a destination that offers something of interest to almost everyone.

Most people go to Graham Island where Queen Charlotte City is located. The town is an adventure to explore. There is a campsite, many B & Bs and a few hotels. Cycling on these islands is a popular mode of transportation as is hitch hiking. This is one of the few places in North America where it is still safe and easy to hitch a ride.

Those wanting more information about the islands, the history, the people or the trails, can visit **Bill Ellis Books**, across from the playground in Queen Charlotte City, phone 250-559-4681. He has a huge collection that covers just about anything you may want to know about the area. Even if you aren't interested in buying a book, go in and have a look. You won't be able to resist buying something and Bill will mail your books home for you if you don't want to carry them.

There is a ferry that goes between the Charlottes and Prince Rupert six times a week during the summer months. The trip takes about six hours. For exact times visit the web site: www..bcferries.com/schedules/inside/.

Graham Island

Sleeping Beauty Trail

Time: Two or three hours return.

Distance: Short but steep.

Difficulty: Class two.

The route: This steep but short walk up Mt. Genevieve will give you spectacular views of the city and of the ocean around the island.

Trail access: In Queen Charlotte City, follow the road north from the Forest Service office at 1229 Cemetery Road. When you come to Honna Forest Road, follow it for 5 km (3 mi). The trailhead is well marked.

The trail: I highly recommend walking this trail even if you are in the city for just a short time as the views are spectacular.

Naikoon Provincial Park

Naikoon Provincial Park encompasses 72,640 hectares of land on Graham Island. The southern border starts at the Tlell River and crosses the island almost to Port Clements. The northern border is near Rose Point, also an ecological reserve. The northern border reaches beyond the Skonun River and then curves south again.

The name of the park comes from the Haida word "Nai-kum" a place that we now call Rose Spit, that piece of land that separates Hecate Strait from Dixon Entrance. The highest point on the island is Argonaut Hill and it stands at 150 m (500 ft) above sea level. Tow Hill, another popular destination stands at109 m (450 ft).

The hiking trails in the park include Tlell River, Cape Fife, Tow Hill, North Beach and East Beach Trails. The most important thing to remember while hiking here is that the ecosystem is extremely delicate. When root systems of plants are broken (from boots walking on them), the wind causes erosion and shifting of the dunes. This movement of the dunes buries other vegetation and destroys campsites and trails. Always be aware that there are undertows at the mouths of rivers and along the beaches. It is highly recommended to use a camp stove rather than build a fire when camping. There is camping in the park at five different locations with four of them being walk-in wilderness camps. Those wanting to hike the 95 km (59 mi) of **East Beach**, from Tlell River to Rose Spit, should see the park office for detailed information. It would take anywhere from four to six days to complete and knowledge of tide schedules would be essential.

Tlell River

Time: Three hours.

Distance: 5 km (3 mi) one-way.

Difficulty: Class two.

The route: This walk is along the Tlell River to the Pesuta boat that was shipwrecked on the island in 1928. This is a photographer's dream stop. You may camp around the boat but you must carry water. Otherwise, there is a hotel about a kilometer from the boat.

Trail access: Drive north along the highway to the Tlell River Bridge and park at the park headquarters. The bridge is 35 km (22 mi) north of Skidegate Mission.

The trail: This is one of the most popular day-hikes on the islands. Follow the north side of the river through forest for 5 km (3 mi) to the ocean. This is a pleasant walk with no elevation change. Walking over some of the dunes near the water look more inviting than along the packed trail beside the river but please refrain from doing so. There are sandhill cranes, Canada geese and whistler swans along this stretch of island.

The Pesuta was a 2150-ton boat that was wrecked by a storm in December 1928, just north of the Tlell River. This is a great subject for those wanting to do some photography. However, unless shooting black and white, color is needed. Bring a colorful scarf, pack, or other object that will brighten up the wreck. Should you wish to see more dunes, go south along the beach, past the Tlell River mouth. These are also a popular destination.

Tow Hill

Time: One to two hours.

Distance: 1 or 2 km (0.5 to 1 mi) one-way.

Difficulty: Class one.

The route: This destination offers a climb up Tow Hill and a walk to the Blow Hole just a few hundred meters past the hill. I recommend visiting both spots.

Trail access: Drive to the north end of the island, past Rose Spit Reserve to the campground on North Beach. The hill is beside the campsite.

The trail: Follow the west side of the Hiellen River until you come to a junction. The trail to the left goes up the hill for a good view of McIntyre Bay and the surrounding area. This is a steep climb for a short distance. You can rest on the way. The other fork at the bottom of the hill goes to the blowhole, a rock formation that allows ocean water to accumulate and then blow up at great speed and distance - like a fountain. The other rock formations in the area are also interesting to observe/photograph.

Fife

Time: Three to four hours one-way.

Distance: 10 km (6 mi) one-way.

Difficulty: Class two – you must carry water.

The route: This is a very long hike, especially if returning on the same day. The trail crosses the Argonaut Plain and some of the terrain has muskeg, old forest and stunted pines that twist like snakes around other trees.

Trail access: Drive to the north end of the island, past Rose Spit Reserve to the campground on North Beach. The trail is beside the campsite and is marked.

The trail: If you have camping gear, a really nice trip is to take the Fife trail and cross the island to Hecate Strait near Kumara Lake. There is a walk-in campsite there. Follow the East Beach to Rose Point at the tip of Rose Spit and then follow North Beach the 20 km (12.5 mi) back to the campground. The beach is full of driftwood that makes good shelter from the wind. The trip is spectacular and not so long that your legs become paralyzed from walking on the sand. The spit is a must to visit if you are at this end of the island.

The trail follows an old settler's path through spruce, cedar and hemlock. Walking across Argonaut Plain will give you a very different view of the island than the beaches do. Here you will have moss, bog, muskeg, tiny streams and twisted trees trying to eke out a living on the barren land. It is beautiful.

Moresby Island

Gray Bay/Cumshewa Head

Time: Four days.

Distance: 25 km (16 mi) one-way.

Difficulty: Class four – the tides have an 8 m (25 ft) difference in height from low to high tide. You must have tide charts and take note to be away from cliffs where you can be trapped during high tide. Hiking boots are essential.

The route: This is a difficult hike to an abandoned village where there are the remains of some totem poles. It is best to get information about this trail from the park office in Queen Charlotte City before starting out. You must also purchase tide charts.

Trail access: Take the ferry from Queen Charlotte City across to Alliford Bay on Morseby Island. From Alliford bay, drive north to Sandspit and then follow the logging road south for 14.5 km (9 mi) to the road that turns east toward Gray Bay. Follow this road to its end.

The trail: Start this walk after high tide so you won't be caught in an uncomfortable place. The first few kilometers are wide beaches so the walking is easy. However, the coast soon becomes rugged with jagged rocks holding hidden caves. You will pass tide pools and see sea lions along the way. Once at the village, you will find the remains of totems and some burial mounds. Trying to cut through the forest anywhere along this hike is not recommended. It is old growth rain forest that is difficult to bushwhack through. Cutting through will take far longer than walking around along the shore.

The Stewart-Cassiar Highway #37

The Stewart Cassiar Highway (as it is commonly called) runs between the Alaska Highway in the north and Highway 16 West in the south.

Along the highway from south to north (north to south in brackets) you will find:

Km 0 (724) - Junction of Highway 16 West and Highway 37 - gas, groceries, minor repairs and restaurant.

Km 76 (648) - Cranberry Junction.

Km 139 (585) - Meziadin Lake General Store – groceries and gas.

Km 156 (568) – Meziadin Junction - gas, minor repairs, restaurant, camping and turn-off to Stewart/Hyder.

Km 250 (474) - Bell II - gas, minor repairs, accommodations, camping and restaurant.

Km 334 - (390) - Tatogga - gas, minor repairs, accommodations, camping and restaurant.

Km 405 (319) – Iskut - gas and groceries with resorts in the area.

Km 488 (236) – Dease Lake – gas, groceries, accommodations, camping, restaurant and turn-off to Telegraph Creek.

Km 626 (98) – Good Hope Lake – gas and groceries.

Km 724 (0) - Junction #37 and Alaska Highway - gas, accommodations and restaurant.

Old Kuldo Hiking

Time: One hour.

Distance: 3 km (2 mi).

Difficulty: Class one.

Equipment: Water should be carried.

The route: This is a historical trail set in an especially scenic area that has the remains of an Indian village and part of the old Telegraph Trail.

Trail access: From the junction of Highways 16 and 37, drive north about 50 km (31 mi) to the Kuldo Main Forest Service Road. Turn west and follow that road for 51 km (32 mi) where you will come to a bridge over a creek. The trailhead is just past the creek. The Kuldo Forest Road is an active logging road and care should be taken when traveling along it.

The trail: The trail has seven stations in all. The first is in an older forest with some trees being about 150 years old. The standing dead trees are known as snags and house insects loved by birds such as woodpeckers. Also in an area like this the pine marten will be found. Pine marten are drawn by the color red and old trappers used to place tomato-tin labels around their traps to attract the marten. Because there is little sunlight reaching the ground, there is little underbrush in this area.

The second station near the creek is called the riparian zone where the vegetation is much thicker due to the abundance of water. There is a lot of Devil's Club that is a devil to bushwhack through - just look at the stems.

The third station is where the telegraph trail once passed. Built as a communication line between Europe and North America it was replaced by the short wave radio and the Trans Atlantic cable before the telegragh line could be completed. One of the problems along the telegraph trail was maintaining the line, especially during winter.

The forth station has remnants of a man-made canal that was used to carry water from False Creek to the village. It was about 2 km (1.5 mi) long and passed the village before it emptied into the Skeena River.

Station five is the actual Kuldo village site where cache pits (depressions) can still be seen. The pits held food and the bigger pits held humans whenever the village was under attack by enemy tribes. There is still an old halfway cabin in the shrub at the site. Halfway cabins were built half way between two main cabins on the telegraph line. The main cabins were built 50 km (31 mi) apart. Linemen on the telegraph line lived in these cabins. The village of Kuldo was abandoned by 1924.

Station six overlooks one of the canyons on the Skeena River, rich in salmon and steelhead, that were fished by the natives with traps and dip nets.

The last station shows where bears have used the tree to mark their territory.

Stewart/Hyder Alaska

Hyder, often called the friendliest ghost town in Alaska, is officially in the United States. However, the town takes Canadian money, most people speak Canadian and there is no American border crossing when going from Stewart to Hyder. However, there is a Canadian border crossing that you must pass when returning to Canada.

There are numerous fish and chip shops, galleries, gift shops, hotels, and of course bars at both towns. Hotels on either side of the border are not expensive, running between Cdn $42 and US $75 for a double while camping is around $12 per tent.

Hyder, originally called Portland City, was renamed in 1914 after Fredrick Hyder, a Canadian mining engineer who predicted great prosperity for the area. The city's boom was between 1920 and 1930 at which time the Riverside Mine took gold, silver, copper, lead, zinc and tungsten from the mountains. This mine operated until about 1960.

Stewart, on the Canadian side of the border is tucked between the ocean and ice-crowned mountains. During the 1890s people began to flock to the area in search of gold. The town was first named in 1905 after two Scottish prospectors, John and Robert Stewart. At the time there were a total of 10,000 people living there. However, due to the lack of gold, the population had dropped to less than 20 by World War I.

Because the area is highly mineralized, numerous mines have been in production for a number of years. Of these, the Premier Gold Mine, Big Missouri and the Granduc Copper Mines were the biggest. Granduc is the only one still in operation today.

Besides getting "Hyderized" (drunker than a pole cat on local hooch) in Hyder, hikers have a number of interesting trails they can access. Stewart Historical Society Museum is of interest and displays items such as a photo of a horse wearing snowshoes. The biggest draw to the area of course is the wildlife with the famous bear-viewing platform on Fish Creek just north of Hyder. There, from a wooden platform, visitors can watch grizzlies and black bears fish, eat, and play. The eagles, waterfowl and smaller animals like wolf and fox are also in abundance.

To get to Stewart and Hyder, drive north on highway #37 from highway 16 at Kitwanga for 220 km (137 m) or drive south from the junction of the Alaska Highway 632 km (393 m) and turn west into Stewart. You will pass the Bear Glacier that spews into a lake shortly after the turn-off.

Fish Creek Wildlife Observation Site

Time: The site is open daily from 6 am to 10 pm during July and August.

Distance: 200 m (600 ft) from the parking lot to the observation tower.

Difficulty: Class one.

Trail access: Follow the Salmon River Road north of Hyder for 6.5 km (4 mi). Once across the bridge over Fish Creek, there is a parking lot that is just a few hundred meters from the observation tower.

The trail: The observation tower can be seen from the parking lot. There is a dike between Fish Creek and Marx Creek that can also be walked but the bears use this as a highway themselves and care should be taken not to frighten one.

The bears fish for chum and pink salmon while at the creek and disturbing them should be avoided as they are wild and protective of their food supply. You as a visitor are forbidden to bring food out of your car. Running, shouting or loud conversation is also not allowed as this could disturb the animals. You must never enter the creeks or sit on the banks as the bears may take this as a threat to their food and territory. At no time may you use a flash as this too can surprise the animals.

Titan

Time: Eight hours.

Distance: 16 km (10 mi) return, part of it a steep uphill and lots of undulating after you are on the ridge.

Difficulty: Class two.

Equipment needed: The views are exceptional and lots of camera equipment and film should be included in your gear.

Trail access: Drive along the Salmon River Road past the observation platform for another half a kilometer (0.25 mile).

The trail: There is a trailhead sign at the start of the trail. The hike starts by fording the creek. Once on the opposite side, follow the trail through the old-growth forest and up the hill. This is an old horse trail that goes for about an hour. Once on the ridge, the views begin. This ridge is the border between Canada and the States. Part way along there is a viewpoint (marked) that allows views of the Salmon River, Stewart Creek and Fish Creek directly below. Salmon River is the big one. But it is the Salmon Glacier that is the real draw. To the north the ice-rimmed Mt. Shorty Stevenson comes into view. It is in Canada.

The trail was built in 1922 and used mostly by prospectors looking for gold. Later, the trail was used by miners working at the Titan Mines. Remains of mining equipment will be seen along the trail. Return by the same route as you came.

Sluice Box

Distance: Less than an hour.

Difficulty: Class one.

Trail access: Follow highway 37A out of Stewart toward Meziadin Junction to the Bear River and take the first right; it is toward the garbage dump. Park before the bridge that leads to the dump and follow the signs to the trailhead.

The trail: This little hike is a leisurely walk that can be done by almost everyone. It is also a good walk for kids. The trail is along the old rail bed that once held the rail line used for hauling ore out of the area. After a bit the trail leaves the rail bed and follows the wooden sluice box that was used by prospectors to sluice the gravel. Eventually you will come to a viewpoint that overlooks Stewart and Portland Canal.

United Empire Loyalists

Time: Two to eight hours.

Distance: 15 km (9 mi) return if going to the alpine. However, it is only 9 km (6 mi) if going just to the mine site and barely 2 km (1.5 mi) return if going to the viewpoint overlooking the town.

Difficulty: Class one/two.

The route: If going beyond the viewpoint you will need good boots. If going early in the season, check with the Forest Service about snow conditions. Be aware that avalanches are common during early June.

Trail access: No vehicle is needed for this hike. Follow the road to the highway service yard at the edge of Stewart. Take the trail that follows the Beaver River.

The trail: The trail starts near the Beaver River and heads up quickly. It is a grunt to the viewpoint overlooking the town and takes about 30 to 45 minutes to reach. The Bear River Valley is left behind as you climb again to the United Empire Loyalist Mine another two hours away. From the mine site you climb onto the ridge and follow it to alpine about 7.5 km (5 mi) from trailhead. Once in the alpine, you may explore more. This is a wonderful hike with good views.

Ore Mountain

Time: Two to eight hours

Distance: 3.5 km (2.2 mi) to viewpoint and 4.0 km (2.5 mi) to alpine.

Difficulty: Class two.

The route: This mountain can be reached from Stewart as a day hike or as an overnight trip with camping at Clements Lake. There is a second lake in the alpines beyond Clements Lake that can also provide good camping.

Trail access: From Stewart drive north along highway 37A toward Meziadin Junction for 13 km (8 mi) to the Bitter Creek Bridge. Take the first right after the bridge and then turn left at the first junction. Veer constantly to the right for another kilometer until you arrive at the Clements Lake

Recreation Site. The site is maintained from May to September. There are no motorized vehicles allowed on the lake. There is a sandy beach near the camping area. From the campsite, walk the old mud road that looks like it is drivable but in fact is not. Walk for about half a kilometer to the trailhead.

The trail: Although less than 4 km (2.5 mi) to the viewpoint over the Bear River Valley, there are some steep and difficult parts along this trail. Tree roots are slippery when wet and so are some rocks. The lookout is at the sub-alpine level and the trail goes for another kilometer before it reaches the alpine.

American Creek

Time: This can be a half-day hike or an overnighter.

Difficulty: Class two/three. The trail follows a creek and because of its gentle ascension, it is not considered difficult. However, wearing good boots and carrying all the things used for a class two hike is recommended. Weather is a big factor in this area and you could run into rain or snow at any time.

Trail access: Drive north from Stewart along highway 37A toward Mezidatin Junction to the Bear River Bridge, 22 km (14 mi) from the center of town. Turn left at the second road and follow the gravel road up a steep hill. Continue along that road, veering to the right for another half a kilometer until you see the trailhead sign.

The trail: This is a trail that follows American Creek. There is almost no elevation gain. It will take about an hour or two to reach Champion Creek at the end of the maintained trail. This is an excellent stretch-your-legs trail that at one time was used by prospectors looking for glitter.

Dease Lake

This is the largest community along the 700-kilometer Stewart-Cassiar Highway. If the unpaved sections of road along the way seem especially slippery during a wet spell that is due to the calcium chloride used on the road to help keep the dust down and stabilize the road base. The chemical also clings to everything it comes in contact with like your clothes, car and camping gear.

The town was originally on Pan-America's Seattle to Fairbanks flyway. This service was used to accommodate Canadian and American forces in the north during World War II. The US Air Force operated the station at Dease Lake after Pearl Harbor and remained around until the end of the war.

Dease Lake offers everything from a good meal to a soft bed and a short hike. The park office has information and maps for the Spatsizi and Edziza parks that are located near here and planes to fly into Edziza can be hired here.

The Northway Motor Inn is clean and reasonable. The owner will go out of his way to accommodate your needs. Their restaurant is also the best in town.

For camping, the Tanzilla Campground, 10 km (6 mi) south of town is a wonderful place to stay. The sites are tucked into a sparsely forested area that is beside a raging creek.

The town also has a small health clinic, an RCMP office and a fairly well equipped grocery and liquor store.

Allan Lake

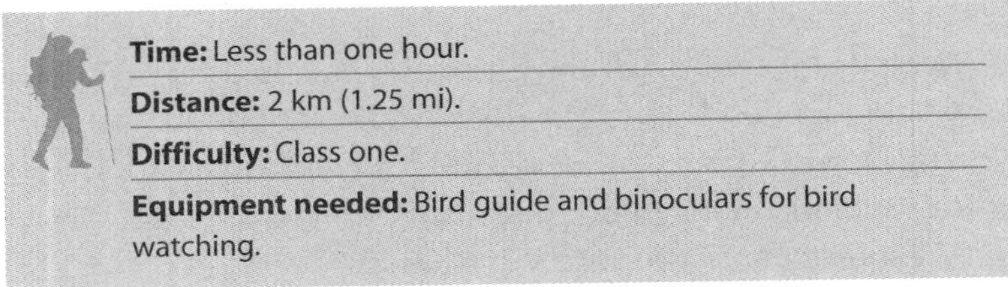

Time: Less than one hour.

Distance: 2 km (1.25 mi).

Difficulty: Class one.

Equipment needed: Bird guide and binoculars for bird watching.

The route: This is a nice walk around a lake, along a groomed trail bordered by forest. The lake supports a large community of birds, many of which are migrating birds.

Trail access: Park at the Northway Motor Inn and walk to the end of the road where the Tanzilla Pub is located. Turn left and then veer to the right when you see the BC Parks sign.

The trail: The gravel walkway follows around the horseshoe shaped lake that is surrounded with forests. This is a nice walk for kids who are tired of riding in the car and need to burn off a bit of steam.

Telegraph Creek

Telegraph Creek is 112 km (70 mi) south of Dease Lake on a narrow gravel road that has a grade of up to 20% in places. The road is not only steep and switch-backed but it is dangerous. Built in 1922, it was the first road ever built in the Cassiar Mountains. It seems to me there has been little upgrading since.

During the 1940s when airports and roadways were necessary for the war effort, Telegraph Creek was a hub of activity. In those days the boats came up the Stikine River bringing food and building supplies needed to build the aerodromes in the north. Once the goods arrived at Telegraph Creek, they would go by truck to Dease Lake and then again by boat toward Watson Lake and surrounding communities. It took the trucks anywhere from eight hours to three days to travel along the road between Telegraph Creek and Dease Lake.

In the 1940s Telegraph Creek had three restaurants, one that often turned into a dance hall during the evenings. There were also two hotels, a bunkhouse and a handful of stores. The town has since declined to 230 permanent residents and it has the atmosphere of a ghost town. The old Hudson's Bay Post from Glenora just south of Telegraph Creek is now the River Song Café, B & B, and General Store. The food in the café is worth stopping for.

From the main street, you will see a two-storey wooden house perched on the hill across the way. It once belonged to the Hyland family. The Hyland River, named after the family, runs west from the Yukon/Northwest Territory border along Highway 10 that goes into Tungsten.

The Anglican Church on the main street was built in 1937 and is a good example of handcrafted carpentry. The property was given to the Anglican Church by Diamond "C" (Frank Callbreath). I am uncertain if this is the same Diamond "C" from the Nahanni legends. One of the great books about the north, *Notes from the Century Before*, by Edward Hoagland, is about Telegraph Creek.

Stikine River Song offers trips up and down the river to the canyons, past the waterfall, and to the glaciers. They are knowledgeable about the local history and are open to making custom trips. You may write to Box 47, Telegraph Creek, V0J 2W0 or phone (250) 235-3196, www.stikineriversong.com/.

Mess Creek Hike

Time: Full day.

Distance: 6 km (3.75 mi) one-way.

Difficulty: Class two.

Equipment needed: You must hire a boat to take you across the river and then bring you back once you have completed the hike. The cost is about $20 each way for the boat (not per person). Ask around town for someone with a boat to take you.

The trail: The well-defined trail undulates along the valley. To see the canyon you must turn right at the forks. Mountain goats are often spotted on this walk. Be sure to carry water.

Taya Lookout

On the way into Telegraph Creek there is a park boundary sign a few kilometers before the village. The trail goes to the lookout of Taya Creek. It is a short walk but the views are worth getting out of the car for. There is also an outhouse five minutes down the trail.

Roadout

At the first pullout south of the 100-kilometer sign and the park boundary sign, there are excellent views of the Stikine Canyon and a waterfall that comes out of the side of the hill. Walk along the trail that is in the center of the hill, veering north to the edge of the cliff where you will be able to see the waterfall. This walk will take less than an hour, including time for photography.

Winter Creek

At 14 km (8.75 mi) south, on the road to Glenora is Winter Creek Campsite. It is on the river beside a clear-water creek. The camping site is clean and well maintained, with outhouses and a shower stall. However the shower is without water. There is also an abandoned building that could offer some shelter should you have bad weather. There are lots of black bears in the area so keep your food locked away. Walking along the creek is recommended.

Glenora

This is the old town site where, during the gold rush, 10,000 tents were pitched. The native graveyard is located about 100 m (300 ft) before the clearing where the town once stood. The older graves from the 1800s are on the river side of the road.

For excellent views of the river, find the first driveway leading to the river. Cross the field and find a path going up the hill. The climb to the top will take about ten minutes. The trail eventually enters private property so once a house comes into view, I would suggest returning down the hill.

At the south end of the clearing, tucked into the bush, is an old log cabin. The cabin was made of thin logs placed in the traditional way; one lying horizontally across the next. The cabin is very tiny, less than 500 square feet. The inside of the cabin was decorated with smaller sticks placed vertically, in geometric designs, kept in place with tiny hand made nails. The roof was made from flattened Klem Milk cans.

The man who built this cabin put all his love into the home while waiting for his bride to arrive from China. It was during the gold rush in the 1800s and most men didn't have the energy or the time for such intricate work. When his wife arrived from China, she took one look and left. Another woman never got the opportunity to live in this cabin.

To get to the old Hudson Bay Company site, you must walk down the riverbank for about half an hour. This walk is not possible during high water. The foundation is the only thing that is left of the old post.

Highway #37

from Stewart/Hyder turnoff to Alaska Border

Stikine River Canyons

This spectacular run of canyons follows the river from the bridge on the Stewart Cassiar Highway all the way past Telegraph Creek and part way to Wrangell, Alaska.

There is good camping on the north side of the river, under the bridge along the Stewart Cassiar Highway. However, it is noisy when the vehicles travel across the metal decking of the bridge. There is a road at the west end of the camping area that leads to Willie William's place a few kilometers farther in. He offers trips with packhorses through Edziza and Spatzizi Provincial Parks, or a full day ride through some of the canyon. If you would like to go only to the start of the canyons, he charges $20 per hour; otherwise his trips are $100 a day. To contact Willie, call (250) 771-4301 or write to Stikine Trail Rides, Dease Lake, V0C 1L0

Stikine River Canyon near Telegraph Creek.

Willie Williams made the trail described below. He and his family have lived on this piece of land for over forty years and they built the buildings. He had six kids; one who became an RCMP officer. He is proud of his lifestyle and accomplishments. Now, much to his chagrin, BC

Parks is claiming his land. If you walk across Willie's fields and use his trails, please leave him a small donation for the use of the place. Be sure to stop and talk to him; he is full of stories.

Mouth of the Canyons

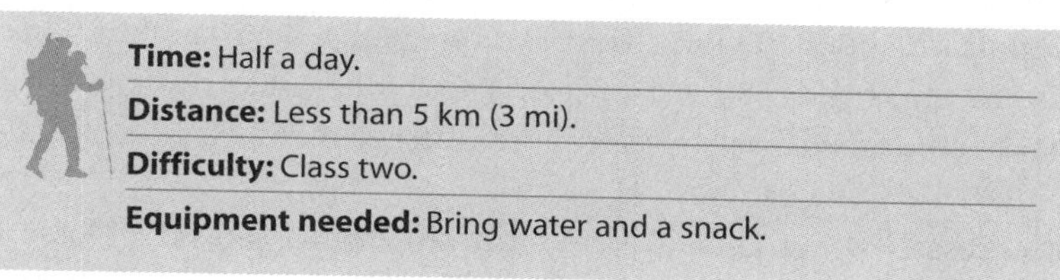

Time: Half a day.

Distance: Less than 5 km (3 mi).

Difficulty: Class two.

Equipment needed: Bring water and a snack.

The route: This trail actually passes across three of Willie Williams's fields. If you do not want to go onto his land you must bushwhack down the river.

Trail access: If you are not going through Willie William's fields, you should leave your vehicle at the bridge and walk along the river or the road to the Williams's gate. At the gate, head into the bush and down to the river.

The trail: Continue along the river until you come to a wide-mouth and swampy creek about half a kilometer past the Williams's field. This section will be a bushwhack through willows and alders. Follow the creek up to a spot where crossing is possible. Once across the creek, look for a well-defined horse trail going up the hill.

The trail can be followed for about half an hour before it opens onto gorgeous views of the canyons. The trail continues along the ridge and you may walk as long or far as you wish. Return by the same way.

BCR Rail Bed

At one time the British Columbia Railway was going to build a line from Vancouver all the way to Dease Lake so the line could haul lumber out of the north. Billions of dollars were spent on the construction of the line from Bulkley House on Takla Lake to Dease Lake. Then one day, the government decided to cancel the project. Within a few months of that decision, they had dismantled everything from microwave towers to bunk houses. All that was left was a million dollar bridge over the Stikine River and the original gravel rail bed of which we cyclists and hikers are willing to take full advantage.

Time: Two days (cycle around the rail bed back to road).

Distance: 135 km (85 mi).

Difficulty: Class four.

Equipment: Bicycle and all repair equipment for the bike.

The route: Although not really a hiking trail, the rail bed offers the biking enthusiast about 135 km (85 mi) of off-road, wilderness fun. There are places where the road is grown over and other places where the gravel has been washed away by mudslides. Passage then becomes a challenge. Otherwise it is a great cycle.

Trail access: Turn at Gnat Lake 26 km (16.25 mi) south of Dease Lake. Drive down to the rail bed that can be seen in the distance and away you go. An alternative to this is to drive to Tatoga Lodge and park there. Then from Tatoga, cycle north 1.8 km (1.1 mi) to Ealue Lake Road. Follow this road for 24.8 km (15.5 mi) down to the rail bed. There are excellent campsites just before the rail bed hits the road.

The trail: There are a number of comfortable campgrounds along this route. Your main concern is water. Hunters have made more than one horse-coral style campsite where you can pitch a tent and enjoy a comfortable evening. Some of these sites are First Nations sites and signs posted on trees indicate that strangers camping at those sites would be unwelcome. Since there are many places to camp, these should be avoided.

If hiking rather than biking in the area, you can drive the 25 km (15 mi) down the Ealue Lake road. If you have no vehicle the owner of Tatoga will drive you for a minimal fee. He also has non-serviced cabins that rent for a reasonable price and you may pitch a tent at Tatoga.

The campsite at the 25 km (15 mi) spot of the Ealue road is established with poles for tarps and rustic camp tables on which to work. It is beside the Kaplin River. To get to the water go down the double tracked trail at the end of the campsite. Take the first single trail to the right. It goes directly to the creek. To get to the Stikine River Bridge or the rail bed farther south, continue along the main road past the campsite and over the bridge that crosses the Kaplin River. At the end of that road you may turn either left (north) or right (south).

The road to the Stikine River Bridge to the left is bumpy but it lends a few good views of the surrounding mountains. It takes about 2.5 hours to reach the bridge by bike and is about 15 kilometers past the Kaplin

River Bridge. The decking on the Stikine River Bridge is deteriorating but the under decks are solid.

The road continues on the north side of the bridge but it is quite grown over. Rain gear is needed as the shrubs can shed a lot of water during one of the day's regular squalls. It is another 15 km (10 mi) to the Stewart Cassiar Highway near Gnat Lake.

Rail Bed to the South

Follow the road from the campsite over the bridge on the Kaplin River and then at the T, turn right and continue south, following the Kaplin River rather than going north to the Stikine. The southern road goes to the headwaters of the Skeena River and to an old coalmine.

Bridge over the Stikine River on the B.C. Rail bed.

The first Coldfish Lake trailhead sign is 3 km (2 mi) down the road bed. From the sign the road bed goes along on a slight up grade, thus making the cycling harder than it appears.

The park boundary sign is another 15 km (10 mi) down the road bed. There are many comfortable places to camp along here. Cabins dot the countryside and most are open so shelter is possible in the event of severe weather.

The second Coldfish Lake trail sign is at 50 km (35 mi) and follows Eaglenest Creek. It is 7 km (4.5 mi) beyond the park boundary sign. The road bed is bumpy but it stays beside the Kaplin River.

Two kilometers farther

along there is a camping spot with a tarp frame that makes the campsite just a bit more comfortable. Water is available.

Three more kilometers will bring you to a nice lake with camping on the west side and off the road. The bird life around the lake is worth taking binoculars for. As you continue up the valley, there are a few old washouts and maybe some new ones too. The road bed washes away quite often. The valley closes in and the mountains seem to rise up higher.

Another 20 km (12 mi) along, a road leading to a cabin on the hill will be reached. The cabin can't be seen from the road. Follow the side road up and you will find the half finished building. Although it would be good to camp here, there is no water. You can continue along the rail bed for another hundred kilometers or so. It is all fun exploration.

Spatzizi Provincial Wilderness Park

This historical wilderness park, encompassing almost 657,000 hectares of land, is a place that, due to its isolation, doesn't attract too many visitors. This is both a blessing and a pity. There are many trails in the park, most made by horses but the most popular by far is the Coldfish Lake – Eaglenest Creek Trail. However, rather than walking, many visitors fly into the plateau and spend all their time exploring up there.

The park name means red goat in the Tahltan Indian Language and was named such because of the many mountain goats living in the area. Besides lots of goats, there are also grizzlies, moose, caribou and wolf. About 150 species of birds have been recorded in the area, including the gyrfalcons.

While hiking this trail, carry Tommy Walker's book on Spatsizi and learn about the interesting history attached to the place. Walker set up a hunting and fishing camp at Coldfish Lake in 1948. Each mud hole and creek crossing he describes will come alive as you hike, albeit under better conditions.

Coldfish Lake

Time: Six days are recommended. Some people fly one way and hike the other. This, for most people, allows time for exploring the plateau. Doing the circle route coming out McEwen Creek takes about ten days. There are four cabins at the lake that are maintained and rented by the Parks Board. Each cabin has a wood stove in it. There is also a shelter at the lake with a woodstove for those not lucky enough to get a cabin.

Distance: 60 km (37.5 mi) to the lake, 137 km (86 mi) for the entire circle.

Difficulty: Class four and five. Bushwhacking and route finding is required if playing on the plateau. Parks BC publishes a map of the route but it is not sufficient if exploring the plateau.

Topo map: 104H/10 and 104H/11.

Equipment needed: Everything that is required for a long hike. Be especially conscious of having extra clothing as the weather can be miserable and extremely wet. Snow in July is not unheard of. Food high in calories is also recommended.

The route: Although this is along a well-used trail, the hike requires good backcountry knowledge because of the isolation of the area. Map and compass skills are essential due to the possibility of bad weather hampering your visibility. There are creeks to cross, canyons to skirt, bush and bog to wade through and mosquitoes to fight off. The area is very isolated and beautiful. There are bridges over some of the creeks and bogs and trail signs are posted in necessary places.

Trail access: The owner of Tatoga Lodge will drive you to trailhead. The recommended direction is to walk from Eaglenest Creek over to the lake and then out McEwan Creek. You may also use a bike to get to trailhead and leave everything else at the lodge. The trail down McEwan Creek is often boggy and wet. Some people prefer to walk in and out by the Eaglenest Creek Trail. That way your bike, if you use one, will also be at trailhead.

The trail: Going in by the McEwan Creek Trail is not recommended. It is much easier to go in by the Eaglenest Trail that starts at the 50-kilometer sign along the BCR Rail bed. There is a park sign at the trailhead. The start of the trail goes up hill for a bit and then flattens out - sort of.

After an hour(about 3 kilometers) of leaving the rail bed a small lake is reached. It is inside the park. There are the remains of a trapper's cabin at the lake and camping here is good. The trail continues and opens up to allow views of the rugged Eaglenest Mountains.

Maintained trail to Coldfish Lake in Spatsizi Provincial Wilderness Park

The trail through the forest is clear and there are logs over the boggy areas. However, there is no clear water available between the lake and Eaglenest Creek. There is a comfortable campsite about four hours (8 km) from the road complete with fire pit and benches.

Continue along the side of the creek. There is a steep uphill section to get around a cut bank that runs down to the river. On the other side of the hill, the trail again follows the river. There are make-shift bridges over most creeks.

Five km (3 mi) beyond the hill is a small campsite – a good place to spend your first night. We saw a cow moose with her calf here. She was quite spooked at our presence. This to me is an indication that she is not accustomed to many visitors.

There is a bridge over Ram Creek, your next landmark. From the creek you continue up Eaglenest Creek. There is a second small campsite on the far side of Ram Creek.

The trail is clear from Ram Creek to an area of open dwarf birch. After that, the trail appears and disappears often – use the blazes and park markers to guide you.

You will again pick up a clear trail near MacDonald Creek. The trail is used by horses and the terrain in this section has been affected by the horses so it is easy to follow and in some places may even be a bit muddy.

An established campsite is at MacDonald Creek and your second night out should be quite comfortable if spent here.

The trail climbs steadily from MacDonald Creek up to Danihue Pass. You have one more crossing of Eaglenest before you see the end of it but the headwaters are nothing like farther below. There is a fork in the trail just after crossing Eaglenest where you may either go to Gladys Lake Ecological Reserve (where you may not spend the night) and then down to Coldfish Lake or you may continue through Danihue Pass to the left. If you have the time, go to Gladys Lake, down Coldfish, back up to Danihue Pass then down Icebox Canyon before reaching the McEwan Creek trail and Cullivan Creek.

When returning, the final leg down McEwan Creek is through a lot of bog. Not fun but it is downhill – sort of. Take protection against the mosquitoes. I didn't go this way out.

Mount Edziza National Park

Mount Edziza has one of the most unique landscapes in British Columbia. However, in order to see it you must either fly in or plan on bushwhacking for days to get up onto the plateau. You may also opt to have an outfitter take you in on horseback. Any of your choices could result in you arriving at the same time as bad weather and thus having to spend days waiting for the clouds to clear. Or worse still, you could be hiking for your entire time in snow. This is an isolated area and self-sufficiency is a prerequisite.

Those wanting to walk in must enter from Telegraph Creek and it would take four to six days of bushwhacking to get to Buckley Lake. You may also choose to go out that way.

The park encompasses 230,000 hectares of high volcanic landscape that includes lava flows, volcanic cones and cinder fields. It is an amazing area. Mt. Edziza, a volcano with basalt flows and a glaciated crater, is the big draw and stands at 2787 m (9058 ft). The crater is 2500 m (8125 ft) in diameter at its base and was created about four million years ago. The volcano became inactive about 10,000 years ago. Other smaller cones surround the main mountain. Two of the more noticeable ones are Coffee and Coco Craters that were formed around 1300 years ago. There is no vegetation on the upper parts of these mountains.

Some of the hills around the main mountain shine brilliant red, yellow, purple and white.

Hiking is permitted in the park between July 1st and September 15th and a permit must be obtained from the park office in Dease Lake before you may enter. Parks, after all, must collect their share of your bank account.

Time: Seven to 10 days if flying in and longer if walking to or from Buckley Lake.

Distance: 85 to 90 km (53 to 56 mi).

Difficulty: Class five.

Topographical Maps: 104/G/7, 8W, 9W, 10/14E/15W and 16W.

Equipment needed: Bear spray is highly recommended. Almost every time I hear of friends flying into Buckley Lake, the welcoming committee consists of a huge old grizzly. Since most of your traveling time will be above tree line, a stove is essential. You must also be prepared for snow and below zero temperatures.

The route: The distance between Buckley Lake and Mowdade is 60 km (37.5 mi). All of this is above the tree line, so when the weather is good the views of the volcanoes, the rainbow-colored mountains and the lava beds are worth the trip in. This route is difficult to follow in places. The lava beds cover an area of about 65 km (41 mi) by 25 km (16 mi). Near the beds are over 30 cones that have formed during small eruptions. You must be skilled in backcountry travel to do this hike. The distances in this description are estimates only.

Trail access: Bush planes may be hired from Tatoga Lodge or from Dease Lake and they fly into either Buckley Lake (the most common starting point) or Mowdade Lake where most people end up. The cost is around $400 to $600 for a plane depending on the size, the cost of which can be shared by your party. You may also start the hike at Kinaskan Lake but you must hire a boat to get you across the Iskut River. Boats may be hired at Iskut, Tatoga or Dease Lake. It is a 24 km (15 mi) hike up the Mowdade Trail from Kinaskan Lake to the campsite at Mowdade Lake.

You may also hike the **Klastline River Trail** that starts at the A-E Guest Ranch near Iskut. This trail follows the river to Buckley Lake. This trail is well over 50 km (30 mi) and if you want to do it, I highly recommend hiring an outfitter with horses to take you.

Most people fly into Buckley Lake and walk to Mowdade Lake 60 km (37.5 mi) away. Flying in means that the week in the park is spent above tree line where the spectacular scenery is located. You must have someone take you across the river from Mowdade Lake. Ask at the park office about this.

The trail: There is a campsite at Buckley Lake where you can spend your first day, especially if you are late getting into the mountains. From the camp follow the creek downstream for about a kilometer, until you come to the boggy flats. Cross them and continue up the valley through arctic birch to timberline. The lava flow will be on your right as you walk away from the lake. Just below timberline is a second campsite that could be reached the same day if you arrive early in the morning.

Buckley Lake is known for the water birds it supports during the summer months. These include the gyrfalcons, ptarmigans, owls, golden eyes, grebes and white winged scooters.

Continue in a southeasterly direction towards the Camel's Hump or Sidas Cone, your first cone about 12 kilometers along the trail. From here on you can expect to see mountain goats, moose, caribou, sheep, grizzlies and black bears. Wolves too, may be heard at any time during your visit to the plateau of Edziza. I often make a howling call when hiking so I can warn wildlife of my presence. I was doing this one time and was rewarded with the howl of a wolf. I answered him and he called back.

The **Camel's Hump** is a classic cone that stands at 1540 m (5005 ft). However some of the crater has been eroded by weather so it isn't as perfect as Eve's Cone that you should see the next day. From here look for the yellowish "Sheep Track Bench Pumice" that, according to geologists, indicates another eruption is possible. The silica found anywhere from the Camel's Hump to Cartoona Peak at the south end indicates that the most violent of eruptions that can be expected have already occurred. If eruptions should happen again it could send an ash cover over northern Canada that would last quite some time. Scientists are unable to predict when or even if this will happen. From the Camel's Hump on, you will be in a moonscape.

Meandering along the route from the Camel's Hump to **Eve's Cone** is most pleasant, especially during good weather. The hump is the start of what is known as Desolation Field and Eve's Cone is in the center. It is not recommended to take short cuts through the lava beds because they are unstable and therefore unsafe. An accident up here would be serious. It is also not recommended to go far off the trail if the weather is bad because the landmarks can't be seen.

The trail goes up a dry creek bed and passes about half a kilometer from the base of Eve's Cone. Eve is a huge black mound with a blown crater top. She stands at 1740 m (5655 ft) and is probably the most classic volcano you will see in North America. Look for obsidian in the area. This is a shiny glass-like black stone that can be sharpened enough to cut the heart out of an enemy (the Maya farther south did this). I wouldn't suggest trying this yourself, even if your hiking mate did eat more of the chocolate bars than rations allowed.

Tsekone Ridge or Black Knight Cone is less than half a day (4 km) from Eve's Cone and is part of the glacier-topped Mount Edziza that stands at 2787 m (9058 ft). The Tsekone Ridge itself is at 1920 m (6240 ft).

Toward the northeast is **Williams Cone** or the Etzerza Crater. It is not too eroded, standing at its mere 2100 m (6825 ft). Along the west flank of Williams cone and down from Tsekone Ridge are a couple of hot springs but I have no description as to where they are exactly.

The next destination should be the established campsite at **Taweh Creek** that overlooks the **Cocoa Crater** on the upper eastern side of the ridge. To get there, you will not have to climb around and over the cliffs on Elwyn Creek (follow the trail going around the crater). Although only 6 or 7 km (3 mi), this is a long day that will be spent walking up and down past the huge mountain after which the park was named. The mountain is a shield volcano that has been eroded by hanging glaciers. The flat wall at the top, so common in the advertising photos, is called Pyramid Dome.

From Taweh Creek you will pass along open ground and between Cocoa Crater and the southern end of Mt. Edzizi. From this point you can see other less impressive craters and the polychromatic hills of the Spectrum Range in the distance.

Leaving the two craters you must again pass a huge moonscape before going up to Raspberry Pass. There are cairns to follow through the moonscapes. Although this is not a long distance day, if you climb any of the craters, it will be a strenuous day. You end at Mowdade Lake the following day and are either picked up or you continue down to Kinaskan Lake where you are taken across by boat. These arrangements must be made before you leave.

Alaska Highway South

From Prince George to Fort Nelson

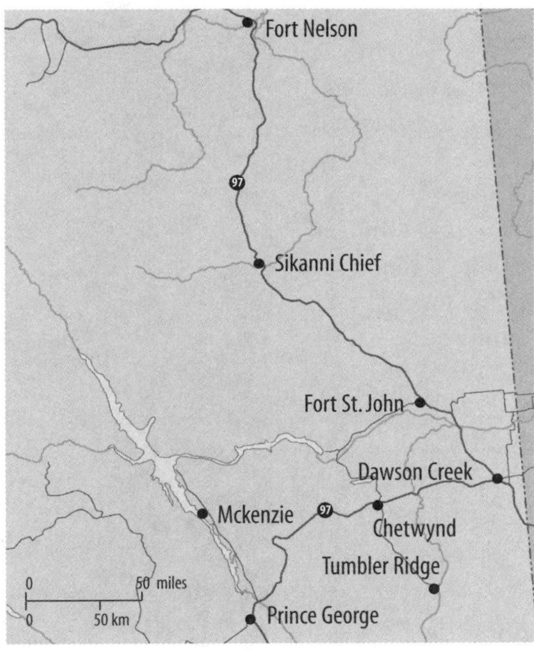

Tea Pot Mountain

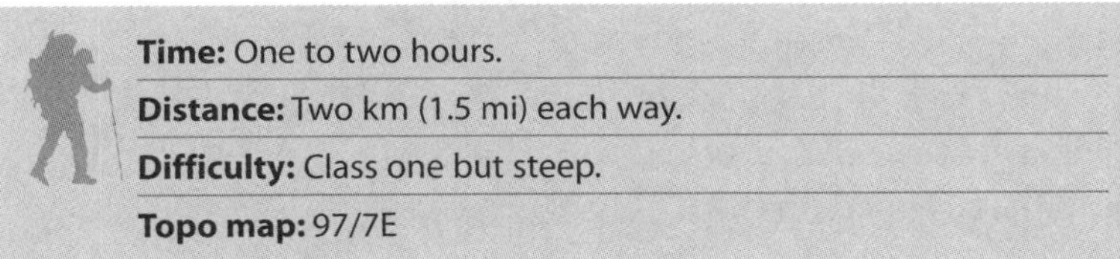

Time: One to two hours.

Distance: Two km (1.5 mi) each way.

Difficulty: Class one but steep.

Topo map: 97/7E

The route: This is a steep climb up the sloping side of a mountain that, from the top, offers views all the way to Fort St. James. This is a great hike for kids. There is no water on the mountain so you must carry it. Once on top, you will see another mountain similar to this one. It is called Coffee Pot Mountain and you need to bushwhack to get to it. For those staying at the campsite at Summit Lake (near the trailhead), Coffee Pot may be fun.

The access: Drive north on Highway 97 from Prince George, past Summit Lake turnoff. Turn north(left) on Tallus Road located 52 km (31 mi) north of Prince George. On Tallus, cross the tracks and follow the road as it veers to the left. Make a right hand turn at the next junction. Continue past the lake and over the Crooked River Bridge and park just beyond the bridge. There are directional signs.

The trail: The trail is clear and goes up the mountain through the woods. You must often climb over rocks and roots that can be slippery when wet. Going to the left at the fork near the top will take you to a campsite of sorts where people often rest and enjoy the view. The trail continues around the top of the mountain and starts back down before returning to the campsite. If you take the right hand fork, you will come to the view point at the backside of the mountain that overlooks the swamp and Crooked River before arriving at the rest/camp spot. You may be lucky to see moose feeding in the swamp below or on the Crooked River itself.

Teapot Mountain, just north of Prince George.

Mackenzie

Located at the south end of Williston Lake, the largest lake in the province, a man-made lake, and just 185 km (115 mi) north of Prince George, this tiny community of 6000 people has excellent hiking opportunities. Besides hiking, the town has a hotel, B & B, restaurants and outfitters to take you into isolated, hard-to-get-to areas.

Since 1966 the town has relied on forestry for its main livelihood and since then has tripled in size. This in turn necessitated other conveniences being present. However, the most endearing feature of Mackenzie is the friendliness of its people. No one is ever too important or busy to give a stranger a helping hand or a bit of conversation.

Mackenzie was also a trading post in the 1800s for the North West Trading Company. The Hudson's Bay Company came in 1820 and continued to trade with those living close by. After the Cariboo gold rush near Barkerville ended, miners started looking for other gold deposits. They went through Mackenzie as they traveled up the Findlay and Parsnip Rivers eventually arriving in Germansen Landing and Manson Creek. Some of the possessions belonging to these miners can still be found on the almost extinct trails between the two communities.

Canty Lake

Time: Four hours.

Distance: 3 km (2 mi) one-way.

Difficulty: Class two with steep sections.

Topo map: Forest recreation maps are available at the Mackenzie Forest District office for a nominal fee. They may be reached at 250-997-2200.

The route: This short hike takes you to an alpine lake and a maintained Forest Service site so there are picnic tables, fire rings and an outhouse. There is also a boat on the lake that can be used. This is not an easy hike and the short distance is deceiving.

Trails access: Travel north from Mackenzie along Highway 39 for 7 km (4 mi). The highway becomes gravel after the Gantahaz subdivision and is then called the West Parsnip Forest Service Road. Follow it to the 90-kilometer sign. The distance from Mackenzie is about 80 km (50 mi).

The trail: There are three steep pitches to this short trail and the estimated hiking time is three hours. This boils down to a single kilometer an hour. There are a couple of wet spots that must be maneuvered around. However, the lake at the top is worth every effort. The lake is tucked into the shadow of Mount Selwyn and surrounded by alpine meadows. It is also stocked with delicious rainbow for anyone carrying a rod.

For the more adventuresome (and experienced) going east from the lake is recommended as there are unique alpine and sub alpine spots to discover. There is part of a trail but it often disappears so navigational skills and a map are required.

This is one of the most favored hikes in the area. Although to date I have not been up here, I was so impressed with the information that was given to me by Gary Hennessy and other dedicated citizens of the community that I surely will do the hike at my earliest opportunity.

Morfee Mountain

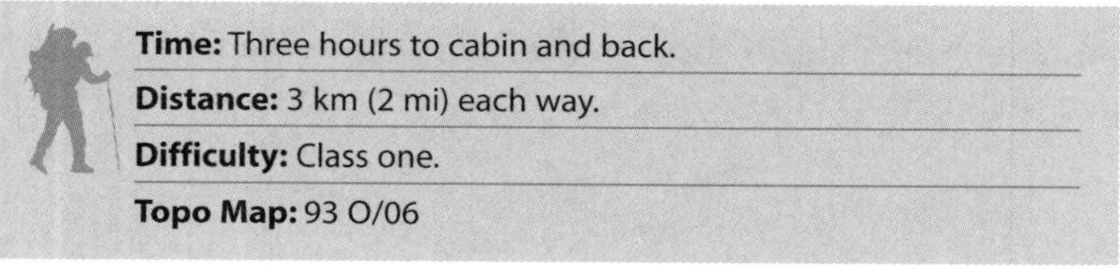

Time: Three hours to cabin and back.

Distance: 3 km (2 mi) each way.

Difficulty: Class one.

Topo Map: 93 O/06

The route: You can drive to the top of Morfee, the mountain seen from town, and walk from there. There is a tiny alpine cabin on the mountain that is maintained by the local snowmobile enthusiasts. They don't mind hikers using it in summer. In winter, you may have to share your sleeping bag.

From the parking lot at the top of the mountain head east across the alpine. You can hike for as long as you like but if you do that carry a map and compass. The cabin is a great destination.

What makes this hike so enchanting is that you can drive through the most difficult section; that climb to the alpine.

Mount Murray and Murray Range

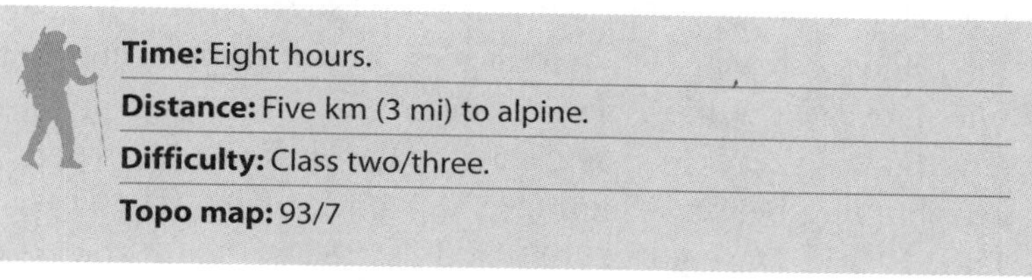

The route: This is a steep climb up to Mount Murray where you can go over the hill to some small lakes and camp. Be certain to have cooking stoves if staying overnight as there are no campfires permitted on the mountain. Or, you may continue walking along the ridge that towers above the highway for miles and camp farther along.

Trail access: Follow Highway 97 to Azouzetta Lake Lodge and service station. Eight km (5 mi) north of the lodge is a road that turns toward the mountains, crosses the Pine River and follows along the railway track. Park at the end of the road.

The trail: Walk south along the track for a quarter of a kilometer. The trailhead is marked. It first crosses the track and then follows a steep gully, through the woods and up for almost half a kilometer. It is a grueling ascent. However, long before the top and just when your legs are giving out, the trail becomes gentle. Once on top, the alpine slopes seem endless.

If there only for the day, you can go to the summit of the mountain and return to your vehicle by the same route. Those staying overnight should continue straight ahead (east) to the lakes. The most appealing walk on this mountain is to continue in a southerly direction, high above the highway until you can walk no farther. There are also more lakes behind (east of) Murray range that can be reached but to find them you must carry a map and compass.

Because this is a high pass, the weather is often unappealing. However, if you get a clear day while in the area, be certain to take advantage of it and climb Murray. The hike will not be forgotten.

Chetwynd

This is a pit stop on the highway that many people miss and that is a pity. The community consists of about 7000 people. The town sits at about 600 meters (2000 ft) in elevation and is tucked in the shadow of Old Baldy, the mountain where the water tower is located. The community has worked hard to develop numerous trails in the area and I suggest you stop at the visitor center and get a map. It is excellent in its descriptions and suggests many alternatives for walking in the vicinity.

Chetwynd was always used as a camp by the First Nations people when they were hunting between Summit and Moberly Lake. They called the place Little Prairie. During the 1700s and the 1800s, the fur traders came following the water routes. Finally, in 1919 a small trading post was built near the present site of the rail yards and a village emerged. When the Pacific Great Eastern arrived half a century later, the town grew. It was renamed after Ralph Chetwynd, director of the PGE and enthusiastic promoter of the Peace River area.

There are numerous hotels in Chetwynd in which to stay, with proprietors that are helpful and pleasant. Some hotels/motels allow pets. The restaurants in town serve international food.

Baldy Mountain

Time: One hour to all day.

Distance: 2 km (1.5 mi) return if going only to the viewpoint.

Difficulty: Class one.

The Route: This is a short leg-stretcher that is not difficult. However, it is possible to continue walking for five km (3 mi) more to the cross country ski trails near Wilkie Creek off Highway 29.

Trail access: Walk or drive to the water tower at the back of town. It is seen from anywhere in town. Follow the trail that leads from there.

The trail: Easy to follow – take the kids, the dog or your grandfather. They will all enjoy it. However, there is some elevation grain and the less able may want to stop at a bench and overlook the city while the rest hike. It is not recommended to hike this trail during a really windy day as there is little protection from the wind once up a bit. Before the top there is a steep section where the elevation gain is about 60 meters (180 ft) in less than 250 meters. Once on top, you can make that your destination or keep going to Windman Falls, another two km (1 mi) away. There are picnic tables close to the falls. From there you can continue down to the cross-country ski trails. I highly recommend this hike in all or in part.

Centurion Creek Hiking

Time: Ten minutes to four hours.

Distance: See below for each section of the trail.

Difficulty: Class one or two.

The route: This set of interconnecting trails goes through parts of town around Centurion Creek. The community has done a lot of exemplary work to develop and maintain these trails.

Trail access: Stop at the visitor center and get a map of the trails and where they go throughout the town. Many trails can be accessed from the highway, some from the rec center, the school, and the railway tracks.

The trails: Below are the names of the trails, their distances and the length of time it takes to walk each one. Some trails are quite rustic but there are signs indicating where you are. This information was provided to me by the Chamber of Commerce in Chetwynd.

Three Culvert Trail	2 km.	25 minutes.
Rodeo Trail	300 meters	10 minutes.
Deer Point	200 meters	5 minutes.
Centurion Trail	4 km	one hour.
Coyote Path	1 km	15 minutes.
Crown Trail	3 km	45 minutes.
Cottonwood Trail	1.5 km	20 minutes.
Windrem Trail	2 km	half an hour.

Tumbler Ridge

This boom-town gone ghost-town is the outdoor adventurer's wish book come true. The mountains are accessible along mining roads no longer used by ore trucks. There are few people in the hills but the wildlife is abundant. It is not uncommon to see a bear, moose or deer walking down the main streets of town or across the golf course. If waterfalls are your thing, there are more here than anywhere else in BC. The hiking is excellent, with few maintained trails but plenty of destinations that have unique landscapes.

During the 1980s, Tumbler was shipping tons of coal out to Japan every day. The BCR spent millions of dollars on building the line plus a huge electrified tunnel to tranport the coal. Then the price of coal fell. The mines shut down. The houses in town sold for less than what a person could build them. A retirement community evolved. But this retirement group is a little different than most. They are an outdoor crowd.

There is a grocery store, restaurants, hotels, a B & B, an Olympic sized swimming pool, a golf course and a campsite in Tumbler. Those going up the Alaska Highway are urged to take the road between Chetwynd and Dawson Creek through Tumbler Ridge and spend a few days checking out the mountains.

The hiking club is called the Wolverine Nordic and Mountain Society and the members work to develop and maintain the trails in the area. Charles Helm, the local doctor, and Kevin Sharman, the local hiking guru are usually the push behind any projects. Helm has written the comprehensive guide to these mountains called *Tumbler Ridge, Enjoying its History, Trails & Wilderness,* and I suggest you purchase it if you wish to do more hiking in this area. Sharman has developed a web site www.pris.bc.ca/wnms/ that you should visit for more ideas about hiking in Tumbler. The hikers from Tumbler are friendly, enthusiastic, skilled and more than welcoming of strangers. Get it touch with them when you arrive or contact the Tumbler Ridge Tourist Office in the center of town to purchase the book.

The trails for the Tumbler Ridge area are taken from the website with permission from the Wolverine Nordic and Mountain Society.

Bergeron Cliffs and/or Falls

Time: To the cliffs is around three or four hours, the falls around five hours and both will take all day.

Distance: 6 km (4 mi) to the cliffs, 10 km (6 mi) to the falls and doing both are about 14 km (8.75 mi) return.

Difficulty: Class three. Because of the steady uphill climb and the dangers of being on the cliff, this is considered a fairly strenuous hike. However, children from age 10 and up should be able to do it.

Topo Map: 93P/02

The route: You have a choice of either going to the cliffs, the falls or combining the two for a long strenuous day. The cliffs overlook Tumbler Ridge and the views beyond include those of the Murray River valley and the Northern Rockies. The falls are the highest in the area and tumble down 100 m (300 ft) into an amphitheatre below. During high water, this is an exceptional view.

Trail access: Drive north from town along Highway 29 toward Chetwynd for 5 km (3 mi). Turn right onto a gravel road; the turn is marked by a sign with a hiker on it. Continue along the road for 8 km (5 mi) until you come to a fairly large gravel pit. The trailhead is at the back and on the right hand side of the pit. There is a sign.

The trail: The trail climbs fairly steeply for half a kilometer or so before reaching a fork. The one to the right goes to the falls, the other to the cliffs. The trail continues up, gives you a bit of respite on a flat area before continuing in an upward direction again. Once you reach a cut line turn left and follow it for half a kilometer or so until you reach a large boulder that has in the past tumbled down off the mountain above. From the rock, go up hill and to the right.

Once on the edge of the cliff, be careful as it is an overhang and a slip could be fatal. The trail darts in and out of the woods until you reach the far end of the cliffs. The views of the town, the mine sites and the surrounding mountains are spectacular.

To the Falls

If going to the falls, return along the trail to the cut line. Follow it until you come to a second trail veering to the left. Follow the left hand trail and continue to the viewpoint across from the falls. Although this section does not have a lot of ups and downs, it is still not an easy trip.

Flatbed Falls and Kevin's Trail

Time: From one to five hours.

Distance: 2 km (1.5 mi) to 16 km (10 mi) return, depending on where you enter or exit.

Difficulty: Class one. This is an easy walk but you can make it a long one.

The route: This trail starts at the Lions Campground and meanders between the road and Flatbed Creek. There are five access trails to or from the highway. This trail is where all the dinosaur tracks have been found. Some are still in their natural state along the trail.

Trail access: You may start walking from the campground, follow a bend in the river and then walk down to Mini Falls. There is also an access to Mini Falls from a trail on the highway. Beyond Tumbler but before the road to Dawson Creek, there is a parking lot on the right and a trail that takes you down to Flatbed Falls.

The trail: Starting at the campground, follow the sign to the trailhead and walk around the bend in the river for about a kilometer. You may then hike down to a small set of falls or up to the highway. Continue along the main trail that follows the river. After about two kilometers, you will come to a switch backed trail that goes down to Flatbed Falls. Coming back up is a bit of a grunt.

Continuing along the main trail for another kilometer and a half, you will arrive at a trail that goes down to Cabin Pool and Overhanging Rock Pool. This trail loops around and returns back at the main trail. From there the trail runs between the river and the highway for about 4 km (2.5 mi) but does not go back to the river again. Instead, it splits into two trails that veer off and lead back to the road.

If you are interested mainly in the dino tracks, you can park at the parking lot between the high road into Tumbler and the road to Dawson Creek and walk directly down to Flatbed Falls where there are tracks.

Spieker Peak

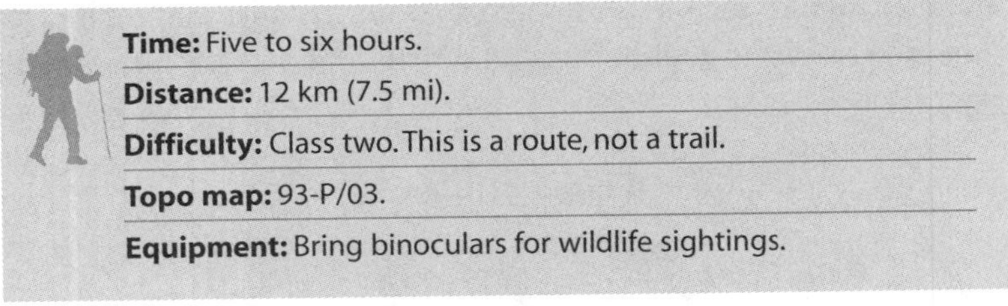

Time: Five to six hours.

Distance: 12 km (7.5 mi).

Difficulty: Class two. This is a route, not a trail.

Topo map: 93-P/03.

Equipment: Bring binoculars for wildlife sightings.

The route: Going to the top of Spieker often results in mountain goat sightings. This hike has very little bush walking. Instead, the alpine is reached within an hour and once there, choosing your own route is easy. If taking the northern peak from the saddle, you may camp at two little lakes tucked just below.

Trail access: Follow Highway 29 north toward Chetwynd for 9 km (6 mi) and turn onto the Wolverine Forest Service Road. Follow it for 12 km (5.6 mi) to the Perry Creek Road. On Perry Creek Road, make a right hand turn at the first fork, a left at the second fork and a right at the third. The first fork is at the 10 km (6 mi) point, the second is at the 12 km (7.5 mi) and the last one is almost at 14 km (8.75 mi). Go to the end of this road.

The trail: Follow the exploration road that goes toward the saddle you can see in the north. Once on the saddle, you have a choice as to where you would like to hike.

A short hike will take you on an animal trail along the ridge that is an extension of the saddle. The peak is barely a kilometer away.

Going to the right (northeast) from the saddle and then east when across from Mt. Spieker, will give you a fairly long day hike. It will take you to the highest point, Mt. Spieker, and the peak that can be seen from Tumbler. This walk is 4 km (2.5 mi) to the peak. For those going farther across the alpines, the distance you cover is up to you.

Continuing north from the saddle will take you onto a long arm that, at the far end, dips and then heads to the peak. This long arm is called the playpen and gets its name from the rock formations where walls form a natural corral. There are many rock crevasses that are wide and filled with snow, even mid summer. The sandstone and conglomerate in this area is quite picturesque. This is a steep but worthwhile climb. After going a bit farther north and down, you will find two little lakes on the eastern side at which you may camp. Bullmoose Mountain can be seen from here.

Roman Mountain/Emperor's Challenge

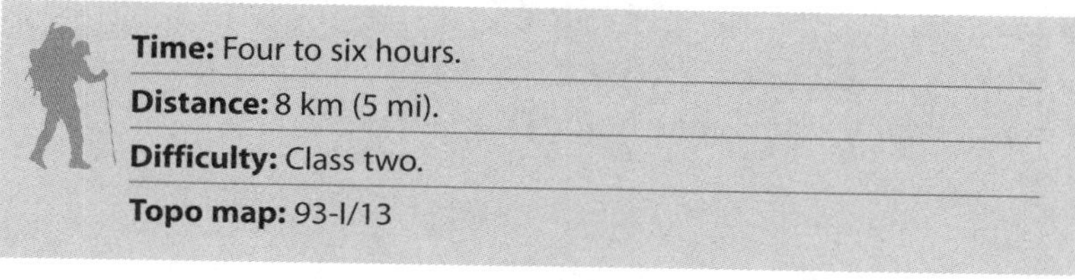

Time: Four to six hours.

Distance: 8 km (5 mi).

Difficulty: Class two.

Topo map: 93-I/13

The route: Looking at the mountains from the window of Core Lodge, a steel shed that has been converted for day-use by the local snowmobile club, Roman Mountain is the one that appears to be the highest.

Trail access: From Tumbler Ridge drive south on Highway 52 (Boundary Road) for 20 km (12 mi) to a side road going to the right. Do not turn toward Dawson Creek. Follow this road (the Core Lodge Rd) for 14.5

km (9.1 mi) to the lodge. Park here and follow the exploration road going toward the mountain. There is a sign where trailhead begins.

The trail: Follow the trail through the sub alpine to the open. The trail is flagged with tape. Once the road leaves the forest you can follow the rock cairns and wooden stakes through the sub alpine to the alpine. There is a little scrambling past some rock outcrops but generally, this is an easy route to follow. Roman has a false summit that is dotted with some coarse conglomerate and quartzite. From this spot you can see the summit. Continuing along the arm, you will come to a dip before finally ascending to the 2027 m (6588 ft) peak. The ascent is the steepest of the day. You may continue along this way for another 3 km (2 mi) before returning along the same route as you came. Views of the Fin come into line along this ridge.

At one point you will come to an intimidating wall where it looks like you can't pass but you can. There are excellent ledges on which to walk.

The mountain is part of the Emperor's Challenge, a running race held in Tumbler each year. The race starts at the Core Lodge and goes up Roman, around the ridges and over to Quintette, ending back at the Core Lodge.

If you wish to follow the Emperor's Challenge, from the summit of Roman, continue to the next peak in the south that is lower than Roman. Pass it and then head down to the creek to the west. Climb back out of the creek for about 25 m (75 ft) and then head due north past the Terminator and through Five Cabin Pass. After the pass, Babcock Creek comes into view. Follow it back to Core Lodge.

The entire circuit of the Emperor's Challenge is 27 km (16.9 mi) and is often walked by the jocks in five or six hours (it took me much longer). The record time to walk this is three hours, 21 minutes and the fastest running time is one hour, 41 minutes.

Tepee Falls

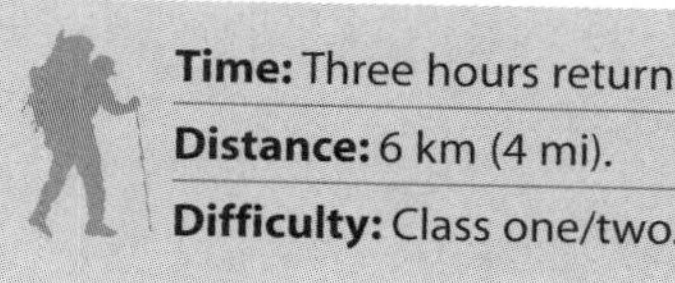

Time: Three hours return.

Distance: 6 km (4 mi).

Difficulty: Class one/two.

The route: This is a nice hike with a moderate ascent to a cliff overlooking the Murray River. There are three maintained viewpoints overlooking waterfalls on the river. One waterfall is very dramatic. The strong and experienced can continue to Windfall Lake from where the Sausage and Caribou Caves can be accessed. Both caves require repelling but are not technically difficult. If you want to do the longer hike, contact the club in town for detailed information.

Trail access: Follow Highway 52 (Boundary Road) but do not turn toward Dawson Creek. After about 35 km (22 mi), you will find a sign-posted parking area on your right. There is a map on the sign at the trailhead located across the highway from the parking area.

The trail: Tepee Creek is about 200 m (600 ft) from the highway. The trail passes through a logging cut before it starts following the creek. There are bridges across some of the smaller creeks along the way.

About 2.5 km (1.5 mi) along the trail is a fork and another map. Take the left-hand fork to a viewing site where there is another branch going to a small waterfall. The main falls are another 100 m (300 ft) downstream. The trail follows the cliff edge – be careful especially if you have kids with you.

The trail climbs to a hill above the falls but this viewpoint is not recommended. Take the staircase to a safer spot with a view of the canyon below. The stairs can be slippery when wet.

Tepee Falls is about 15 m (45 ft) high and plunges off the cliff into a jumble of boulders that have been pushed off the face of the mountain by the force of the water. You may continue along the trail leaving the falls behind, to another viewpoint. To return, follow the trail veering to the left to the sign-posted junction at 2.5 km (1.6 mi) where you reached the first fork.

Pinnacle Peak

Time: Full day but overnight is recommended.
Distance: 7 km (5 mi) one-way.
Topo map: 93-P/04 and 93-I/13
Difficulty: Class three.

The route: This route requires good route-finding skills and lots of strength to reach the peak. I suggest spending the night somewhere near trail-head as the hike will take all day and the drive is over an hour each way. This route is one of the favorites of Kevin Sharman's, the hiking guru of Tumbler Ridge. The steep climb takes you to a dramatic peak that looks ascendable only with 'beaners and ropes. However, this is not so. The summit is accessible for most.

Trail access: Drive north on Highway 29 toward Chetwynd to the Bullmoose Mine turnoff. Follow the mine road for 17 km (10.6 mi) and turn onto the Windfall Creek Forest Road. Follow that road for 23 km (14.4 mi). Turn left and follow this tertiary road for almost 2 km (1.5 mi) to the bridge beside Windfall Creek. Park on either side of the bridge.

The trail: Cross the clear-cut area and start along the path that is marked with flagging tape. The trail climbs through sub-alpine vegetation to an avalanche chute. Climb the chute and get onto the ridge above. This section is very steep.

Once above the chute, follow the rock cairns in a southerly direction along the ridge. This section of the trail goes up and down a lot. Up and down, up and down and then all of a sudden Pinnacle Peak comes into view and takes your breath away. From this point it will appear that you can't get to the top without climbing gear.

Follow the ridge until it narrows and then move to the left. You will need to scramble in a few places between here and the summit. There is a notch in the ridge with a tilted slab of rock that you should go to/around. The views are exceptional. If you started early and it has not taken you too long to get here, you can continue exploring other peaks. Return along the same route as you came.

Fort St. John

This little prairie town of Fort St. John sits on the eastern side of the Rockies and is just a few miles from kilometer/mile zero on the Alaska Highway. There are the usual services in town like restaurants (18), campsites (2) and hotels (9) and B & B's (3). A great coffee shop is called the Cosmic Grounds. There is also shopping available for food and hiking supplies.

Fish Creek Community Forest

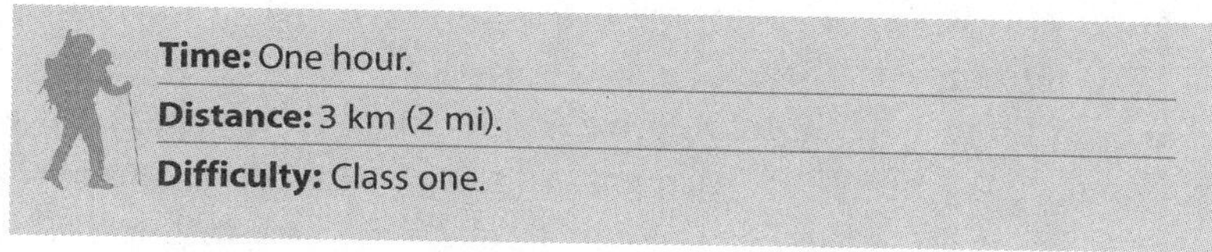

Time: One hour.

Distance: 3 km (2 mi).

Difficulty: Class one.

The route: This maintained interpretive trail can be enjoyed by almost everyone. It is used for hiking in summer and skiing in winter.

The access: The trail starts at the back-side of Northern Lights College on the Bypass (119th Ave). From 100th Street and 100th Ave, in the center of town, drive or walk north to 119th Ave, also known as the Bypass Road. Turn east and you will be in front of the college. Work your way through the grounds to the back end and follow the signs along the interpretive trail. The signs indicate the birds and animals that may be seen on the trail along with trees and flowers.

The trail: The Multipurpose Trail goes for almost 5 km (3 mi) with more than half of it being a loop. This trail goes in a south-west direction and has a total of 17 interpretive signs. For this trail, follow the red signs. **The Anatomy Trail** is half a kilometer and takes about half an hour to complete. It is wheelchair accessible. For this trail, follow the green signs. The **Silviculture Trail** is just under a kilometer in length and takes about 45 minutes to complete. For this trail, follow the blue signs. Anyone wanting a longer walk can complete the Multi-purpose loop to the Disaster Creek bridge and then continue straight ahead to the Silviculture Trail rather than returning from the bridge back to your vehicle.

Sikanni Chief Falls

Time: One hour of hiking but driving to trailhead is a long distance. The trail is 34 km (21 mi) off the Alaska Highway and along a forest service road. If you are ready to pitch tent for the night and would like a quiet spot, this may be a good choice. There is a Forest Service Campsite along the Sikanni Chief River.

Distance: 1.5 km (1 mi) each way.

Difficulty: Class one.

The route: This is a short hike to a nice set of falls that drop about 40 m (125 ft) into the river below.

Trail access: From Fort St. John, drive north along the Alaska Highway to kilometer 230 (mile 170). Turn left onto the Forest Service Road. There is a sign indicating the Sikanni Chief Falls. One fork in the road gives you four choices; take the one to your farthest left.

The trail: Walk from the campsite (follow the sign) and head up the mountain for about 30 to 45 minutes. There are steep drop-offs so be careful.

Alaska Highway North

Between Fort Nelson and the Chilkoot including The Tatshenshini Provincial Park

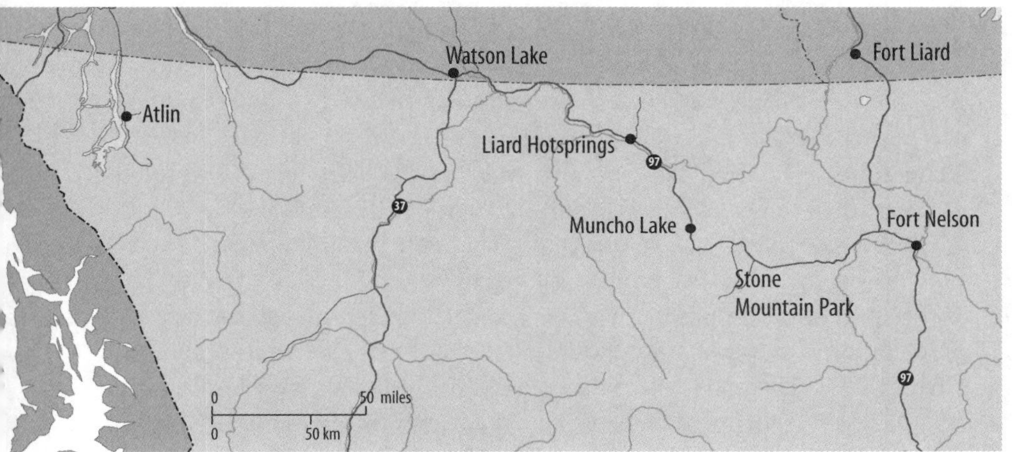

Fort Nelson

Fort Nelson is a tiny town that has an enthusiastic hiking group. They have charted many of the trails, they help with the maintenance and they have produced a book about the area. For more information about hiking in the area, visit the Northern Rockies Regional District in town or phone (250) 774-2541. For information before arriving, visit the web site www.northernrockies.org.

At time of writing there was a hiking book for the area, written by Heather MacRae and her partner, Peter Goetz, in the production/publishing stage. The book is accurate and complete.

There is a motor home/tenting campsite at the west end of town with a few tent spaces that are in the open but segregated from the motor homes. For places to eat, Fort Nelson caters to everyone from the fast food lover to those seeking European and Oriental cuisines.

Flower Springs

Time: Five to six hours, to the lakes, four hours to the radio tower.

Distance: 13.6 km (8.5 mi) to the lakes and 10.2 km (6.4 mi) to the radio tower.

Difficulty: Class two/three.

Equipment: If staying overnight be aware that fires are not permitted in the alpine and a stove should be taken.

The route: This trail takes you to three alpine lakes with views of the Terminal Range to the west and the Sentinel Range to the east. It does not take long to get above tree line and into the alpine where the trail levels out considerably and walking is easier. The lake farthest in is tucked into a cirque and has alpine vegetation growing all the way to its shore. Going to the tower offers great views to the north, east and west.

Trail access: The trail is at the south end of Summit Lake near km 600 (mile 373) along the Alaska Highway. Turn into the Summit Lake campground and park in the day-use area. The trail is directly across from the Summit Peak Trail.

The trail: There are two routes to the kiosk where the trail splits and goes either to the lakes or the tower. The first is the trail following the lake edge located across from the Summit Peak Trail. This has more ups and downs but is also more scenic than the other. The second trailhead is found at the end of the campground and to the left of the parking lot. Follow the radio tower road just over the gravel bar. This trail is faster and more gradual.

Whichever route you take, once at the kiosk, sign the registration form put there by BC Parks. The more people using the trails the better chance we have of getting more maintained trails and parkland. There are no trees beyond this area so follow the wooden stakes with yellow markers on them.

During the first half hour you pass over land that is a bit boggy. The next hour will take you over a series of moraines. The lake comes into view and you stroll down to it. If the day is calm, look to the opposite end of the lake where you should see some bubbles. This is the spring for which the trail is named.

The trail continues on the right hand side of the lake to a creek at the far end. From here there are no more markers. To continue, follow the creek bed to a path that goes up a steep embankment next to a waterfall. Continue up the valley until you come to the end where a little lake is tucked under a hanging valley. This destination adds 5.4 km (3.4 mi) to your hike.

Camping is permitted near the lakes but fires are prohibited.

This trail description was given to me by Heather MacRae and her partner, Peter Goetz. For further information about hiking in the area, please visit the tourist office and/or purchase their book.

Summit Peak

Distance: 10 km (6 mi).

Difficulty: Class two

The route: This is a strenuous hike that goes over rocky terrain to Summit Peak. Wildlife is abundant, especially birds. However, this is not a trail to do early in the year as it is high and snow may impede walking.

Trail access: The trail is at the south end of Summit Lake near km 600 (mile 373) along the Alaska Highway. There is some confusion as to the mile-post number; the historical mile post number is 393 but the newer (more accurate) numbers are now used. The trail is directly across from the Flower Springs Trail. There are signs. There is a huge washout near trailhead.

The trail: This hike starts by slogging up the creek bed around the bend and beyond. It is difficult walking but the main draws are the hoodoos so common in this area. The views also, on a clear day are worth every pant it takes to get here. If you are not in shape or accustomed to route finding, I suggest you take the Flower Springs trail instead.

Wokkpash Hiking

Time: To Wokkpash Lake is two to four days. To Wokkpash Valley returning by MacDonald Creek is four to seven days.

Distance: To the lake is 25 km (16 mi) and the circuit is 70 km (44 mi) of back country hiking along an isolated route.

Difficulty: This is a class five hike with orienteering skills being essential as the area is often fogged over. Using landmarks is not always possible.

Topo maps: 94K/7 and 94K/10.

Equipment: Pepper spray should be carried by each member of the team. Stove and fuel are necessary as there is not always wood available to make a fire. Only the most skilled should attempt this hike.

The route: This route takes you through some of the most dramatic landscape in British Columbia. However, there are numerous creek crossings; MacDonald Creek is often too high to cross and waiting for the water to recede may be necessary. There are some cairns and markers and part of the route is along game trails. There are no bridges or official signs. This route is not for the amateur hiker. The distances shown in this trail description are approximate.

Trail access: Drive 140 km (87 miles) west of Fort Nelson to about km 615 on the Alaska Highway to the Old Churchill Mine Road. If coming from Muncho, drive 35 km (22 mi) southeast toward Fort Nelson. Turn onto Churchill Mine Road and follow it for 19 km (11.8 mi) to a campsite and the Wokkpash Creek Bridge. The road is for 4 X 4 vehicles only. If it rains while you are in without a four-wheel drive, you may not get out. The hike starts on the east side of the creek. If you do not have a four-wheel drive to go that last 19 km, ask at the lodge on Muncho Lake for a shuttle. If they are unable to help, they may be able to direct you to someone who can.

The trail: Cross the creek and hike upstream along the creek bed for a bit. You will find a horse camp after about two hours of walking at a spot called the Canyon of Teetering Rocks.

From Teetering rocks, the horse trail continues along the side of the creek. Follow it for about 9 km (5.6 mi) more to the entrance of Wokkpash Gorge. Leave the creek here and go above the gorge. The next possible campsite is at the end of the gorge, 5 km (3 mi) farther along so if you are tired and don't feel you can go for another few hours, camp here. Photography of the hoodoos in the canyons is recommended so getting the soft morning or evening light is another reason to stay at this spot.

Shortly after the end of the gorge, you will come to Forlorn Creek. This too is a recommended spot to stop because there are soft, flat spots for tenting and some clear water.

The next notable landmark is the Forlorn Gorge that is considered by some more dramatic than Wokkpash Gorge. This gorge is 25 m (75 ft) across and 150 m (500 ft) deep and has Blashford and Bensla Peaks standing sentry to the southwest while Mt. St. Magnus watches from the southeast. The two mountains directly to the west are Bastion and Sandhurst peaks. Once past Forlorn Gorge, you will be heading to Wokkpash Lake, bright blue/green under the sun and grey under clouds.

When leaving Forlorn Gorge, walk past Blashford and Bensla Peaks. This is a pleasant section although it will take quite a few hours (it is about 8 km (5 mi)). The next landmark is Wokkpash Lake. Once at the lake, go over and follow the east side of the lake to the far end. There is no comfortable camping along the lake. The color of the water is due to copper oxide being ground by ice out of the rock and settling into the water. Plug Creek is at the far end of the lake and where you may camp. It will take five to six hours to get from Forlorn Gorge to Plug Creek. Wokkpash Lake has a family of Northern Loons living on it. With luck, they will perform for you.

To get from Plug Creek to Lost Call Lake, follow the northwest side of Plug. There are some markers and cairns along this section of the trail. The walk in the alpine will contour the valley and you will travel east of the White Stone Ridge.

There is a good campsite just before Lost Call Lake. It will take five or six hours to reach it from Plug Creek. At the lake itself there is no comfortable camping. The big peak to the west is Angel Peak.

From Lost Call Lake stay high and on the east side of the gully. Walk to the northeast for about two hours until MacDonald Creek comes into view. Go down to the creek and cross. Do not camp in the creek bed as the creek is subject to flash floods.

Follow the creek for about 2 km (1.5 mi) and then start looking for a horse trail. It will go for about 4 km (2.5 mi) into the bush and then lead you down to the creek again. Cross the creek and hook up with the trail once more on the other side. The Alaska Highway can now be seen. There are numerous horse camps where you may camp before reaching the highway. This is your last night out.

Salt Licks

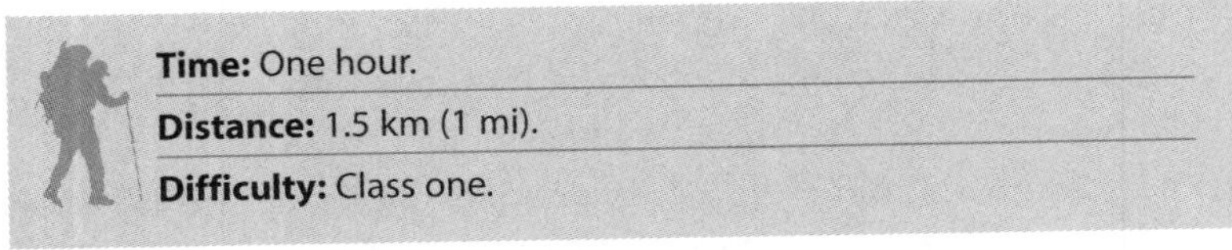

Trail access: Drive west of Muncho Lake to Kilometer 732 (mile 455). There is a sign indicating the hike and a parking lot to pull into.

The trail: This is a good place to spot wildlife; sheep especially like to come and lick the salt. The trail meanders through the landscape to a lookout over the Trout River. This is a worthwhile walk, easy for even young kids.

Liard Hotsprings

The springs are located at kilometer 794 (mile 496) along the Alaska Highway, between Muncho Lake and Watson Lake.

Although this isn't really what you would call a hiking trail, it is a stop that should not be missed; a stop to sooth sore muscles regardless of whether they are sore from sitting in the car too long or from carrying a 27 kg (60 lb) pack for a week.

The hot springs are one of the hottest in the world with temperatures between 42°C (107.6°F) and 52°C (125.6°F). The springs are in pristine condition with very little development except that which is necessary to protect the environment. Other than a bit of gravel on the bottom, stairs to enter and a few wooden seats in the water, the springs are in their natural state with lush vegetation framing the surrounding rocks. There are two levels to the springs, called the Alpha and the Beta pools, both with change rooms for public use. The Beta pool is the hotter one and is located above the Alpha pool. The bathroom here is a multi-million dollar structure erected with conservation of the springs in mind. It was not in operation the last time I was here.

The hot springs have always been used by native communities living in the area. Robert Campbell, the first European explorer to come through here, arrived in 1835. This is recorded in the journals of the Hudson Bay Company. But it wasn't until 1920 that a European by the name of Tom Smith built a cabin at the springs and lived here with his daughter. One spring they were headed down the Liard toward Fort Nelson when their boat overturned and Tom drowned but the daughter was saved by locals who happened to see the accident from shore. They took the girl to the Anglican Church that in turn sent her to Hay River to get an education. She never returned to the Liard area.

The area was made into a park in 1957.

The campsite has 52 sites, all tucked into the trees with no power or water hookups. There is wood for campfires and a day area for those not wanting to stay for the night. There is a restaurant and a private campsite across the highway from the campsite entrance.

The half-kilometer walk along the boardwalk that is over a swamp heated by run-off water from the springs is wheel chair accessible. Often there are moose enjoying the vegetation of the swamp. To date there have been 14 species of orchids identified, 104 species of birds and 28 species of mammals.

Atlin

Located in the northwest corner of BC, the town of Atlin sits on Atlin Lake, the headwaters of the Yukon River. A Tlingit word, Atlin means "big water," an apt name for the largest natural lake in the province.

With a population of 400 this tiny community is about 180 km (112.5 mi) south-east of Whitehorse. The last 93 km (58 mi) of road leading to Atlin branches off the Alaska Highway and was built in 1949 by the Canadian Army Engineers.

Although not as grand as the Klondike Gold Rush, the Atlin Gold Rush in 1898 occurred after the discovery of the yellow glitter on Pine Creek. Today the museum, housed in a 1902 schoolhouse, contains many artifacts from the rush.

Atlin's second rush came during the roaring twenties when rich tourists made this scenic wilderness a popular destination, not for gold but for pleasure.

Atlin is a pretty town with two good restaurants and many historical buildings. Pine Creek Campsite, just 2.4 km (1.5 mi) down Warm Bay Road, is clean and comfortable and believe it or not, the tent pegs go into the flat ground easily. You can pay for your stay at any business establishment in town and payment is on an honor system; it's up to you to be honest because no one will check.

The **Llewellin Glacier** lookout is 11.5 km (7.2 mi) from the start of Warm Bay Road. There is a small sign indicating the lookout. Binoculars are needed to see the glacier well. It is an impressive one and can be seen from both hikes recommended in this book or by hiring a boat to take you down the lake to its toe.

Warm Springs is 24 km (15 mi) down Warm Bay Road and is a small but warm pool that is fed by underground springs. Rimmed with wild watercress, the spring was used by the Tlingit for ceremonial and medicinal purposes. Tlingit tradition required that the men bathed before the women and children. Luckily, times have changed.

Monkeyflower Adventures take interested visitors on guided hikes in the area. They pepper their vast knowledge of the area with interesting anecdotal stories. The prices for the trips are reasonable. You may phone (250) 651-2211 or email www.backwoods benny@hotmail.com. for more information about times and dates or to book a special hike.

Although the mountains in the area are not bare and rugged, they are fun. If you have any questions or need any help while hiking, please contact Wayne Merry at wmerry@atlin.net. or telephone him; the number is in the phone book. Very knowledgeable, Wayne is the author of St. John's Ambulance 1st Aid Guide and Basic Ground Search and Rescue in Canada. Take along one of his books for signing!

Monarch Mountain

Time: Four to six hours.

Distance: 8 km (5 mi) return.

Difficulty: Class two.

Topo maps: Not needed except for interest's sake. They can be purchased at a store in the village.

Equipment: This is a dry hike so water must be carried as there are no creeks or lakes where it can be obtained. A walking stick would be beneficial as parts of the trail are steep.

The route: This route ascends out of tree line within forty-five minutes. At the beginning, it passes through residential area but soon elevates to spectacular views of Atlin Lake and the Llewellen Glacier. During the gold rush days, miners and movie stars often climbed up to have a picnic or spark a romance on this mountain. Today it is hikers doing the same thing.

Trail access: Turn south off Discovery Avenue down Warm Bay Road and drive for 3.4 km (2.1 mi). There is a parking area on the lakeside of the road. Cross the road to the sign indicating the start of the hike.

The trail: The trail crosses the road twice while passing the residential area of the mountain. The route is well marked. There are both open areas and forested spots for the first hour or so. Sage can be smelled once out of the pine trees. Continue to the top where there is a 360º view of the area. Because you are out of the trees quickly, (within forty-five minutes), this is a popular walk for locals.

Fireweed is abundant on the mountain. Rich in vitamin A and C, the young spring shoots can be eaten like asparagus. Fireweed is a mild laxative and the First Nations people used it to get rid of worms. The juice when the stems are squeezed can be used as a cream for dry skin.

Ruby Mountain

Time: Eight hours.

Distance: 6 km (4 mi).

Difficulty: Class three.

Topo maps: Surprise Lake; 104 N/11. Although not needed, it is recommended and can be purchased in the village of Atlin.

Equipment: Water must be carried as there is no water on the mountain. It is a dry lava cone with sharp loose rocks so boots are essential.

The route: Although there are other options, I recommend going to the west side of Ruby Mountain, along Ruby Creek. The hike to the tree line requires about 1.5 hours of fairly easy bushwhacking. From there you must start climbing over the lava rocks to the summit where there is a cairn with a tin hidden under some stones. Sign your name.

Trail access: Drive 18.8 km (11.8 mi) to Surprise Lake Campsite maintained by BC Forest Service. Continue along the road to a fork at 20.3 km (12.8 mi) from town. Take the right fork and follow the lake for 5.3 km (3.3 mi), past Boulder Creek turn off. The road is gravel and has just one creek flowing across it. A car with a bit of clearance can get through although I would think the road could be slimy during a wet season. At Ruby Creek there is a pullout where you may park. From this point, if you are unsure of bushwhacking, take a compass reading so that you end up back at your car when returning.

The trail: Start up the mountain just behind your car. Try to choose a route through the Spruce trees as they choke out the underbrush making the thrash fairly easy. Willows are horrid, especially uphill. It takes about 1.5 hours to get out of the trees.

Once on the lava flows, the walking becomes steeper but easier. Head for the one large pile of boulders on the top where it is flat. The pile looks like a medieval fortress. It should take about another 1.5 hours to reach the fortress from the tree line. Then, go to the cairn on the summit and follow instruction located in the tobacco tin.

The Llewellin Glacier is visible from the summit as are numerous exploration roads that could be fun to explore on a bike. Although not extremely rugged this landscape is stunning.

On the way down, pick your route carefully. It is much more fun arriving back at the road near your vehicle rather than five miles away.

Tatshenshini-Alsek Provincial Park

Although the Tatshenshini Provincial Park is primarily accessible from the Yukon, it is actually located in British Columbia. Mostly known for the river after which it got its name, the park, with almost 9500 square kilometers of protected land, is also a haven of charted and uncharted hiking routes. Some of the routes in the park were used by First Nations people for centuries and others were explored by mining companies. We love the bulldozer, especially when it cuts a swath through willow and alder!

The Tatshenshini has an exciting history starting with the fight against Windy Craggy Mines to make the area a park. Kwaday Dan Sinchi, a Tlignit/Tutchone man who had died on a glacier in the park was found in 1999, 500 years after his death, by some hunters. The find caused many hikers to linger in the area hoping to find another hopefully ancient body.

The park is also known for the rare, blue glacier bear that is thought to be a variation of the black bear. This species is found nowhere else in Canada. Half the province's Dall sheep is also reported to live in this park. Peregrine falcons, great grey owls and bald eagles are just a few of the bird species known to haunt the area's quiet forests.

Klehini-Tkope area.

Hiking in the Tatshenshini is best done after mid-July when the snow has melted and the water levels have gone down. We crossed the Tat in early July and found the levels almost too high to manage. There are no bridges in the park to make creek crossings easy.

Parton River

Time: Three to six days.

Distance: 50 km (31 mi) round trip.

Difficulty: Class five.

Topo maps: 114P/15, 114P/10, 114P/11 - maps are a must.

Equipment: Bicycles can be used for some of this trail but I found that during a wet year they were more trouble than they were worth. We ended up abandoning them and continuing on foot.

The route: Crossing the Tatshenshini River can be difficult due to its width (four minutes across) rather than the depth or swiftness of the water. The Parton River route follows a road up to a pass. The valley eventually leads to an abandoned airstrip. There is a wonderful side trip up Mount Scottie that could be an ultimate destination if time is short. The return trip is by the same route as going in.

Trail access: Follow the Haines Highway past the Blanchard River Bridge for 9.3 km (5.8 mi) to a gravel road that turns south and leads to the Tat River. The distance down the road is 1.3 km (0.8 mi). Camping is possible along the road, near the river but wood is almost nonexistent and the river water, although clean, is silty. We did leave our vehicle here for ten days with no ill effects.

The trail: This hike starts with the crossing of the Tatshenshini River that can be difficult if done early in the year or during a wet spell when water levels are high. We crossed right at the road and side-stepped to a gravel bar that is about 2 m (6 ft) from the far bank. We had to follow the gravel bar up river for about 20 m (60 ft) before we could step across onto the land. Use your pole to feel the depth of the water on the far side of the bar. The current is not extremely strong on this section of the river but the water is cold.

The road on the south side of the Tatshenshini is mucky, especially if the weather has been wet. However, follow it to a second creek crossing, through more muck and to the Parton River, a gravel washout that carries the runoff water from the mountains into the Tat.

If you do not want to stay by the Tatshenshini River for the night, the Parton River washout is a good spot to camp and it is just two kilometers up the trail. There is some wood, lots of flat spots and the water is clear. The crossing is not technical. You should be able to see the road continue on the other side.

The road is mud, gravel, mud, and more gravel, from the washout to the end. Just as you start to think you have good traveling, it turns to mud again. However, after 3 km (2 mi) you will be in forest and camping anywhere along the side of the road is fairly good. There were wolf, moose and bear tracks on the road when I was there.

About six kilometers in there is a large flat washout area along the Parton River where camping is excellent. Flat spots and wood seem to be the beckoning call. However, you must climb down the bank to get to the flats. If the bugs are bad, camping here is recommended because there is always breeze along the river.

Just past the river camp is a creek coming from the west that has hoodoos at its entrance. Camping is good here also. The creek is a nice place to go for a day hike. Follow the ridge above the creek for excellent views of the hoodoos. You can continue to Scottie Mountain from this spot by weaving in and around the non-vegetated trails that lie between the oceans of willow. Continue in the direction of Scottie Mountain.

There is an old wagon or flat bed truck at the side of Scottie Mountain (about three km (2 mi) farther) and the road splits, with one fork going uphill. If you do not want to go to the top of Scottie Mountain, do not go up hill but follow the road along the valley. If going up Scottie, you can follow the road to the alpines and then onto the ridge that leads to the peak of Scottie. Once up there you should be able to see your vehicle parked at the Tatshenshini River. High winds are common so bring warm clothing even if it seems fairly warm in the valley. There is a golden eagle who lives and hunts around Scottie Mountain.

Back on the mining road, you will find that it deteriorates more the farther you go. There are numerous mudslides that must be maneuvered. The plywood cabin, about 10 km (6 mi) in, is used by outfitters, but it is not much of a comfort. It has been invaded by small critters and is filthy. However, it will give a bit of shelter in the event of really bad weather. Also, the fire ring can be used to make a smudge to keep the bugs off when there is no breeze. There is a creek with clear water just below the cabin along the road.

After leaving the cabin and crossing the creek, the hill proceeds steeply toward the upper valley. The landscape becomes more attractive with each passing kilometer. There is a mudslide at 15.5 km (9.7 mi) that must be climbed above in order to be gotten around. If you have bikes, this may be where you decide to leave them, although there are patches of road beyond that could be cycled. A huge floodplain full of glacial silt is below. The silt is from the Samuel Glacier.

Within the next kilometer, the road leaves the Parton River Valley and swings up toward the airstrip. Going down to the Parton River near its mouth is not recommended because of the glacial silt in the riverbed.

The road appears and disappears flowing through the alpine for over 12 km (8 mi) before it drops back into the forest. Eventually, it leads to the airstrip. We did not go that far. However, we did climb all the ridges and even of the peaks on the mountains on the east side of the valley. We could see the St. Elias Range on the far side of the Tat and we watched some sheep playing nearby. There are some excellent camp spots along this section of the trip.

The return trip is downhill so it is a few (quite a few) hours shorter.

Nadahini Creek

Time: Eight to ten hours.

Distance: 6 km (3.75 mi) to glacier, 9 km (5.6 mi) to the pass.

Difficulty: Class three.

Topo maps: Nadahini Creek, 114P/10

Equipment: If going to the pass, creek-crossing footwear is needed.

The route: The Nadahini Creek was part of the Dalton Trail during the Klondike gold rush. Doug Sias of Kluane B & B found a cow horn on the creek. He believes the horn was from the days when they herded cattle up the Dalton Trail to the miners in Dawson City. This is a boulder-hopping walk along a creek bed. When the creek hugs the bank, you must scramble up the side of the hill. It is really worth going all the way to the pass. The view of the Nadahini glacier is spectacular when looked at from above. It is a steep climb to the pass.

Trail access: Drive south on the Haines highway, 36.0 km (22.5 mi) past the Blanchard River Bridge. There is a large gravel washout on the north side of the road where you may park. If camping near the road overnight, go a little way up the creek where you are away from the traffic and where there is water. However willow is the only wood available for burning so a stove is recommended.

The trail: Stay on the south side of the creek. We had to scramble up the side of the hill three times before reaching the upper end of the creek. The scramble was not difficult but the bushwhacking along the bank was a bit unpleasant. The willows are old and well established on the lower end of the creek valley.

The Nadahini Glacier has receded beyond the curve. The last kilometer up the valley is a moonscape. The side hills are often ice covered with mud and slides are a constant threat.

The rare whitish rush and the purple-haired groundsel are found on this creek for all you wild plant lovers.

To go to the pass, continue around the corner to the toe of the glacier, cross the stream and walk up the side, heading for a light brown outcrop with a green patch above it. At the outcrop turn right and follow that creek up to the pass. It is steep in places. The snow is wet and heavy making it firmly packed and safe to walk upon.

You may cross the pass and go down the other side to the Samuel Glacier and then around, coming out another 3 km (2 mi) south on the Haines Highway. See Samuel Glacier hike.

Samuel Glacier

Time: Three to five days.

Distance: 36.5 km (22.8 mi) return.

Difficulty: Class five.

Topo maps: Nadahini Creek 114P/10.

Equipment: Warm clothing due to the winds off the ice and a stove with fuel are essential.

The route: This is not a difficult route to follow except for crossing the pass. The change in elevation is minimal if going to the glacier and across to the Parton River Valley. The hike over the pass to the Nadahini Glacier is steep but not so steep as to make it dangerous. The circular walk can be done in three long, hard days but I suggest taking longer (minimum of four days) and enjoying the land.

Trail access: Drive south on the Haines Highway 38.3 km (23.4 mi) past the Blanchard River Bridge and just past Chuck Creek. Turn right off the highway when traveling south. There is a large gravel washout for camping, clear water in the creek but no wood for a fire.

The trail: There is a mining road at the start of this hike. The road works its way gently up the valley, above Clear Creek. After about four hours, you will arrive at the creek. Although not a difficult crossing, boots must be removed before going into the water. Once on the other side of the creek the road becomes dubious.

Just under 10 km (6 mi) into the valley, you must cross the swampy valley to the gravel bed. This is a good spot for your first night's camping. The gravel is dry, level and comfortable. Staying on the bottom end of the hill would be wet and unpleasant. There is no wood anywhere in the valley so a stove must be used. You will get to the gravel bed early in the day leaving time to make camp and climb a peak or two to see the surrounding landscape. The creek that feeds the gravel washout has a huge canyon just a short way up. Walk on the west side of the creek and then on the hill above.

Samuel Glacier in the Tatshenshini Provincial Park.

From the gravel bed walk toward the Samuel Glacier along the side of the hill. It is pleasant walking for the next five km (3 mi). You may come to a sinkhole big enough to hold a twelve-storey building. It is close to the spot where, at one time, an arm of the Nadahini reached across and held onto the Samuel. The arm is shown on the map but has disappeared from the landscape.

Since this glacier is known to attract bad weather, be careful if the mist is dense. Falling into the sinkhole would be disastrous.

Although walking on the glacier looks inviting, I suggest you stay on the moraine and the hill. The Samuel is not a crevassed glacier but there are cracks, some fairly wide. Walking too close to the glacier will result in you sinking into the wet glacial flour and often sinking above your boot. Better to walk a bit up the hill where the earth has drained and dried itself.

As you descend into the next valley, you will come to the glacier-fed lake, its green color visible for miles. The first creek coming from the east is the creek leading to the pass if going to the Nadahini Glacier. The creek is wide and not too steep. The snow can be intimidating but staying in the creek bed is far better than walking on the side of the hill for the first part of this section.

Continue due east until you can see the Nadahini Glacier and then head down the side of the glacier. This is a great crossing although steep. It will take you a few hours to get to the pass where there is lots of ice and snow. Once across and at the toe of the Nadahini, the walk down the creek is not difficult. There are camping spots along the way, especially near the toe of the glacier.

At the end of the creek you will have to walk the last 3.5 km (2.2 mi) along the road back to your car.

Should you decide not to go over the pass to the Nadahini you may return by the same way you came. Stay on the north side of the swamp and Clear Creek until you hook up with the road. It will take about five hours to walk from the center of the Samuel back to the car (you will be going downhill).

Walking down the east side of the Parton River looked like fairly dense willow so it is not a recommended option. Walking in the riverbed would mean trying to get through a lot of silt. This can be dangerous. Crossing over to the other side of the Parton River Valley where there is a road would also be difficult because of the silt in the riverbed.

Schultz Creek/Oil Pipeline

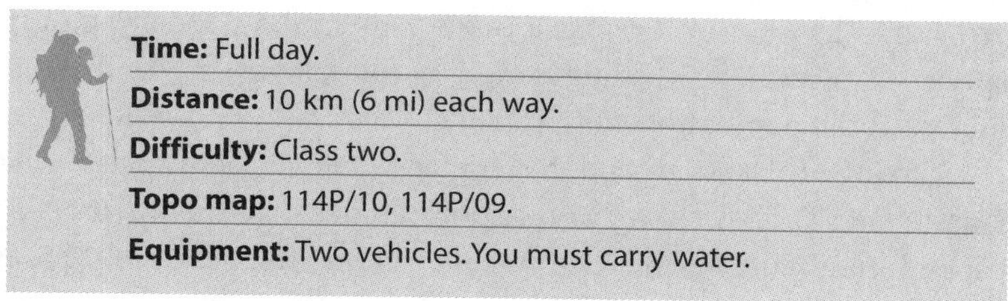

Time: Full day.

Distance: 10 km (6 mi) each way.

Difficulty: Class two.

Topo map: 114P/10, 114P/09.

Equipment: Two vehicles. You must carry water.

The route: This day hike can be done in either direction. Two vehicles are needed unless you return by the same route as you came or you hitch-hike back to your vehicle. It is easiest to hike from Three Guardsman Pass down to the end of the trail as it is mostly downhill. There are many bird watchers haunting this area. Wildlife is also abundant. The walk passes through thick forests of coastal western hemlock. The area is undisturbed for the most part.

Trail access: Drive south on the Haines Highway to Schultz Creek less than 5 km (3 mi) past Tina Creek and park one vehicle. Continue south with the second vehicle to Five Mile Creek (just five miles from the border) and turn right on the first road after the bridge. Continue down this road for about 3 km (2 mi). You will not be able to go any farther as the bridge is not crossable with a vehicle. It is recommended to leave the first car at Five Mile Creek and start at Three Guardsman Pass as the hike is downhill. However, I have described the trail in the opposite direction (going up to the pass). For day hikes, I prefer exercise.

The trail: The road is the abandoned pipeline. If starting at Five Mile Creek, the most scenic part of the trail is at the beginning, through thick rain forest, so thick that bushwhacking would be impossible without a machete or power saw. The trail has deadfalls that must be maneuvered but there are no creek crossings. There are a few places to fill water bottles but they require plunging through the forest in order to reach the trickles.

For plant lovers, the rare mountain Sheldon Butterweed and the Iceland koenigia are both found near the Three Guardsmen Pass/Lake region.

This corridor supports about 180 bird species. Watch for the rare peregrine falcon or its close relative the gyrfalcon. The peregrine likes to live in sub alpine areas, close to lakes and where other birds that it uses for fodder can be found. Because of the use of DDT and other pesticides, falcons' eggshells have become too thin to permit the chick to grow to full gestation. This has caused a fall in the population of many species. However a breeding program for falcons in the Yukon has increased the population substantially.

Starting at the south end, the trail goes up all the way to the Three Guardsmen Pass. It curves at one point and, as you climb, the glacier-capped mountains in the Klehini Valley come into view. On the opposite side of the landscape, Three Guardsmen Pass appears. If the day is sunny, this is a spectacular hike.

Klehini River Valley

Time: Four days.

Distance: 37 km (23 mi).

Difficulty: Class five.

Topo map: 114P/10, 114P/09.

Equipment: Extra film as the scenery warrants a few more shots than usual.

The route: This is a spectacular four-day hike that goes up the valley, over a pass and down to the Mineral Lakes. There is no bushwhacking; the entire hike is in alpine. The crossing of Inspector Creek should be taken seriously as there is a huge canyon and waterfall just below the crossing. Although the map indicates numerous roads winding through the landscape, we found only one.

Trail access: Drive south along the Haines Highway for 53.7 km (33.5 mi) beyond the Blanchard River Bridge. Park in the shadow of Three Guardsmen Mountain, off the highway and along the old pipeline.

The trail: Start on the south side of the creek beside which you have parked and head west up the hills. There are tiny lakes and huge boulders dotting the flowered landscape.

Once you have gone about a kilometer, start veering slightly to the south. It is pleasant walking. If hiking early in the year, there will be snow on the shaded sides of the hills. Boot ski. When Copper Butte, an appropriately named mountain comes into view, head for the south face of it. The last hill you come to before reaching the Butte is steep but vegetated so it is stable. There are two lakes at the east side of Copper Butte and an open mine shaft just above. Some people have gone inside to explore. Others have removed artifacts.

Head straight south from Copper Butte until you reach the old mining road. Follow it to its end up the Klehini Valley. This area is important habitat for the Tundra Shrew. This is 800 km (500 mi) farther south than the shrew's previously known limits. Shrews are small mammals that eat insects. They are about 3 to 5 inches in length, grayish-brown in color, with pointed noses, long whiskers and short legs. If handled they give off a strong odor. Some predators find this distasteful and leave the shrews uneaten. Shrews live in the grass or dead-leaf mounds and are active all year. Shrews mate between March and August and have two to

Klehini River hike in the Tatshenshi Provincial Park.

10 offspring. These youngsters are born blind and naked and are weaned within three weeks. The lifespan of a shrew is between 12 and 18 months.

There is an abandoned miner's cabin on the west side of Copper Butte. It is not recommended for staying inside but it is nice to see. Beyond the cabin is Inspector Creek, not an easy crossing. Be careful not to fall in – use all caution because there is a canyon and waterfall about 70 m (200 ft) down stream. Once on the other side of the creek, leave the road and go down to see the canyon.

The next 11 km (7 mi) is a nice walk up valley that is best done right at the Klehini River rather than side-hill gouging. Continue past the glacier that is spewing flour and rock down the side of the hill. The flour is forming mountainous peaks that make the runoff look like a relief map.

Continue on to the next moraine that reaches the valley. This is where the river changes direction. The split makes it an interesting land formation because it is not at the top of a pass. Camping is not too great here. You will need a stove.

Getting to the pass will take about three hours from the center of the river-splitting moraine. Walk along the Klehini and then head up toward the craggy mountain to the right, starting up on the green arms that lead to the top. Carry water. Once on top the O'Connor River comes into view as do the snow-capped mountains to the south and west.

The next 2 km (1.5 mi) are downhill toward the Mineral Lakes. The walking is easy. Stay on the east side of the pass. Get onto the rocks and follow them down. There are tiny ponds that will have to be maneuvered. Camping is splendid above the Mineral Lakes on the arm leading down from the pass. If you are early in the year, the land around the lakes could be quite soggy.

The next 12 km (8 mi) is pleasant alpine walking, past little lakes and boulders that give shade to ground critters, with no real vegetation to battle. Go down the hill and past the Mineral Lakes on their south end, cross Inspector Creek again and follow the valley in a south easterly fashion until you are back at the highway. The walk can be a bit wet early in the season.

Skagway, Alaska or Whitehorse, Yukon

Both Whitehorse and Skagway are tourist friendly towns with every amenity a backpacking and/or motor home visitor could desire. Backpackers staying in Whitehorse usually stay at the Robert Service Campground that is within walking distance from the center.

The campground is the place to go if you need a hiking partner, a ride to trailhead or just ideas for other things to do while in the area. There are numerous restaurants, hotels, bars and gift shops in Whitehorse. The bookstore on Main Street carries a large selection of books about the Yukon.

Skagway is located along the Pacific coast and on the Lynn Canal. Originally founded by Captain William Moore it can be reached by road along the Klondike Highway or by boat from southern ports. Captain Moore, who was in the area as part of the Canadian survey crew headed by William Ogilvie to map the American/Canadian boundary, also discovered the lower route to the Yukon through the White Pass. He named it after the Minister of the Interior, Sir Thomas White. Eventually the railway took this route.

Skagway, a town with many restored buildings from its boom days in the 1890s, is now a cruise ship stop so the tourist population varies anywhere from ten to 10,000, depending on the time and day. Like Whitehorse, all amenities are available. This is where park headquarters is located for the Chilkoot Trail. Parks issue the mandatory registration pass.

Chilkoot

Time: Four days.

Distance: 53.1 km (33.2 mi).

Difficulty: Class four.

Topo maps: If you want maps for identification purposes, they can be purchased both in Skagway or in Whitehorse.

Equipment: A passport is recommended as you must travel from the United States back into Canada. You must also make arrangements for getting to and from the trailhead. Parks Canada has published an excellent trail description.

Permits: A maximum of 50 hikers will be permitted to enter Canada over the Chilkoot Pass on any given day and forty-two reservations will be accepted at park headquarters, leaving eight for walk-ins. Groups must be limited to twelve or less people. For reservations call: 1-800-661-0486 (from Canada and US) or 1-867-667-3910 (local and overseas). Permits may be picked up at the Trail Center in Skagway, on Broadway near 2nd Ave. The cost of permits is as follows: $35 in Canadian currency for one adult for the full trip. Youth between 6 and 15 pay $17.50 each. A season pass is $105 for adults. Reservation fee is $10 per hiker over and above the permit costs. Day permits are $5 for adults and $2.50 for youth. Reserved permits must be paid for at time of reservation and picked up by noon on the day of the planned departure.

The route: The Chilkoot trail can be hiked in either direction although the most common is the direction the Klondikers took: from the south, starting in Skagway to the north ending (for you not the Klondikers) at Bennett Lake or Log Cabin. The Chilkoot Trail is an historical hike with many artifacts from the gold rush still on or near the trail. It is illegal to deface or remove any of these objects. The hike up to and over the pass from the American side is steep and intimidating making it much easier to go up rather than down. The weather can be horrid and snow, sleet, hail or fog should be expected at all times of the year. However, sunny days are not uncommon either and when it is hot, the weather is just as difficult to deal with because the sun shines for about 20 hours a day leaving little relief. Because of this, the sun warms the land quickly. There is little shade going up to the pass or going down on the Canadian side of the mountain before Bennett Lake where the tree line begins.

Both black and grizzly bears haunt the route. Hypothermia is possible and should be prevented by always keeping dry. During years of heavy snow pack, avalanches are possible between Sheep and Happy Camp throughout the summer. Water tablets or a filter are needed as giardia has been reported. Camping is restricted to designated areas in order to keep the environmental impact to a minimum.

Trail access: The hiking trail starts at Dyea, 16 km (10 mi) from Skagway. There are shuttles and taxis available in Skagway to take you to trailhead. Check at the Trail Center for information. If driving, there are signs from Skagway to Dyea that go along the Klondike Highway, around Nahku Bay and up Taiya Inlet.

If crossing Bennett Lake, a boat can be hired at Carcross. The White Pass and Yukon Route Railway can be taken to/from Skagway and/or Fraser where Canadian Customs is located. You may also hike to Log Cabin and flag a bus heading for either Whitehorse or Skagway. If this is your plan, check on bus schedules before starting.

If you have vehicles, one may be left at Dyea and the other at Log Cabin parking lot. Lock all vehicles and leave nothing of value visible.

The trail: Prior to the Klondikers, the early Tlingits used this glacier-free corridor (one of three) through the Coast Range so they could trade with the interior peoples. By 1880, explorers and prospectors started to cross the trail looking for gold and in 1896 they found it. This in turn brought thousands of miners to the Chilkoot, then the easiest and shortest route to the gold fields. Restoration of this trail began in the 1960s but it does not always follow the original route. According to the Seattle Post-Intelligencer in 1897, the route actually crossed the Taiya River eight times. Today hikers stay on the east side of the river and climb over a hill instead.

During the gold rush, Dyea sported a transient population that was between 8000 and 10,000 people. Over 150 businesses offered services and supplies where the travelers could purchase anything from immoral and illegal items to a hot meal or a forgotten piece of equipment that would be needed farther north. The town disappeared after the White Pass and Yukon Route Railroad was completed in 1899. There is a shelter, toilets, a campsite and parking lot at Dyea.

The trail climbs a steep hill, drops down the other side and then follows a logging road to the braided channels of the floodplain and the ruins of a small sawmill that was in operation in the 1950s.

Finnegan's Point at the mouth of the Taiya River, eight kilometers from trailhead, is where some Klondikers dragged their canoes full of supplies during the summer. This allowed them a few extra kilometers of canoe travel rather than packing. Pat Finnegan and his sons charged a toll for the use of their bridge and road. In 1897 there were about seventy-five tents at the site, some of which were restaurants and saloons. The camp was abandoned by 1898. Today the site has a tenting spot and toilets.

Canyon City campsite, another four kilometers along, is across the river from the old tenting site. The location of the old city, a natural camping spot, had been used by First Nation people going to and from the interior for many centuries before the prospectors came. Today, the ruins contain a boiler from the Dyea Klondike Transportation Company, one of the two companies that had equipment here. The boiler powered the first section of an aerial freight tram over the pass. During the height of its existence, Canyon City had over 1500 residents and 24 businesses. It seems that they even had a town planner as the town was laid out in an organized system of lots, blocks and streets.

Pleasant Camp, at the head of Taiya Canyon, got its name from the level ground that is available. During the stampede, the tents between Pleasant and Sheep Camps were almost solid. There was also a toll bridge here that took the men to the other side of the river where walking was better. Today the toll is paid in Skagway!

Sheep Camp, at tree line, is the most popular place to stay before crossing the pass. There are campsites, toilets, a warden's cabin and a canvass covered shelter complete with stove. Originally a camp for sheep hunters, this spot became a stopping point for Klondikers if winter storms caused people to wait it out before crossing the pass. During its height, Sheep Camp had everything from a post office to a hospital, ready to serve the 6000 to 8000 transient residents who were on their way north.

The Scales, 26 kilometers from trailhead, is where packers would re-weigh their loads and re-adjust their prices, always charging higher rates for the steep climb to the summit. This was often the turn-around point for many not so hardy prospectors.

The Golden Stairs starts shortly after the Scales and goes for half a kilometer at a steep, forty-five degree angle. This is the spot where the famous photo of the human rope of prospectors trudging up the mountain in the snow, one directly behind another, was taken. The half-kilometer of hiking is difficult with huge rocks to maneuver around and over, often in rain or fog that in turn, makes the rocks slippery. The Klondikers took up to six hours to get to the top and had to make as many as thirty trips to get all their gear over to the other side.

The Chilkoot Pass is what you have come for; to cross this legendary piece of land with so much history attached. You have come almost 27 kilometers with about fifty pounds on your back. How do you compare to the Klondiker? During the days that the North West Mounted Police collected a customs duty here, their small hut would get so wet from melting snow off the men's feet that the customs forms would dissolve. There were two bunks in the shack. One of the bunks often had up to $90,000 in duties lying in a bag under the bed. Since you have already paid your fees there is no longer any money to be found in the cabin. However, when occupied, the Parks Canada officers often have a hot or cool drink waiting for those crossing. Be certain to stop here, regardless of the weather, and while gazing over Crater Lake imagine the prospectors during the rush entering this desolate land. To get across the ice fields, follow the rods with the orange flags fluttering. Once across the snow there are stone cairns to show the way.

Remnants of the tramways, built to carry goods for the Klondikers, can be seen along this part of the trail. There were three companies in the old days with trams. The longest one extended from Canyon City to this spot just above Crater Lake. It was called Stone Crib. There is a great box of rocks that anchored this end of the tramway. Klondikers rich enough to use this system paid about seven cents a pound for their goods. In summer, up to 150 horses and mules could be seen grazing in the meadows beside the lake. Wagons were available to carry goods from Crater Lake to Lindeman Lake down the valley.

Your first stopping place in British Columbia, Happy Camp, has tenting sites, a cooking shelter and an outhouse. Even though the terrain is sparse it is a welcome sight after your seven-kilometer haul from the top of the pass. Luckily, you need to carry less than one hundred pounds of supplies, unlike the Klondikers who had to have 1000 pounds (450 kg) with them before the NWMP would allow them to cross the pass. If this camp is full, it is only another 4 km (2.5 mi) to the next one at Deep Lake.

Deep Lake campsite and facilities is on the lake and some think it is more picturesque than beside the river at Happy Camp. But it's 4 km

(2.5 mi) farther (or closer to the end). The river falls 200 m (600 ft) through a series of rapids and a rock canyon between here and Lindeman Lake.

Lindeman Lake/City in 1898 had thousands of tents pitched around its shores. Now Parks Canada allows only a few. The lake was named by Lt. Fredrick Schwatka in 1883 when he passed this way on his journey north. Schwatka named it after the secretary of the Bremen Geographical Society. Although there are only tenting facilities and a warden's cabin here now, the atmosphere, sparkling with excitement and adventure is still the same as it was during the rush. An old boat frame from the Klondike days can also be seen close to the site.

Bare Loon Lake is a pretty spot but most people prefer to stay at Lindeman City. However, all needed facilities are at Bare Loon Lake. Look for artifacts (if you have any energy left). Just past the campsite is the turn off trail for those going directly to Log Cabin on the Klondike Highway rather than to Bennett Lake.

Bennett Lake is the end of the trail for hikers. The lake was named by Lt. Frederick Schwatka of the U.S. army after the editor of the New York Herald. Besides the excellent facilities, there is a Presbyterian Church where you can give thanks that you made it. There are also the graves of those who were not as lucky as you. At the lake, pilings can be found where the steamers docked and tied up. In 1898, the ice broke on May 29th and within a week, 7000 boats departed from this spot.

From Bennett you may catch the White Pass and Yukon Route Railway trains or you can continue walking along the track for about 15 km (9.5 mi) to Log Cabin on the highway. There are no camping facilities at Log Cabin. At one time this was a thriving community of about twenty buildings that catered mostly to the railway workers.

The White Pass Rail line was first surveyed in 1892 and then again four years later when it was decided that there were no serious problems visible to impede building of the line. The initial cost was estimated to be $1.5 million. After 27 months of battling the snows, winds, minus 50ºC temperatures and the winter darkness, the line cost $10 million.

However, the profits expected from carrying freight and passengers was estimated to be $3 million for the first five month period. There were days after the line was in operation that produced as much as $11,436 in earnings. It didn't take long for the investors to earn back their capital.

Hiking tips

Laws of the land: Low impact camping is the recommended philosophy when going onto the trails of northern British Columbia. This means leaving nothing behind. New markers or cairns should not be put in where there are none. When walking in the alpine stay on the trails. If there are no trails, then spread out so a trail does not form. Whenever possible and when there is no trail, stay on rocks in creek beds. Avoid loose or steep terrain as it will slide.

- Cover all excretions with natural products such as moss or leaves and burn or carry out your used toilet paper. Use a stove instead of a campfire and, if using a campfire, remove the ring and ashes before leaving unless in a designated campsite and there was one there before.
- If making a new campsite and having a fire, remove all fire scars before leaving. One man I met used to cut a spot for his campfire in the turf, removed the turf and then make his fire on the bare ground. When he was finished, he made certain the fire was out, returned the piece of turf to the campfire spot and then watered it before heading down the trail. He certainly left no mark. If you must make a campfire in a grassy area, use the above method or better still, use a stove.
- Never cut vegetation to make room for your tent and never cut vegetation to make shelters. Place a tent on sand or gravel whenever possible; the romantic vision of sleeping on a knoll in the alpines is not much fun. I have seldom found a flat spot in the alpines.
- Wash water should be dumped at least 30 meters (100 feet) away from water sources. If possible, have used dishwater filter through gravel and stones instead of pouring it onto vegetation as soap kills vegetation. Gravel helps filter water before it finds its way back to the stream. When I had a bear encounter a few years ago, I was going to throw my porridge into the creek but instinctively stopped myself. Instead, I put the porridge (still in the cooking pot) into my backpack. That way, I left no pollution and the bear did not get any of the food. He did, however, follow me and the smell of porridge down the trail. Luckily, I met some park workers who were able to scare the bear away.

- Do not plan on going into the backcountry in British India's fashion, with 300 porters and helpers. Keep your groups small. Four or five people are the most desirable number. If there are more than five in your party, break into two groups, using different routes. Safety wise, four or five people is recommended; if there is an accident there are two to go out and get help while one or more persons can stay with the injured.
- Carry out all garbage. "Leave only your tracks, take only your snaps." If you see pieces of garbage dropped along the trail, pick them up and carry them out. Become fastidious.
- Do not pick, move, remove or change anything natural that is in the environment. This includes flowers, rocks, horns or berries. Although delicious to eat, adding berries to your food supply is hard on the environment. Over-picking of any wild plant could result in extinction of the species. Bring your own food supply.
- Take food that does not smell. If using tinned food, burn the tin after emptying it in order to burn out the smell. Flatten the tin and carry it out with you.
- When breaking camp, make certain all traces of your presence are gone. That plastic bag will not disappear from under a rock nor will the toilet paper. Carry the bag. Burn or carry the paper.
- Never leave garbage buried in the ground or dumped in the rivers or streams. The fish do not eat our garbage! Animals will eat plastic bags but their digestive systems have not evolved enough to benefit from the bag.
- Human waste should be buried at least 30 meters (100 feet) from any water and all toilet paper should be burned or carried out. You may feel that a low-use area can accommodate some garbage and it probably can but this is poor practice. Don't be the first to leave a mark.
- Make certain that the campfire is out. Be aware that moss is dry and can smolder for long periods of time (years) before starting a fire. Seven and a half centimeters (3 inches) of peat takes 100 years to form and only minutes to destroy.
- Unnecessary use of firewood will end in shortage. This has happened in many Canadian and American Parks. Make fires only if necessary. Lightweight stoves are recommended.

- If possible, use bear canisters to carry and store food as the canisters prevent all animals from associating food with humans. Feeding any animals including pesky ground squirrels is illegal.
- Wear boots with good grip but shallow treads.
- Use light runners or sport sandals while in camp. This minimizes the impact in a highly used area.
- View wildlife only from a distance. Never follow animals as you may be separating a mother from her young. It is against the law to harass or harm wildlife and if an offender is caught fines can be up to $150,000.

Bear Country

In Northern British Columbia, there are both black and grizzly bears. The grizzly is a majestic animal (when observed from a distance) but can be more aggressive than any other animal in the wilderness, especially if it associates humans with food.

- There are more differences between grizzlies and black bears than their size. They have different habits and, when encountered, they must be treated differently. Learn these differences and habits and enjoy one of Canada's greatest treasures.
- Some people, usually foreigners, are so intent on getting photos of bears that they set baits for them. This is illegal and any known incidents should be reported to the authorities.
- Due to the high profits, poaching is a problem in Canada. According to the Canadian Wildlife Federation, bear gallbladders have sold for as much as $18,000 in Asia. If you see anything suspicious that could indicate poaching of wild animals call the authorities. Convicted offenders can face fines of up to $150,000. Refusing to purchase products made from animal parts will also help eliminate the practice. I encourage those interested in preserving our wildlife to financially support the nonprofit organization, The Canadian Wildlife Federation, 2740 Queensview Dr., Ottawa, Ont. K2B 1A2.
- Most native groups believe bears deserve respect and these groups have interesting methods of showing their respect. Some groups never walk over bear scat as this is considered disrespectful and if the act is com-

mitted, they believe an unpleasant bear encounter will ensue. Some people also speak gently when they see a bear and they never look directly into its eye. Many native groups of Northern British Columbia never hunted bear and killed bears only if attacked.

Identification

Identification of the species is essential for your safety. The following hints may help.

- Mature grizzlies can be anywhere from 90 - 360 kilograms (200 - 800 pounds). Generally they are larger than black bears. In the north, grizzlies are usually smaller than those living farther south. Bears inhabiting the Pacific moisture rim are generally bigger than those in other parts of Canada. If the vegetation is thick and lush, the bears will be the same.
- Grizzlies have a hump on the back of the neck where black bears do not. This is not always easy to spot, especially in a young grizzly.
- Grizzly prints have toes close together and almost straight across; they are not arched. The claws may be 4 inches long.
- The black bear's toes are farther apart and the toes lay in an arch. Their claws are shorter than a grizzly's.
- The grizzly's nose is concave (a pug nose) and the black bear has a straighter, Roman style nose.
- Grizzly scat is usually in large piles. If it is fresh, the animal may be near.
- Grizzly and black bears may be any shade of color from albino white to sandy brown to black. Grizzlies sometimes have light-tipped hair with darker fur on the inside but I hope you never get close enough to check this out. Both species may have a white blaze on their chests. Grizzlies have grizzled fur, thus the name. Black bears have smooth, shiny coats. This is good to know if you see hair on a scratching tree; the hair left behind will indicate which type of bear is in the vicinity.
- Males of both species are larger than females, but up close even the youngster looks big.
- Some grizzlies can climb trees and all black bears can.
- If in doubt, assume the bear is a grizzly.

Habits

- Grizzlies seldom attack on sight. However, if the animal's ears are up and the hair is standing up on the back of the neck, this indicates a charge is coming. If the bear is snorting, whoofing and growling, this also means an attack is possible. Whoofing is a sign that the bear knows you are there. A bear standing sideways, showing his size with his head down and chomping his jaws, is a threatening sign. Bears standing on their hind legs are sniffing the air trying to get your scent.
- Any bear near a carcass or carrion is dangerous. He will protect his food supply from anything threatening. Hovering ravens are an indication that garbage or carrion may be present. Circle away from this sign, or back off.
- Grizzlies usually hunt at night while the black bears usually hunt during the day. However, I have often seen grazing grizzlies during the day.
- Bears accustomed to garbage are a nuisance and are dangerous. Do not feed bears. Use a canister to carry your food. Some municipalities are addressing the problem of garbage dump bears by putting electric fences around their dumps.
- Bears do not stumble when running downhill nor do they run on their hind legs but they can outrun any Olympic sprinter.
- Bears, especially young teenagers, are curious. They may check your camp just to see what it is. There was a bear I came across one year who found a sleeping bag hanging on a tent. The bear played with the tent and masticated the sleeping bag for hours before he got bored and moved on. For the four days before returning to civilization, the owner had to sleep in the bag scented with bear breath. It was pretty ugly.
- In July, bears hang around hillsides where fresh green shoots grow, moving up as the snow melts. By August they move down to ripe berry patches, or streams where there are fish. Bears like moist areas because more young vegetation will be available in these areas. Bears eat cow parsnip and horsetails and they love soap berries or buffalo berries. They also like bear berries (hence the name), low bush cranberries and crow berries. Bears nip the flowers off some plants. This is often evident in the fireweed patches so abundant in Northern BC. If the flowers have been recently nipped, be wary.

- Bears turn over rocks, claw deadfall and dig up turf looking for insects. They are capable of massive excavations. Look for these signs. A bear stomp is where bears leave tracks going to and from a favorite tree that they rub against. A bear stomp is a good sign that a bear is living in the area.
- Bears like dense bush for cover but they also like to graze in the alpines. September is their most aggressive month, when their daily food intake increases from 8000 kilocalories to 15,000 or 20,000 kilocals.
- By October, grizzlies den on mountain slopes at about 1200 meters/4000 feet and black bears usually den on forest floors. During winter, their heart rate falls from fifty beats per minute to eight. They keep their body temperatures close to summer levels. During their sleeping period, they lose 35% of their body weight. Although they sleep most of the time they are known to come out for a romp in the snow on a sunny day.
- Bears mate in June and July but the embryo does not develop until November and then only if the female is fat and healthy. If she is too thin or sick to sustain the development of a healthy embryo, she aborts. Their rule is "If you can't support, abort." With a healthy female, the young are born during the winter and live off the female's fat-rich milk (25-30% fat) until spring. A litter usually consists of one or two cubs but a sow may have up to four cubs in one year.
- Black bears do not usually inflict the same degree of injury as grizzlies but they can do just as much damage to gear or cabins.

Things to do

- I believe sex between humans in bear country is dangerous because of the resulting smell. Seminal fluid mixed with vaginal fluid causes an odor that could be attractive to bears. Although no studies have been done on this topic, Steven Herrero, bear biologist and author of *Bear Attack*, agrees that my hypothesis is reasonable. Until this hypothesis is disproved, girls especially should never take the chance of having the odor of sex left on their bodies, in their sleeping bags or in their tents.
- Girls should use tampons instead of napkins during a menstrual cycle as tampons smell less and are easier to discard. Be certain to change often to prevent any odor. Burn all used tampons. Never bury them.

- Keep a clean (odorless) campsite. Bears smell food and garbage from a long distance away. The natives claim that when a pine needle falls, the deer hears it, the eagle sees it and the bear smells it.
- Travel in a group; the more the safer. Like humans, a bear will approach a single person before it will approach a group.
- If you come around a corner and see a bear, back up slowly, move your hands up and down and speak in a soft calm voice.
- Always photograph bears from at least 300 meters (1000 ft) away. Any closer may be considered harassment. Some natives believe that if you step over bear scat an unhappy bear will visit your camp. If you see people rolling in scat, you can be certain they are intent on getting a close-up photo.
- If you are retreating and a bear is following, drop an object (not food) to distract him but do not drop your pack. Your pack may be protection a few feet down the trail when the bear catches up.
- If suddenly attacked by a grizzly, play dead. Do not fight, yell or make any aggressive moves. PLAY DEAD!!! Cover your neck with your hands, and bring your knees up over your stomach and remain in this fetal position until the bear leaves or help arrives. Be prepared to assume this position for hours.
- On close confrontation, scream, shout and intimidate a black bear but never a grizzly. However, the latest theory states that if you are confronted with a predatory bear, you should be aggressive. I think this new term"predatory bear" is a euphemism for bear encounters that have not been explained. Most unpleasant bear encounters can be traced to human error. We may not yet know all the parameters of human error. From my own experience, I know that it is almost impossible to remain passive if encountering a bear. During my only close encounter, I kept throwing rocks and screaming at a grizzly (acting aggressive). This drove him off long enough for me to find a safe place, but he followed me.
- Before going on a hike, try to find out if there are any bears in the area. Find out the animal's habits and avoid attracting it.
- Take binoculars in order to scan an open area before entering. Make noise to let bears know where you are. Also be aware that even if all rules

are stringently kept, you still may have bad luck. It is the same as driving down the highway; you could be hit by an oncoming truck. Likewise, you could encounter a curious, angry or sick bear.

- Always place your tent upwind from your cooking spot. Do not use someone's tent that may have food (or sex) odors on it. If you borrow equipment, make certain it is from persons fastidious about keeping their gear odor free.
- Cook only needed amounts of food or over eat. It is hard to burn unused food. Besides, it smells.
- For sleeping, wear clothes not worn during the day. Do not sleep in clothes worn while cooking.
- Camp in open areas, and off trails. Like humans, animals prefer trails for walking. If you are in the open, the animal may see and therefore avoid you. If near trees, keep a climbable one in mind.
- Look for digging signs, claw marks on the trees, uprooted stumps, fresh bear scats, fresh prints and hair rubbed onto trees. If you see fresh signs, make noise and try to leave the area.
- Every member of your party should carry pepper spray and it should be where it can be reached in a second, never inside your backpack. Keep it in the tent at night. If a bear is sprayed once, it will not be able to attack for five minutes. If it is sprayed by three people, there is little chance it will return. However, if it does, it will be one angry critter. Be certain to always have a couple of shots left in your sprayer. All used or expired spray containers should be replaced immediately.
- Never hike alone. More than half of the recorded injuries inflicted by bears occur to lone hikers.
- Place everything with an odor into your bear canister. Feeding a bear almost guarantees his death as he will associate all people with food and eventually meet someone who refuses to give him some. In that case the bear will become aggressive and cause death or injury to the person. The result of this will be death to the bear.
- Do not use make-up, deodorant, perfumes, after-shave lotion, perfumed soap or anything else that smells, especially near or in the tent.

- Scented toothpaste, when spit onto the ground, smells. Dilute the spit with copious amounts of water or swallow it. Some third-world countries sell unscented toothpaste but I know of none sold in North America. Using baking soda as a tooth powder is an unpleasant alternative.
- Do not camp where someone has left garbage. Do take out any garbage you find and report the incident to the club in the area or if in a park, to the authorities.
- Never run from a bear. Bears run faster than humans. Running may be interpreted as aggression.
- These hints are for the prevention of an unpleasant encounter with a bear. Use all caution when in the bush, not only for your own sake but for the sake of the animal as well. Should a bear learn that humans mean food (food and sleep is all they are really interested in once mating is finished) then they will want yours. If a bear harasses a human, the bear is the one that pays and usually with its life. This is not fair. Please mitigate this injustice by acting responsibly.
- Although your chances of being hit by lightning are greater than those of being attacked by a bear, an attack is so violent that it seems worse than other types of deaths. I hope that you do everything possible to prevent a serious encounter.

More Things to do

The following hints may seem repetitious but I cannot stress enough the importance of safety for both you and the bear.

- Carry a pair of long johns that are used only for sleeping. Put your day clothes in your pack and leave the pack 20 or 30 meters (65 or 100 feet) away from the tent or, if available, in a bear cache. Do not leave your pack in the vestibule of your tent.
- Pitch your tent upwind from your campfire. This will keep the smell of food off the tent. Also, put all sleeping gear in a safe place before making supper thus preventing food from spilling on the gear. No sex in the tent; no sex in the backcountry.
- Use dehydrated food because it does not smell as much when it is being carried.

- Keep your sleeping bag and tent as far away from the food bag and/or garbage bag as possible while it is in your pack.
- Do not cook more food than you can eat. Burning uneaten food may be difficult, especially in the alpine. Food smoke smells.
- Never take food or garbage, deodorants, perfumes or toothpaste into the tent.
- Never take your pack into the tent. In the case of bad weather, take a plastic bag or pack fly to cover your pack.
- Always store food away from camp. Hang it in a tree if you are not carrying a canister. One girl had her food in a canister and she actually heard a bear knocking it around while she slept (actually while she lay in her tent with her eyes wide open) but the bear was unable to get into the canister so it left.
- If a bear gets food from you, it may stalk you believing it can get more. Do not let a bear get any food.
- Read Steven Herrero's book, *Bear Attacks* published by Hurtig, Edmonton in 1985. The updated version should be released soon.

Creek Crossings

Most trails in this book do not require the fording of creeks. However, the crossings that are in the book require skill. Some of the creeks are wide, some are deep, most are swift and all are cold. Proper crossing knowledge is essential.

- Crossing early in the morning is the first general rule. The snow on the mountaintop melts less when the sun is set so the creeks become substantially lower during the night. However, if you happen to have a bad night of rain, the water level may rise. During spring runoff, northern rivers crest between the beginning of June and the end of July. The farther north you go, the later the waters crest.
- Wearing shoes to cross creeks is recommended. Neoprine canoe booties or socks are warmer than runners and do not weigh much. Booties have a sturdy bottom and keep your feet warm. However, they take longer to dry than runners. The best combination I have found is neoprene socks under sport sandals. The socks keep your feet warm and wring almost

dry thus making them lightweight for carrying. The sandals are light and double as evening slippers. Use bonzo rings on the Velcro of the sandals to prevent them from being pulled open in the current. Cheap sport sandals do not have a stiff enough sole to keep from bending when in swift water.

- Remove long pants before crossing a creek because the extra material will create resistance in the current.
- While crossing, use a stick or ski pole to lean into. When in the water, there should always be two out of three points on the ground. The three points are your two feet and the stick. Move one foot, then move the stick and then move the second foot. In murky water, the stick should be used to feel the depth of the water before moving a foot.
- Always face upstream. The current would soon whip your feet from under you if you were leaning down stream. When approaching the far bank, do not turn sideways until your feet are on dry ground. It does not take much current to whip you off your feet.
- ALWAYS undo the waist and chest buckle on your pack when crossing a creek. If you fall, you must be able to get out of your pack. When on your back and strapped into a pack, you are as immobile as a turtle. There have been deaths from people not undoing their packs during a stream crossing. One of the wardens told me about a girl who fell while strapped into her pack and died in about eight inches of water. Tie an empty water bottle to a rope and then secure the rope to the outside of your pack. This will give you a buoy to grab in the event that your pack does go under water.
- Choose the widest, thus the shallowest spot on the creek. Walk up and down the creek a bit to find the best spot. Usually, the creek widens as it reaches its mouth.
- Look for a flat area where the drop is not significant as this will result in a slower current.
- Once you have chosen a spot, move upstream a few feet. When crossing, do not move directly across or upstream. Allow the current to move your foot slightly backward while you move it to the side, using the same physics as a reaction ferry. This method will be quicker and safer than

trying to fight the current by going directly across.

- If there is a group crossing, you may link arms and cross together. This forms a human chain. Put the stronger members upstream thus forming an eddy. The weakest should be farther downstream. One person should co-ordinate the movement by giving a command and then everyone should move at the same time.
- If there are only two or three people crossing deep water, have the people form a triangle with the shorter ones moving behind the taller one. The front person will shield the shorter one from some of the current. Cross in unison with the front person giving commands. The person at the back will not be able to use a stick but can lightly hold onto the front person's pack or waist.

River crossings are difficult and cold.

- If reconoitering difficult water, secure the person who is in the water to a rope and hold the other end. In the event of an accident, the current will force the one in the water toward the bank as long as the person on shore pulls the rope. Note however that if the crossing is wide, a long rope will eventually drag in the water and possibly force the crosser off balance.

Giardias and Hanta Virus

Commonly known as Beaver Fever, the giardias flagellate is present in northern BC and comes from water contaminated with human or animal excretions. I always drink the water straight from the creeks and eat the glacial ice with no bad effects but most parks in the north have official warnings about giardias. The closer you are to glacial water, the safer it is.

- Symptoms of giardias infection appear anywhere from 7 - 21 days after ingestion. Explosive diarrhea, flatulence, cramps, bloating, fatigue and weight loss are common symptoms. Depression or lack of interest is also a symptom. Curing the condition usually requires a doctor and drugs. If you think you have it, get out of the bush and see a doctor.
- There are three ways to purify water in the wilderness. One is to boil it for ten minutes and a second is to dissolve a heavy-metal tablet containing iodine or silver. The tablets must be dissolved in the water for ten minutes before the water is safe to use. Chlorine tablets are not strong enough to rid the water of parasites. The third method of purifying water is by using a water filter. Light-weight, reliable purifiers are available at most sports shops.
- Bury all feces at least 30 meters (100 ft) from the high water level of any body of water and 15 cm. (6 in.) below the surface. This speeds decomposition and is aesthetically more appealing. Burying feces helps prevent the spread of giardias.
- If you become obsessed with personal excretions, a good book to read for sound information and humorous entertainment is Kathleen Meyer's book *How to Shit in the Woods* by Ten Speed Press, P.O. Box 7123, Berkley, Ca. 94707
- Hanta virus is a virus that lives in rodents, particularly deer mice. The virus is passed to humans by inhalation of air where the rodent's saliva, urine or feces has dried. Some of the cabins in the backcountry have rodent feces in them so this could be a nesting place for the virus. If a cabin you come across has lots of animal feces, it may be better to stay outside. A precaution against rodents getting into your food bag and exchanging fresh meals for digested ones is using the food canisters.
- Signs of hanta virus are flu-like symptoms that cannot be explained in any other way. These symptoms can lead to cardiopulmonary failure. If you think you have been exposed to the virus, get medical help immediately.

Hypothermia

Hypothermia is one of the most dangerous health hazards in the mountains. Hypothermia is a condition where the body loses heat faster than it is produced. The body compensates, trying to keep warm by shivering. Because of sudden winds, rain, snow or sleet and because of the glacial-fed streams, the high mountain passes, and the possibility of exhaustion, hypothermia is a constant danger, even in July or August. This condition often occurs at fairly mild temperatures, but when a person is wet and exposed to the wind.

Symptoms:

- Uncontrolled shivering
- Slurred speech
- Stumbling
- Stupor
- Collapse that may result in death.

Some cool off by dipping in the water.

- Treatment includes removing wet clothing and getting the person out of the wind. Then, warm the person by putting heat to the head, neck, chest and groin.
- If a fire is not possible, place the person in a sleeping bag. Remove your clothing and climb in too. Your partner will get your body heat quicker this way.
- The latest research indicates that moving so the body can create its own heat is most successful in bringing the body temperature up to normal. If the hypothermic person is conscious and in a dry sleeping bag, start him/her doing some exercise such as sit-ups to generate heat.
- If there is a problem with the person's breathing, give mouth-to-mouth resuscitation thus transferring some of your hot air into the victim's body.

- Give the person warm tea with sugar or any other sweet, warm (not hot) drink. Never give the person alcohol as it causes decreased sensitivity and lowers the body's heat production.
- Always carry all extra clothing in a sealed plastic bag so it will not get wet. Most packs will leak under extreme conditions.
- Wear waterproof clothing during wet weather.
- Wear a toque - 40% of your body heat is lost through the head.
- Eat high calorie foods *before* becoming tired.
- Even when on an easy day hike, always carry some type of shelter such as a bivy-sack, piece of tarp or survival blanket.
- Understand the symptoms of hypothermia and never be blind to the possibility of this condition either in someone else or yourself. A shivering person is not a wimp!
- Stop hiking before you get tired. If you are tired and conditions become difficult, you are more susceptible to hypothermia and to accidents.
- Don't eat snow or drink cold water if you are chilled or wet. Make warm tea! Eat food containing fats or carbos.
- If everyone in your party is shivering, don't pretend nothing is wrong. You must help your mates before they become unreasonable. Once someone passes to the second stage of hypothermia where reasoning becomes difficult, getting him/her into a safe place, especially if s/he is bigger than you, may not be possible - especially if you too are starting to lose it.

Sun Burn

Be certain to take sunscreen while hiking. During June, July and August, the days in the north are much longer than they are in the south, which in turn makes exposure to the sun much longer. Higher elevations also increase the amount of radiation being endured. Being on or near snow doubles the amount of sunrays you will get. If you have become sun burned, cover the burned area, place cool water or cool wet cloths on the skin, drink lots of cool liquid and rest. Heat exhaustion may seem unlikely in northern BC but do not be fooled. Both extremes, hypothermia and heat exhaustion, are possible.

Equipment

The equipment section of this book has been revised and edited by Rik Shedden of Vancouver, B.C. who has worked in the sports retail business for a number of years. Rik has also done extensive back packing in southern Australia, Africa and Nepal. At the time of his research, he was working for Coast Mountain in Vancouver. I respect Rik's vast knowledge and thank him for his input.

Equipment can make or break a person when on a trip of any duration. Cheap gear is not safe and is usually heavy. As a general guide line, the better the equipment, the lighter the weight.

The better thought-out a trip is, the more pleasurable the experience. Before purchasing an item, make certain that it is needed. The more important an item is relative to your personal safety, the better the quality should be. For example, boots must be excellent whereas you can get away with an okay dish or set of pots. Rain gear must keep you dry and sleeping bags must be warm but it really does not matter if you have climbing rope or binder twine for a clothesline. Tents must be waterproof but you need not purchase expensive Kalvin Klein t-shirts or shorts to wear. Personally, I have to compromise weight in the luxury section of my pack because I must have a warm sleeping bag that will give me heat, even if it gets wet. Get to know your body, your limitations and your needs. Then decide what you really need and why.

Shoes

This is the most important item for any type of hiking trip. If just going off the road and onto a short trail for twenty minutes, running shoes will usually suffice. If the terrain is difficult or wet, runners are dangerously slippery and an accident would almost be inevitable so boots are recommended. Any footwear less sturdy than runners is only for the fifteen minute stroll along a boardwalk. Any trip longer than a day hike or more difficult than a dry, level trail requires boots.

- Hiking boots come in as many shapes, sizes and colors as people do so choosing the best for you will require research. The perfect all-round boot does not exist. Light breathable boots are good for day hikes but a solid, all-leather boot is needed for long backcountry trips. Leather boots prevent feet from being cut on the rocks and many hikes involve walking up rocky creeks into the alpines.

- When looking for a boot, eliminate the ones that feel soft in your hand. Flex them checking for rigidity in the sole and lateral support. Look for a pair that come well above the ankle; generally the taller a boot, the more support it will give. Make certain the tongue and gussets are all leather, otherwise waterproofing becomes difficult. Ask for boots with a full shank to give the needed support. Good grip on the sole of the boot helps your footing in slippery places and on steep slopes. Also, when traveling with a heavy pack in hot weather, leather boots help keep the bottoms of your feet from burning.
- Suede and Cordura boots are good for short hikes. Such boots will leak faster than leather but they also dry faster. Another attractive feature is that these boots are less expensive than leather.
- When fitting boots bring along your own socks. Use your largest foot (both feet are seldom the same size) and size your boots accordingly. Keep in mind that after a few hours of backpacking, feet swell so a little extra room in a boot is better than tight boots. It is critical that the length of your boot is sufficient. Once your boots are laced, you should be able to splay and wiggle your toes comfortably. Try your boots with a pack and step on a downhill slope. Your toes should not cram up at the end.
- You may adjust the volume of a boot by changing the thickness of the insole, especially if wearing an orthopedic insert. If strong arch support is needed, do not use a spongy insole. Try"Superfeet", a generic fitting orthopedic insert originally designed for ski boots but excellent in hiking boots as well.
- When you first purchase boots, take them home and wear them in the house for a few hours or even a few days. If there are pressure points or any heel rubbing, you should return the boots. If you have chosen leather boots, rub a silicone snow or water sealer on them and then sit the boots near a warm draft or in the sun so the sealant soaks into the leather. Avoid waxes as they corrode the stitching. Some leathers are impregnated with silicone so treatment only at the end of the season is needed.
- Sport sandals are excellent to carry as a second shoe. They provide foot protection for creek crossings (thus keeping boots dry), they double at

the end of the day as a slipper and they are not heavy to carry. The Velcro attachments often come with Bonzo rings so the Velcro, which loses 30% of its stick power when wet, will stay fastened. However, if bush-whacking, don't Velcro the sandals to the outside of your pack. Stuff them inside as the Velcro comes undone when snagged by branches. Short neoprene canoe booties are excellent for warmth when creek crossing and they easily fit inside sport sandals.

- One of the most important things to remember when thinking about your feet is to clip your toenails. This will prevent"black-toe syndrome" which is painful and ugly. And, it takes a year to disappear. When hiking downhill with a heavy pack, your feet are pushed to the front of the boot. This causes bruising of the toes if the toenails are too long. So, clip your toenails - it also makes your feet that much lighter!! Another precaution against the dreaded"black-toe" is to tighten the laces near the toe of your boots before descending steep hills. This helps keep your foot where it belongs, preventing it from slipping too far forward. Undo them again when on the flat or going up hill.

Socks

Choose a"hiking" sock that is padded in the sole and heel and lighter on the top. Natural fibers like cotton and wool absorb and retain moisture while synthetics do not. The higher the wool content the warmer the sock. At all times, you should have two pairs of socks for day time use and a third lighter pair for night time. Gortex socks are expensive but they will keep feet dry even if the boots become soaked. Wearing a thin silk sock (sock liner) inside your main sock often prevents blisters. Frequently washing your socks is essential as the salt from sweat will cause foot burning, especially during hot weather.

Gaiters

Gaiters are highly recommended. They help keep stones out of your boots and protect your legs from mud and scratches. I like the style that has Velcro up the front and a leather strap that fits under the boot. Gaiters that must be put on before boots are on are inconvenient. Gaiters are hot when worn in hot weather but they help keep you warm in colder times.

Backpack

Should you become an avid backpacker, you will eventually find it necessary to have a closet full of packs, one for every type of trip. There are numerous styles of packs with different convenience gadgets or materials from which to choose.

For backpacking on longer trips, the external frame packs are not as popular as the internal frames because the internal frames seem to produce fewer rub spots. Unless you can afford an expensive external frame pack, like the Kelty, I would suggest staying away from them. I like the type of pack that has many pockets so that I can keep things organized. For example items such as bug lotion, spare glasses, or camera should be easily accessible. The duffel type packs that were in style a few years ago have been modified with side zippers so that everything in the pack is easily accessible.

- Wearing a well-fitted pack allows about 80% of the weight to be transferred to the hips and large rump muscles. The hip belt should fit snugly leaving the shoulder straps for stability with the pressure at the front of the shoulder, not the top. A strap across the sternum helps keep the pack from jiggling when trying to make precarious moves over logs and rocks.
- The pack should be worn close to your back yet low enough that it does not hit your head. Frequent adjustments should be made as weight and terrain changes.
- Do not purchase a pack that is too big for your frame. A pack should have some torso length adjustment capabilities. A 70-liter pack for men and a 60-liter pack for women are the average sizes needed for longer trips. Carry your heaviest objects in the middle of the pack close to your back to minimize offsetting your center of balance.
- A cup attached with a shower curtain hook or carabineer to the front strap makes obtaining water a simple matter. When attaching tents, bags or bear canisters to your pack, pile them above or to the sides rather than behind. This helps maintain your center of balance. Make certain everything is well attached. If bushwhacking, an article that has been snagged off your pack by a branch would be impossible to find.
- I advocate proportional weight distribution. In other words, bigger peo-

ple should carry more weight than smaller people. When adjusting for weight distribution, use the formula, weight of pack over weight of body is equal to unknown weight of pack over second weight of body. For example: 45/150 = X/100. Cross multiply and"X" becomes 30. This means that if a 150-pound (68 kilograms) man is carrying 45 pounds (20 kilograms), then a hundred pound man carrying the same weight would have a stress level equal to carrying 67.5 pounds (31 kilograms). Therefore, the 100-pound (45 kilogram) man should carry 30 pounds (13.6 kilograms) to be equal to the man carrying 45 pounds (20 kilograms). Of course the formula must be adjusted to compensate for disabilities like weak knees or age.

- If purchasing a new pack, be certain that the construction is sturdy, the belts and straps are well padded and the material is of good quality. From there, look at the size and organizational capability of the pack. After you have those few things figured out for your style of travel, look at the price. The main rule for a pack, as for your boots, is that it must fit perfectly. You will not be able to carry a large weight for many days if the pack is uncomfortable or if it cannot be adjusted to sit comfortably in different positions on your body.
- As for color, my suggestion may seem flippant, but I like a bright (usually red or yellow) colored pack because it looks nicer in photos. Bright colors are also easier to spot should you become lost. Greens, blues or browns blend in with the landscape.

Pack Fly

Pack flies are nice to have and they do help keep gear dry. I always use mine to cover my pack at night, rain or shine. Whether using one or not, keep your clothes and sleeping bag protected with heavy-duty plastic bags. I also recommend purchasing the orange or yellow garbage bags to be used as flags in the event that you become lost or injured. Bright colors are easier to spot from the air.

Tents

There are more styles and makes of tents than there are backpacks and boots. So, again, care must be taken in choosing what is suitable for your needs. The first and most important thing to remember is that the tent must be waterproof. There is little value in a tent that lets in the elements. After choosing a good quality material, (which translates into a mid to high-end cost and brand name) you must decide on size and weight. If you will travel only in a caravan of six or more people, a big tent is more efficient. If traveling with only one other person, a small tent is in order. I once met a couple who were carrying around seventy pounds each on a four-day hike because they had a tent in which to sleep and another one in which to cook and both tents were big enough to hold a wedding reception. You are in the mountains in order to be outdoors and you need shelter only when sleeping or to protect yourself from bad weather.

There is also a choice between the free-standing tent or the peg-type tent. The free-standing does not need to be secured to the ground where the peg type does. Often with the peg type, it is difficult to get the pegs into the ground or once in they will not stay there. However, free-standing tents need to be secured with weight as winds can carry them a long way.

- If looking for a good three-season tent, make sure it is well ventilated with mesh side panels to prevent condensation from accumulating. Also, a functional vestibule for boot storage is recommended. Do not put your pack in the vestibule as it will more than likely have odors on it that are attractive to bears.

- Tents with aluminum poles are lighter than those with fiberglass poles. Tents with pole clips are easier and quicker to set up than those with pole sleeves.

- Single wall tents are very light but expensive. Four-season tents are designed for winter season or mountaineering use and are usually too heavy for average backpacking trips.

- All tents should have a waterproof floor and fly. In the morning, be certain that the tent is dry before packing it. A damp tent can produce mould that will ruin the tent's fabric. Better tents are mould resistant but not mould-proof.

- Some people use a plastic ground sheet under the tent to protect the bottom from sharp objects. I prefer to carry a nylon tarp to eat under or to use as instant shelter if the weather is bad. This tarp can double as a ground sheet when camping on sharp rocks.

- Zippers in tents occasionally need a silicone covering in order to prevent the zipper from sticking. This can be done with official silicone zipper stuff, a wax candle or a tube of lip protection. The candle and lip protection do the same trick as the silicone but at a much cheaper price. Zippers stick and break when sand gets blown into the teeth. If camping in this type of terrain, wash your tent when you get home.

- Some people like to carry a Bivouac Sack instead of a tent. This keeps the weight down but at the cost of comfort. A bivy-sack slips over a sleeping bag and has a small tent-like area for the person's head. These sacks weigh around a pound. I have seen them used and the biggest problem was that the users had a difficult time keeping their sleeping bags dry inside due to condensation. A bivy-sack is good to carry on day hikes in the event of sudden bad weather or an accident.
- If you borrow a tent, be certain that the tent is good quality and it does not have food smells on it.

Sleeping Bags

A good night's sleep is necessary if you are going to enjoy your days in the wilderness. A three-season sleeping bag is good enough to keep you warm in the event that an unexpected snowstorm (which is possible at any time in the north) or if you have become wet and need to warm up before hypothermia sets in.

- Down bags require extra care and if they do become wet, they are useless. However, down is comfortable to sleep in. They are also the lightest in weight and the most compact of all bags. If carrying a down bag in a waterproof stuff sack, which is lined with a heavy plastic bag, you should be able to keep the bag dry. The final drawback is that down bags are expensive.
- If choosing a down bag, remember that the higher the loft, the lighter the bag. High loft (700 fill) means that less down is needed to fill a bag and achieve the same temperature rating as low loft (550 fill). High loft results in a compact bag with greater longevity.
- If your adventuring often takes you in close contact with water then synthetic fill would be more appropriate. A synthetic bag keeps its loft when wet thus it keeps you warm in potentially life threatening situations. The -5° to the -10°C category is all you will need for summer hiking in the north.

- Synthetic bags dry quicker than down bags.
- Sleeping bag stuff sacks should be lined with a plastic bag. Because of the seams and draw cord system, no stuff sack is completely watertight.
- The style of a bag is also important. There is no need to get a square bag when a mummy bag, shaped narrower at the feet than the shoulders, is less weight and bulk. Learning to sleep in a mummy bag takes a few tries because you must move the bag with your body when turning over rather than moving inside the bag like you do when sleeping under a blanket. Mummy bags with hoods will help keep you even warmer (40% of body heat is lost through the head). Be certain to purchase a bag that is complimentary to your height. Good bags come in short, medium or tall sizes.

Mattresses

A mattress certainly helps at the end of a long day when the body is tired. I recommend carrying a good one. The blue Airolite foams are made from a closed-cell foam and are hard to sleep on but they keep the cold from coming up beneath you. There are also closed-cell foams called Ridge Rests that are lighter and more comfortable than Airolites but bulky when rolled up.

- Therm-a-rests are great. Undo the valve and the mattress blows itself up. This is an added benefit when you have little or no energy left at the end of the day. It is in the morning, after you are rested, that a tiny bit of energy is needed to push the air out of the mattress. Therm-a-rests add warmth and padding for your hips and shoulders. With care, Therm-a-rests last for years and are easy to repair so the high price is well worth the comfort. Therm-a-rests are also heavier (weighing about one pound) than Airolite foams.
- Therm-a-rests come in two lengths, the full body length and the shorter three-quarter length. Choosing a three-quarter length mattress means saving on weight but skimping on insulation for your feet. A full-length mattress keeps your bag off the tent floor that may get damp. Get the mattress with a non-slip surface so your bag does not slide.
- Some Therm-a-rests are up to 50mm (2 inches) thick but again they are much heavier. Full-length, 50mm Therm-a-rests weigh 1.1 kg (2 .5 pounds).

- Taking a sponge, open-cell foam mattress is out of the question. They are bulky and, if wet, they are cold, heavy and useless. Because of the bulk they don't fit well into a pack and when carried on the outside of your back while bushwhacking, they get caught on branches and tear.

Stove

In low impact camping areas stoves are essential. The alpine, where much of your hiking will be done, has little wood. Alpine trees that are available do not burn.

At lower elevations, there is still wood available in Northern BC but it is best to use it sparingly. A hiking book, written in the early 1970's stated that it would be approximately 300 years before wood shortages would be noticeable in our forests. In heavily populated areas such as National Parks, wood shortages are a problem only twenty years after that prediction was made.

Finally, in the north, the fire hazard is often high which results in the prohibition of campfires. Stove cooking should be assumed from the outset. Be certain that your stove works and you know how to fix minor problems that may occur while in the backcountry.

The type of stove chosen is again a matter of preference. There are stoves that burn white gas, automobile gasoline, diesel fuel, butane or methyl hydrate. Some stoves can burn a number of fuels.

- Methyl hydrate stoves use alcohol and are the simplest, safest stoves of all. No priming is needed and they burn clean. However, the BTUs (measure of heat) produced by burning alcohol are the lowest of all fuels.
- Butane Canister stoves can be light, but when these canisters are empty, they must be packed out of the bush. This is added weight. There is also no indication as to how much fuel is left in the containers. Butane stoves do not put out as many BTUs as white gas or kerosene stoves.
- White gas stoves are excellent because they put out a lot of heat and fuel is easy to obtain in North America, but you must carry the liquid fuel. Weight again. There are many variations to the white gas stove. One thing to consider is that the base of the stove should be big enough to hold the pot when cooking. If the base is too small, the pot will tip.

- Multi-fuel stoves may burn kerosene, car gas or white gas and some new ones burn just about anything found in the bush. The advantages of kerosene over white gas are that it may be more available in foreign countries, it produces more BTUs and it is not as volatile as white gas. However, kerosene is not as readily available in Canada and it does not burn as clean.
- Stoves that must be primed may have a pump that requires frequent oiling and maintenance. Some self-priming stoves do cause problems when temperatures are below freezing because they do not build up enough pressure to light the stove.
- With butane and white gas, extra fuel must be carried for longer trips. A butane canister will last about three hours. White gas should be carried in aluminum bottles that are specially made so they do not leak or puncture easily. One liter of white gas will last about four hours burning time. The newer stoves are becoming noticeably energy efficient that in turn makes the overall weight of fuel much less.
- The most important considerations after purchasing a stove are that the stove be in good working order, you know how to use and repair it and that you have enough fuel to last the duration of the trip.

Fuel Containers

These can be purchased in lightweight aluminum with excellent, safe screw tops. They also come in different colors for easy identification. These containers may also be used as water or booze containers but should always be labeled. MSR stoves fit Sigg aluminum containers but Sigg containers are not guaranteed for use under pressure on the stoves. Use only the recommended containers for your stove. Plastic bottles may have contaminants in them and should not be used to pack fuel.

Booze Bottles

Booze should not be carried in standard plastic containers because alcohol reacts with some plastics to create a poison. In Canada, small bottles of distilled alcohol stored in non-reacting plastic can be purchased in the liquor stores. These are ideal for hiking. Do not carry liquid in glass bottles because they can and usually will break. If your pack develops a medicinal odor during the trip, you can be certain the booze is leaking. This is a form of alcohol abuse.

Pots

Aluminum pots are light in weight, durable, and quick-heating. Some people prefer the stainless steel pots because it is rumored that too much aluminum in the diet contributes to memory disorders. This is a matter of preference, weight versus health.

The most popular pots fit one inside the other. I put things like my salt, pepper, spoon, stove, dish soap, tea-towel/dish-rag/pot-holder and other spices inside my smallest pot in order to make the condiments easy to find. This is like organizing a kitchen.

Compass/GPS

A map is useless without a compass. Know how to use both before doing any of the longer hikes or routes. A GPS is not a substitute for a map and compass. It is an added piece of equipment that will help with your safety. All GPSs use the same chips and shock resistant electronics. You don't need one that will let you down load a map from the US government to be read on a thumb-sized screen. A GPS should never be the only method of navigation you use for a long trip. The accuracy of a GPS is said to be up to 10 meters for 90% of the time and five meters for 50% of the time. Altimeter readings on a GPS are unreliable.

Swiss Army Knife

These handy gadgets are of the utmost value and are like a badge of honor among hikers. The knives come with many attachments including tweezers to remove rose thorns, magnifying glasses to start a fire when your water proof-matches get lost, tooth picks to replace the dental floss you forgot to put into the comfort kit and cork screws to drool over when the mirage of a wine bottle appears. The only warning I have is that there is a cheap "Made in China" model that just does not compare to the real Swiss model. I advise you to pay the extra money and get something that will last (as long as you don't loose it).

Another piece of equipment used by many is the Leather-man multi-tool. Although heavy, it has items that may be needed when on a long trip.

Bear Resistant Food Canisters

These cylindrical canisters are made of hard plastic so that a bear cannot get a grip on the container with his teeth or his claws. The containers come in two sizes; 8" x 12" (20 cm x 31 cm) or 8" x 18" (20 cm x 46 cm) and the smaller one weighs about 3/4 of a pound (0.35 kilos). The small container holds 9.6 liters or about 38 cups (4.2 kg) of granola. I had a bear encounter one year, and ever since I have carried my own canister when hiking.

Studies have shown that the canisters are useful in decreasing the aggressiveness of bears towards people. If a bear does not get the reward of food when he approaches humans, he will not bother them. And a fed bear is a dead bear. We want to keep the bear population healthy in BC so please, whenever possible, use the canisters.

We sprayed our black canister with fluorescent paint thus making it easier to find in the event that a bear swats it into the bush.

Bear Spray

Pepper sprays are legal in Canada and a must when going into the backcountry. If a bear comes close, the spray can buy you time to find safety. Some bears will give up after one spray. If hiking with a number of people, the combined force of spray power can drive off even the most persistent bear.

Some spray containers come with holsters that can be attached to your waist and worn comfortably at all times. This is the only piece of equipment I ever take into my tent at night. Although not a guarantee that it will prevent a bear attack, it is one more measure to make your backcountry experience safer. However, spray is not a guaranteed safety tool.

Some researchers claim that if a wild animal is intent on attacking, even sprays will not deter it. You must not develop a false sense of security when carrying a spray. It is to be used only after everything else has failed and an attack is imminent. Basic rules should never be ignored because you have a spray.

Although I have had many sightings, I have had only one high-risk encounter in more than thirty years of hiking. On that encounter I did not have a spray but did everything else to prevent an attack. However, I now carry a spray because had I had it during my encounter, I may have made the experience for the young bear so unpleasant he would have avoided people for the rest of his life.

Binoculars

Although not essential, binoculars are handy. They enable you to observe, from a distance, wild animals and birds. This way, the wildlife is not disturbed but the thrill of watching them go about their daily activities in their natural environment is enjoyed. The binoculars are also excellent for locating landmarks while reconnoitering or checking for bears before entering a meadow. I highly recommend taking binoculars if weight permits. Small, compact sets are available for a reasonable price.

Dishes

I like to carry a tin cup on the outside of my pack, attached to the front harness with a shower-curtain hook or a spring-loaded carabineer. First of all, the tin makes a bit of noise that will help warn bears that someone is in their territory. Second, it is handy if you wish to stop at a stream and have a quick cup of water. Tin does not break or burn; you can even use a tin cup for cooking things like soup or reheating coffee in the morning. Plastic is a bit lighter but if put too close to the fire, it is gone.

For utensils, I usually take a metal spoon and a Swiss army knife. I know a fork is more elegant when eating spaghetti, but the spoon sort of matches the old sock I use for a napkin after I've used it for a potholder. I also take a tin bowl for my meals. The bowl has a lip around the rim for holding safely when it and the food is hot. Some people eat out of the pots to lessen weight.

First Aid Kit

This need not be elaborate but some precautions should be taken in the event of accidents or even normal body wear and tear. I take only small quantities of medicines and often use labeled film containers for pills.

- Antibiotic powder like Neosporin or"Cicatrin" are good for any oozing (wet) skin disorder. The powder does not deteriorate as rapidly as a liquid antibiotic.
- Antihistamine cream prevents itching and thus keeps you from scratching the many mosquito bites you will get.

- Antihistamine tablets are useful in the event of allergies, an unexpected cold or a reaction to a sting. Wasps abound in the north during dry periods. Natives say this indicates a cold winter. One sting leads to another because pheromones released by the stinging insect in turn, attracts other insects. Keeping food under cover helps keep wasps away.
- Aspirin or any analgesic needs no explaining. A few in a film container, well labeled, will be sufficient. However, should you forget them, you may find the active ingredient, ASA that is used in Aspirin, by chewing on willow leaves. They taste awful; better to carry pills.
- Band-aids with elastic material on the outside are the best. The plastic ones come off too easily. A few butterfly band-aids are recommended in the event of a deeper cut.
- Burn ointment is a must. Get a cream recommended by your druggist. Burns can occur from the fire, the stove or the sun.
- Topic disinfectant such as rubbing alcohol or Detol is recommended for cleaning cuts or infected spots. Film containers leak so use a plastic container with a screw-top lid for liquids.
- Laxatives and plugger-uppers should be carried in the event of stomach problems. If this should occur three days from the road, it could be an unpleasant slide back. Giardia is a fact of life. Flagel, Tineba or Immodium may keep these problems under control for a day or so but be aware that using them on an unknown infection can occasionally cause more problems. Tineba causes side effects more uncomfortable than a mild case of Giardia so should be your last choice. If constipated, drinking more water will usually do the trick.
- Liniment. I have gone steady with Ben Gay for years.
- Moleskin should be the first item put into the kit. It is always better to put moleskin on before a blister appears. If the blister has already appeared, make a donut-style cover so the blister can sit in the hole of the donut. Never break a blister to relieve the pressure. Blisters are nature's natural band-aids. If the blister does break an infection is possible so use some powdered disinfectant as a precaution.
- A tensor bandage is necessary in the case of a sprain or shin splint. It can also double as a sling in the event of an arm injury.

- Duct tape can be used to secure a sprain or reinforce a piece of moleskin that has been used over blisters. It does not come off when wet where moleskin does.

Comfort Kit

A comfort kit is what I call my bag of personal belongings. There must be some privacy and personal space even on a hiking trip and if you feel justified in carrying something personal or frivolous, then this is the place for it. I once met a fellow who thought it would be a blast to put a plastic blow-up doll on a mountain and photograph the reaction of other hikers. The following items are more serious suggestions for a comfort kit.

- Biodegradable soap is recommended but it should never be used in the rivers, lakes or creeks. These soaps degrade faster than ordinary soap but they still take a long time.
- Toothpaste can be carried in a film container or you may purchase small tubes that are great for hiking.
- Hair comb or brush helps you look and feel good for ten minutes every day.
- Lips become chapped and sore from the sun, the wind, and heavy breathing (when hiking) so chap stick is recommended.
- Skin becomes dry and chapped from silty water. Bring a skin cream that has no perfume.
- I would hate to be eaten by a bear with hair on my legs!! Men occasionally want to shave although a beard provides protection from mosquitoes. Taking a razor is up to you.
- A lightweight metal mirror can be purchased in most sports shops. However, a good compass with mirror will double as a dressing-table mirror.
- Sports towels are light-weight and soft. Lufa scrubs help keep sore feet and sun-burned faces in good condition.
- Other personal items can include things like contact lens cleaner, extra glasses or anything that you may need to make the hike better. My husband never goes without a book - just in case he gets lost and must wait

for a rescue. I have a friend who carries more candy than the corner store but she feels she needs the security of extra energy.

Camera

There are many lightweight cameras on the market today. Many do an excellent job. Those with a 35-80 ml zoom lens make for a good range. This provides a large format for scenery plus it does a nice job in camp, of friends falling in the river or any other memorable data you may wish to record. It will not take good flower, bird or animal pictures. Digital cameras weigh almost nothing and there is no film to carry.

Never try to photograph an animal from close range becauuse the animal may attack. Once an animal loses its fear of humans, its life is in danger.

However, if you are an avid photographer and have a particular subject or style in mind, you know what you must carry.

Candle, Fire starter, Matches

I keep a candle for survival purposes. The heat from a small candle can be enough to keep you alive under some circumstances. Dry fire starter that is manufactured for lighting barbecues is excellent. However, in a pinch, spruce pitch can be used to start a fire. Wooden matches (not paper ones) are the only type to take. Place matches in a plastic, screw cap bottle. Since some matches will ignite only with special material, put some of the striker material from the side of the box in which the matches came into the lid of your plastic match container. The striker will stay dry and always be near the matches. Lighters are dangerous because they must be held upside down in order to light the fire or stove. The lighter could ignite causing a serious burn.

Survival Blanket

This is a soft silver-foil blanket that is lightweight and can fit into a first aid kit. Some tarps have one side covered with silver foil. With those you then have the advantage of having a tarp (or ground sheet) along with a survival blanket. Whatever you choose, be certain to have one at all times, even on short day hikes.

Insect Repellent

This is essential when traveling in the north. Repellent with more than 20% DEET is toxic. Repellent with 95% DEET is supposed to be diluted before use and even then it should be used for dipping clothes into, not for placing directly on skin. Citronella is a beautiful smelling repellent but not all that effective. Light colored clothing is said to help keep bugs away, especially if the clothes help keep you free from sweat. Choose places where there is a breeze for camping or rest stops as the bugs do not like wind.

Toilet Paper

Use a biodegradable paper (bleach free). The bleach-free paper takes longer to burn but there is less residue left after burning. Never leave excretions exposed to the environment.

Rope

Rope is useful. It may be used to lower packs down steep inclines or as a harness for reconnoitering creek crossings. A rope is needed to hang food bags or to dry clothes. If your bootlaces break, a piece of rope will replace the lace.

Clothes

Warm clothing is necessary in Canadian mountains. Layering is of course the best way to stay warm. To keep your skin dry, wear a wicking material next to your body.

Rain gear is essential. Rubber will make you wet on the inside from sweat; poor quality rain gear will make you wet on the inside from leaks. Gortex has improved over the years. It does keep one dry, even in moderate downpours. Some people hike with an umbrella though it is useless in heavy bush. It may sound ridiculous but give it a try. Besides, statistics show that no person carrying an umbrella has ever been mauled by a bear. (This is a joke).

Long underwear is necessary in the cold and shorts are needed for warmer weather. Rather than carrying long pants, some people have two pairs of long johns, and wear shorts overtop one pair. Shorts and pants should have zippered pockets. Never wear jeans. They are heavy, take a long time to dry and actually, when wet, pull body heat out of your body. The light, synthetic, wind-resistant materials are excellent.

I wear a cotton neck scarf for warmth. It doubles as a headband, a wash-cloth, a hanky, a tea towel, and a bandage. Finally it adds color and flair for photos. A toque is also necessary. It may even be used while sleeping in colder weather. These items are light and compact. Waterproof mitts may keep your hands warm during cold, windy days.

Whatever packing you do, always be prepared for wind, snow and sub-zero temperatures. It is easy to pack for warm, sunny weather. If you can stay warm and dry under difficult conditions, you will have great hiking experiences.

When **packing for a day hike**, always carry a tarp, first aid kit, matches, fire starter and a rain jacket. Even if just going for a couple of hours, an accident could happen. If you must wait for help and bad weather sets in, you could be in trouble without some emergency supplies.

Nutrition

I cannot emphasize enough the need for proper nutrition while hiking in Northern BC. Every day will be a new and difficult challenge and your body must be in excellent condition in order to supply the needed power. During a long hike is not the time to diet. Food must be of good quality and sufficient quantity. Do not use foods that are 90% chemicals and 10% filler. Home-prepared foods high in protein and carbohydrates are the best as they have what the body needs (see Food, below). Calcium found in milk and cheese is needed for muscles and joints and as a soother to the nervous system. Potassium is needed to make muscles move. Protein is needed for muscle repair and water is needed to prevent both kidney problems and dehydration. If suffering from a headache in the heat of the day, your body is probably lacking water. When exerting physical strength, the body breaks down stored fat. This produces chemical by-products that require water to flush out. Without water, kidney damage may occur. Once stored fat is depleted, the body breaks down muscle. If calcium is not replenished, the body draws the mineral from your bones.

Foods high in proteins that are easy to carry on the trail include nuts, Parmesan cheese and soybean products. Carob is high in potassium, calcium and phosphorus. Wheat germ is high in vitamin B necessary for the nervous system. Vitamin B is also reputed to help repel mosquitoes. Pasta, instant potatoes, rice, and couscous are good sources of carbohydrate needed for energy. There should be one meal a day that is loaded with carbos.

Food

Not only must food be nutritious and sufficient to keep your body in top shape but it should also taste good.

If hiking for more than a single overnighter, planning the menu involves considerations of weight, unless, of course, you have a personal supply of Sherpas with you. I don't have a Sherpa but I do need good meals. So I pack dehydrated foods and I mainly dehydrate my own food. Below are a few sample meals, but I urge you to be creative and try some of your own favorites. Dehydrators can be purchased for around US $100 and they last with heavy use for at least 15 years.

Fruits

Overripe fruits are wonderful when dehydrated because they have higher sugar content and the fruits often come on sale at the grocery store thus making them cheaper. For example, bananas that have turned black or peaches that are mushy are excellent when dehydrated. Because bananas are high in potassium they are good for muscle movement. Avoid non-ripened dehydrated bananas as they taste like sawdust.

Dried strawberries are another good idea. They keep their tartness, a treat when thirsty. They make an excellent dessert if you add a touch of sugar and boil them for a few minutes. As a power snack however, they do not have much bulk and I did not find them very satisfying. On the other hand, dehydrated pineapple is great and apples are delicious. I also like dried pears because they keep their flavor. I have tried some exotic fruits like papaya and honeydew melon, and I found that they also keep their flavor. Peaches should be dehydrated with their skins on. Because they do not give much bulk, fruits like peaches and strawberries should be considered a dessert to be hydrated with sugar rather than eaten as snacks.

Fruit Leathers

Fruit leathers are lightweight, nutritional and tasty. Rhubarb stewed with raspberries and then dehydrated make a great fruit leather. When dry, cut the leather into eatable chunks, separate each chunk with plastic and bag it.

Dehydrated yogurt makes another good leather. Often a store will sell outdated yogurt for pennies. Yogurt also fills your calcium requirement.

Suppers

Stew, spaghetti, curries and sweet-and-sour meals, cooked according to your favorite recipes, are excellent when dehydrated. The meat used must be fat free because fat does not dehydrate. Instead, it becomes rancid. It is also unpalatable. The best meat to use is very lean hamburger.

Since meals seem to lose some flavor on dehydrating, add a bit more spice, sugar or vinegar than you normally would thus making the flavor stronger. After cooking these meals, thicken the sauces and dehydrate. Place some plastic sandwich wrap on the tray and spread the food over top. Once the top is dried, flip the meal over, pull off the sandwich wrap and finish dehydrating. Package in the sizes you need and label the bags. This is important because all meals look the same (like dog food) after they've been packaged. Nothing bugs me more when I am tired and cranky than to have my taste buds lined up for spaghetti that turns out to be stew.

- Macaroni and cheese is another great meal on the trail. A tin of corned beef adds the needed flavor. The beef is salty, filling and even has a bit of nutrition.

- Mashed turnips and potatoes dehydrate well as do onions and celery. Asparagus is another excellent vegetable that seems to get more flavor after dehydrating. Be creative. Try anything. However, I suggest a test at home before taking a new meal on a long hike.

- Onions dehydrate well and add flavor to most meals but onions are a horror to dehydrate at home because the flavor scents the entire house for days. Tinned salmon leaves the same unpleasant odor in the house while it is being dehydrated.

- Some white sauces are tasty when combined with noodles and fish. Thick pea soup can be dehydrated but plan on lots of biscuits if this is to be the final meal of the day. Pea soup's big advantage is that it rehydrates quickly and is light weight. It can be used for lunch breaks or as an emergency meal. When making soups, make them thick before dehydrating and thin them out on the trail.

- A single pot dinner allows you to use one pot for everything. The dried soups, Knorr brand from Switzerland or the Maggi brand from Latin America, make a great base for this type of meal and, when added to some noodles, some dehydrated veggies and even some dehydrated meat, you have an instant stew.

Breakfasts

This is always an important meal because most people like to cover their longest distance in the morning. Being well fuelled permits this. Also, because it is often chilly in the mountains in the mornings, a hot meal will help kick-start you for the day.

- Oatmeal is an all time favorite going back to the gold rush days and even before. Adding raisins gives extra energy and flavor. Use powdered milk. Instant porridge is quick to prepare and uses less fuel but it does not have the bulk that the real stuff does.
- Cream of wheat with dates and cinnamon is tasty. Cream of wheat is quicker to prepare than some cereals and it provides more energy than dry cereals.
- Granola is a fast breakfast that produces lots of energy. It is also tasty when warmed with hot water and then flavored with powdered milk and dehydrated fruits.
- Pancakes make an excellent meal for the start of a long day. You must carry fat for frying. Syrup needed to make them palatable may be heavy.

Lunches

A hard cracker is good for lunch, combined with some hard, non-colored cheese and a spiced, heavy sausage. You must also carry fat for frying.

Some people prefer to have their large meal at mid-day followed by a long rest. They then have a snack before hitting the sack in the evening. Others prefer to have a snack mid-day and a large meal when reaching camp for the night. I have used both methods and I find it depends on the circumstances on that particular day. If hiking in the north during mid summer, there is about eighteen hours of daylight so eating at weird times is possible. However, if doing an overnight ski trip in the winter anywhere in Canada there are only six to eight hours of daylight. A snack would be in order mid-day and the large meal would have to be eaten in the dark after camp is set up.

Index